The Complete

BOOK OF
THE CAT

The Complete

BOOK OF
THE CAT

CHARTWELL
BOOKS, INC.

A QUINTET BOOK

Published by Chartwell Books
A Division of Book Sales, Inc.
110 Enterprise Avenue
Secaucus, New Jersey 07094

ISBN 1-55521-491-6

This book was designed and produced by
Quintet Publishing Limited
6 Blundell Street
London N7 9BH

Creative Director: Peter Bridgewater
Art Director: Ian Hunt
Designers: Stuart Walden, Vince Murphy
Project Editor: Amanda O'Neill
Editor: Belinda Giles

Typeset in Great Britain by
Central Southern Typesetters, Eastbourne
Manufactured in Hong Kong by
Regent Publishing Services Limited
Printed in Hong Kong by
South Sea Int'l Press Ltd

The material in this publication appeared
previously in THE CAT, UNDERSTANDING
YOUR CAT and THE CAT CARE MANUAL.

CONTENTS

WHAT MAKES A CAT?

INTRODUCING THE CAT

The cat has a mystique of its own. Despite its veneer of domestication, it is never just a pet but rather a co-habitee with humans, living its own life in our world. Although man has kept the cat in his home for thousands of years, his influence has affected its outward appearance and its essentially wild nature far less than any other domesticated animal: the cat is still astonishingly close to its wild cousins.

Man has always recognized this special quality of the cat, and this small independent carnivore has occupied a special place in his affairs – worshipped as a god, feared as an agent of the devil, but never ignored. In every country where they are known, cats have been supposed to wield mystical powers, both for good and for evil purposes.

The Ancient Egyptians were the world's first great cat lovers. They worshipped a cat-headed goddess called Bast or Pasht, from which the word Puss probably comes. In addition to this, they made many beautiful figures and talismans representing cats, and these can be seen in museums all over the world. The Egyptian preoccupation with the cat went a great deal further than art, for to kill or eat one was a crime punishable by death.

With the spread of Christianity, cat worship declined, and its association with non-Christian religions led to a sinister view of the cat as a creature linked with the occult world. Nonetheless, the cat's association with man was deep-rooted and, although many cats were cruelly destroyed by witch-hunters, it continued to co-exist with humans. People still kept cats as companions and mousers; an Italian legend telling of a cat that gave birth to her kittens in the manger where Mary laid the infant Jesus inspired many artists, most notably Leonard da Vinci, who included a cat and kittens as a part of many of his studies of the Madonna and Child. In 1504, Albrecht Dürer produced an engraving of the Garden of Eden, which showed a cat sitting at the foot of the Tree of Life, its tail curled around Eve's legs. The undoubted virtues of cats have continued to inspire artists throughout the centuries, from Rembrandt to Renoir, and Gainsborough to Gauguin.

Today we no longer worship or dread the cat, but feelings still run strong about it. Cat-lovers are totally committed in favour of the one animal that appears to share our lives voluntarily, without dependence, and without losing the ability to walk out of the door into its own world. Those who dislike cats find that same independence disconcerting. The cat will always treat the human with whom it lives as an equal, never as a master, and this is perhaps the key to its fascination.

THE EVOLUTION AND ORIGINS OF THE CAT

The line of descent of the modern cats goes back some 70 million years, to about the time when the dinosaurs became extinct. Amongst the fossilized remains of the earliest placental mammals are those of a weasel-like, climbing carnivore called *Miacis*, thought to be the ancestor of all modern carnivorous mammals, including dogs, bears and cats. It had already begun to develop the specialized carnivore's dentition that we see in our modern cats, with the large carnassial teeth designed for cutting and shearing; it may also have possessed claws on its feet.

It took another 10 million years for the first cat-like carnivore to appear (and yet another 10 million before the dog made its bow). This first cat is known as *Dinictis* and was about the same size as the lynx. It looked very much like the modern cat. However, although its canine teeth were larger, its brain was considerably smaller.

It is believed that the descendants of *Dinictis* gradually diverged into two groups which gave rise on the one hand to the family *Viverridae*, which includes the modern civets, genets and mongooses, and on the other hand to the family

THE CATS' COUSINS
The ancestor of the cat also gave rise to the viverrids, including the civets, genets and mongooses. These are small or medium-sized animals, longer in body and shorter in leg than the cats, and with longer faces to accommodate a larger number of teeth. They are nonetheless recognizable as cousins to the cat family, with their sinuous grace. Mongooses, such as the small Indian mongoose (Herpestes auropunctatus) **(BELOW FAR LEFT)**, *were kept by the Greeks and Romans as household mousers before the domestic cat became established in*

this role outside Egypt. The civet (Viverra civetta) **(BELOW LEFT)** *is another member of the Viverridae, notable for its highly-developed scent glands which have been used in the manufacture of perfume. The blotched genet* (Genetta tigrina) **(LEFT)** *is the most cat-like of this family, as the picture clearly shows. The resemblance between the cats and the viverrids is particularly marked in the case of such wild members of the cat family as the jaguarundi and the flat-headed cat, two species whose appearance is distinctly reminiscent of the viverrids.*

Felidae – the modern cats, big and small.

Many of the early recognizable cats were large and dangerous creatures which have now become extinct. The European cave lion was a fearsome example. Perhaps the most notorious of the cat's ancestors was the sabre-toothed tiger (Smilodon), which had a wide distribution over much of the earth's surface apart from Australia. These tigers were ferocious hunters, capable of hacking prey down with their elongated upper canine teeth. They are believed to have fed on mastodons, or primeval elephants. Unlike contemporary cats, sabre-toothed tigers used their canines for stabbing rather than biting, sinking them deep through the tough hide of the mastodon. Their line finally died out about 13,000 years ago, which is recent in geological terms, and they left no immediate descendants. The cave lion outlasted the sabre-tooth until perhaps as late as the 5th century BC, to be succeeded by the modern lion.

Smaller cat-like animals began to emerge about 12 million years ago; the history of the present wild cats can be traced back through fossilized remains for some three million years. The distribution of these cats was directly influenced by the movements of the various land masses. Australia separated from the major land mass called Gondwanaland about 180 million years ago, which was long before cats had evolved. The South American continent

did the same but linked up again with its northern neighbour approximately two million years ago. This event afforded cats on the northern land mass an opportunity to spread southwards into new territory, whereas cats have never been native to Australia. Meanwhile, in the absence of 'true' cats, as they are classified today, marsupials had evolved to fill the same predatory niche in Australia and South America. Such creatures are often described as 'cats', although they differ significantly, not only by the presence of a pouch where the young are reared, but also in their pattern of dentition. The tiger cat, or large spotted-tailed native cat (Dasywrops naculatus), found in eastern parts of Australia, is a typical member of this group.

The contemporary members of the cat family have adapted and diversified to meet the wide range of climate and environment they are likely to find. They are all carnivores and highly efficient hunters. Some prefer the solitary life on the prowl, while others – the lion is a notable example – like to live and hunt in groups.

Similarities between certain subspecies of the Wildcat (Felis silvestris) and our domestic cat are so obvious that it seems highly probable that the Wild Cat, now extinct outside Europe and Asia, was the last stop on the evolutionary train before arriving at the cuddly creature purring in front of the fire.

AFRICAN CATS

The continent of Africa boasts two of the 'big four' amongst the Felidaw, the lion (1) and the leopard (2) as well as the cheetah (3), which is classed in a genus of its own. Other African cats include the caracal (4), sometimes called the desert lynx from its lynx-like features, the sand-dune cat (5), a small desert-adapted species, and the long-legged and large-eared serval (6).

THE WILD CATS

The modern family *Felidae* comprises many variants on the theme of cat. There is a dramatic range of sizes, from the tiger, which can weigh up to 800lb (360kg), to the smallest wildcat of the world, the African black-footed cat, which weighs in at only 4½lb (2kg). The range of colours runs from plain to striped, spotted or blotched.

The wild cats have adapted to habitats as diverse as the hot arid deserts of Africa and the frozen wastes of the north; they have adapted their lifestyles to suit their territory. Lions have developed social hunting groups to increase their chances of survival; the cheetah has evolved as a specialist racing machine to become the world's fastest land mammal, capable of speeds up to 65mph (90kph) over short distances. Cats such as the jaguar and the fishing cat have overcome the innate feline distaste for water and make use of the rivers in their territory to supply much of their food. As a family, the cats owe much of their success to their ability to adapt to a wide variety of environments.

The family *Felidae* is usually subdivided into three genera, *Acinonyx*, *Panthera* and *Felis*, although recently zoologists are tending to go further and break down the latter genus into as many as ten distinct genera. There is some disagreement about the number of species, but somewhere between thirty and forty species are recognized.

THE CHEETAH

The genus *Acinonyx* comprises just one species, the cheetah (*Acinonyx jubatus*), which is so different from all other cats as to merit this distinction.

The cheetah's ancestors evolved separately from other cats at least three million years ago. It differs from the other cats in its build, with its long legs, slender body and small head, and in the fact that its claws are non-retractile, like a dog's.

Cheetahs are also unique amongst cats in having a long tradition of being kept by man for hunting purposes, from about 3000 BC up to the eighteenth century. According to the writings of Marco Polo, 1,000 hunting cheetahs were housed at the court of the Great Khan, while later in Europe they were used to catch hares and roe-deer. More recently, attempts have been made to utilize the cheetah's speed in the entertainment world by setting up cheetah race tracks, but these attempts have foundered simply because the cheetah is still a cat, with all the cat's characteristic independence, and, unlike the greyhound, cannot be persuaded to co-operate in competitive racing after an electric hare.

THE BIG CATS

The genus *Panthera* comprises the big cats, the lion (*Panthera leo*), the tiger (*Panthera tigris*), the leopard (*Panthera pardus*) and the jaguar (*Panthera uncia*). Essentially, the big cats are characterized by their size and by a specialized voice box which enables them to roar. Some zoologists would also include the clouded leopard (*Neofelis (Panthera) nebulosa*) and the snow leopard (*Uncia (Panthera) uncia*) in this genus, despite their smaller size and inability to roar, on the basis of some skeletal and behavioural resemblances.

The big cats are familiar to every schoolchild, with their size, beauty and dramatic presence. The lion has long borne the title of 'King of Beasts' from its majestic demeanour and from its practice of living in family groups, called 'prides', within which the magnificent male with his unique long flowing mane appears as if surrounded by courtiers. The lion is the only truly gregarious cat, living in large social groups which can be comprised of as many as 35 females overseen by a dominant male. The task of providing food for the whole pride falls to the lionesses, with the male generally being content to feed from their kills. He may consume 60lb (27kg) at one time and then will fast for several days.

The lion's coat is a golden colour, the actual shade varying from buff to ochre. In 1975 great interest was aroused amongs zoologists when white lions – not albinos, but yellow-eyed – appeared in the Transvaal.

The lion occurs widely over Africa south of the Sahara, while in India a small population of the Asian subspecies *persica* survives in the Gir Forest reserve.

The tiger is the largest of the big cats, a massive and powerful hunter characterized by its striking pattern of dark stripes on a reddish-orange ground. No two individuals carry exactly the same pattern or stripes. Although many species of cat produce a melanistic (black) form, reports of black tigers have never been authenticated, but various white forms are fairly well known. Some are genuine albinos, pure white with pink eyes, while others have a pale body colour and lighter markings than normal.

Unlike the plains-dwelling lion, the tiger is a denizen of the jungle and tends to be a solitary hunter. Its range covers India and south-east Asia, but pressure from man has reduced its numbers to the point where several subspecies are already extinct and concern has been expressed for the tiger's continuing survival in the wild.

The leopard is another endangered species, partly because of the demand for its pelt to make leopardskin coats. Its black spots are arranged in rosettes of varying sizes on a golden background ranging in depth of hue from straw-colour to rich ochre. Black leopards are not uncommon, especially in densely forested areas.

These cats live and hunt alone, stalking prey determinedly with maximum stealth before pouncing and killing their victims by suffocation. They can leap 22ft (6.6m) in exceptional circumstances, and clear 10ft (3m) without difficulty.

The leopard is an adaptable species, equally at home in jungle, plains or even snowy mountain ranges – indeed, it is often found at high altitudes and has been reported at up to 15,000ft (4572m). A million years ago its distribution included Europe, but today its range is restricted to parts of Africa and Asia, extending into China and Siberia.

The last of the 'big four', the jaguar, is the only American representative of the genus. Like the leopard, it has black spots on a tawny ground, but the spots are larger and fewer and the cat itself is more massively, even clumsily, built, with its barrel-shaped body, short thick legs and large blunt head. Black jaguars, like black leopards, occur from time to time, again most commonly in areas of dense forest.

The jaguar's range features few large prey animals such as abound in Africa, and much of its hunting is for relatively small game – rodents such as capybara, small wild pigs, and fish. It is rarely found far from water and will wade into rivers to take heavy fish such as the pirarcu, which can weigh 450lb (200kg) and grow up to 13ft (4m) in length. It will also take turtle eggs and the turtles themselves, its powerful jaws breaking open a turtle's shell with ease; it has even been known to take caimans.

Its range today covers much of South America and the southernmost United States, but the demand for pelts for the fur trade has eradicated it in many areas: it is already extinct in Uruguay and rapidly disappearing from Argentina.

THE SNOW LEOPARD AND CLOUDED LEOPARD

The snow leopard and clouded leopard fall somewhere between the big and the lesser cats and are sometimes included in the genus *Panthera*.

The snow leopard, or ounce, inhabits some of the most remote areas of central Asia. Somewhat smaller than the true leopard, it carries dark irregular streaks and blotches on a muted yellowish-grey ground. Its very dense, rather woolly coat is an adaptation to the bleak climate of the mountainous regions where it is found.

The remoteness and inaccessibility of this cat's range has made study of its lifestyle in the wild difficult: it is known to be a solitary hunter roaming widely over large territories, and to migrate down to lower ground in winter. Its prey includes deer, gazelles, ibex and wild boar. Like other spotted cats, it has suffered at the hands of the fur trade and in 1971 concern for its survival led the International Fur Trade Federation to agree a ban on the further use of snow leopard pelts.

The clouded leopard, another Asian species, is one of the most beautifully marked of cats. The ground colour is tawny: the limbs and face are spotted, but on the body the spots are drawn out into large cloudy blotches outlined in black. Its Chinese name of 'mint leopard' derives from the fancy that these markings resemble mint leaves, as distinct from the round coin-shaped spots of the true leopard, which is known as 'golden cash leopard'.

A forest dweller, the clouded leopard spends much of its time in trees; it is secretive and rarely seen. Blending characteristics of the big and small cats, it is unique in its dentition, with elongated canine teeth longer, for its size, than those of any other living cat and recalling the extinct sabre-toothed tiger.

ASIAN CATS

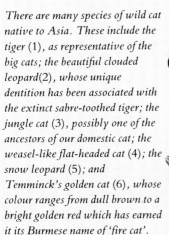

There are many species of wild cat native to Asia. These include the tiger (1), as representative of the big cats; the beautiful clouded leopard(2), whose unique dentition has been associated with the extinct sabre-toothed tiger; the jungle cat (3), possibly one of the ancestors of our domestic cat; the weasel-like flat-headed cat (4); the snow leopard (5); and Temminck's golden cat (6), whose colour ranges from dull brown to a bright golden red which has earned it its Burmese name of 'fire cat'.

MEDIUM-SIZED CATS

Amongst the lesser cats comprising the genus *Felis* there is a wide range of sizes. The American puma, cougar or mountain lion, as it is variously called *(Felis (Puma) concolor)*, is the largest, although it is quite distinct from the true big cats. In appearance it is not unlike a smaller, small-headed and maneless lion. Its coloration consists of variations on the theme of tawny, with colour phases ranging from red to grey.

Originally ranging across much of North and South America, the cougar has been pushed back from many areas by man but remains widely distributed across a variety of habitats from jungle to savannah, preying on creatures as diverse as deer and grasshoppers, and wandering widely over large areas.

The lynxes are sometimes regarded as a distinct group. The lynx *(Felis (Lynx) lynx)* is a large and beautiful cat with a dense coat adapted to cold climates, tufted ears, short tail and paws so thickly furred as to serve as snow shoes. Its keen sight is proverbial – it can spot a mouse 250ft (75m) away, and a deer over 1,650ft (500m) away, and it takes its name from the mythical figure Linceus who with his sharp eyes, safely piloted the ship Argo.

In Europe, human persecution has reduced the lynx's range until today it no longer occurs in most of western Europe, apart from Spain and Portugal, although it still extends into the northern areas such as Scandinavia, Russia and Czechoslovakia. In America its range covers northern areas of the United States and Canada.

A close relative is the North American bobcat *(Felis (Lynx) rufus)*, smaller and less densely coated, while in Asia and Africa a form of lynx is found in the caracal *(Felis (Caracal) caracal)*, which shares the long legs and tufted ears but not the short tail of the true lynxes.

Other medium-sized cats include the South American jaguarundi *(Felis (Herpailurus) yagouarundi)*, an oddly weasel-like species, and the serval *(Felis (Leptailurus) serval)*, a graceful and agile African species whose leggy build and fairly short tail recall the lynxes.

SMALL CATS

Amongst the smaller members of the genus *Felis*, the wild cat *(Felis silvestris)* is noteworthy both for its wide range and for its relationship to our domestic cat. Somewhat larger than the house cat, with tabby markings and a bushy, ringed tail, it has a number of subspecies including our own Scottish wildcat *(Felis silvestris grampia)*, the only wild feline of the British Isles, now confined to remote areas of Scotland.

Wildcats occur in much of southern Europe, as well as parts of Russia and neighbouring countries. Asia has its Asiatic steppe wildcat or Indian desert cat *(Felis silvestris ornata)*, while the African subspecies *(Felis silvestris libyca)* is the form most closely related to the house cat, and is generally credited with being its direct ancestor.

Like many other felines, the wildcat has adapted successfully to a variety of terrains. Solitary and nocturnal, it preys largely on small mammals but will also take insects, lizards

AMERICAN AND EUROPEAN CATS

These cats include the puma (1), the American 'lion'; the margay (2), a small American species resembling the ocelot (5); and the bobcat (3), another American cat, this time of the lynx family. The European wild cat (4) is widely distributed across Europe, with the Scottish subspecies the only wild feline of the British Isles. The lynx (6) is found in both Europe and North America, where it is well adapted to cold and mountainous terrain. The jaguar (7) is the only big cat found in the New World, for the smaller puma, despite its lion-like appearance, is not classed amongst the 'big four'.

and birds. The Scottish wildcat is noted for its ferocity and has usually proved untameable in captivity. The African subspecies is more docile, a trait which surely contributed towards the domestication of early cats.

There are many small species of cat. It lies beyond the scope of this book to describe all of them, but a selection is mentioned to give some idea of the range of species.

The sand-dune cat *(Felis margarita)* of Africa and Asia has adapted to life in arid deserts. It survives in areas where there is no water at all, making full use of the liquid supplied by its prey, and its feet have developed thickly padded soles for protection from the burning sand.

At the opposite extreme, Pallas's cat *(Felis (Otocolobus) manul)* has adapted to life in snow-covered mountains, developing an enormous coat to protect itself from the cold. A native of the frozen wastelands of central Asia, it lacks the graceful morphology associated with other cats, possessing a broad head with flat ears and eyes positioned high in the skull, and short, stocky legs. Living in an environment where there is little vegetative cover it has adapted to observe without being seen itself.

The fishing cat *(Felis (Prionailurus) viverrinus)* inhabits marshland areas in south-east Asia and, as its name suggests, makes full use of its watery environment. It is said to dive into water to catch fish but also feeds on crustaceans and molluscs, as well as land mammals. Its claws are much longer than those of other cats and appear to be adapted for scooping fish out of the water.

The smallest of all wild cats is the black-footed cat *(Felis nigripes)* of Africa, said also to be one of the fiercest despite its lack of size. Native folklore credits this little cat with attacks on sheep and even on giraffes, in which it is claimed to seize them by the neck and bite through the jugular vein. More reliably, it is believed to prey on small rodents, birds and reptiles.

COATS OF MANY COLOURS

Camouflage is important to any predator, and the beautiful coats of most cats are designed to enable them to merge into their surroundings. Cats inhabiting dry country tend to rely on coats which are plain-coloured or only faintly marked, like the pale or Chinese desert cat *(Felis bieti)*, with its yellowish-grey fur and the 'King of Beasts', the lion itself.

Forest dwellers tend to break up their outline with spots and streaks and tabby markings, often of great beauty. The marbled cat *(Felis (Pardofelis) marmorata)* has markings very like those of its larger cousin the clouded leopard, while the ocelot *(Felis (Leopardus) pardalis)* is wonderfully patterned with a whole range of spots and stripes, no two individuals featuring the same arrangement.

The beauty of their coats has led to many of these smaller cats, as well as the big cats like the leopard and jaguar, being slaughtered for their fashionable pelts. Many species of wild cat are endangered today, either because their needs conflict with man's as he takes in more and more of the wild places, or because of the insatiable greed of the fashion world for their beautiful pelts.

TOP: *The jungle cat* (Felis chaus) *was domesticated by the ancient Egyptians alongside the African wildcat* (Felis silvestris lybica) *and may share with it some of the credit for the ancestry of the domestic cat. Like the African wild cat, it played an important part in religious ritual.*

ABOVE: *The modern house cat is not a very different creature from the animal worshipped by the ancient Egyptians.*

LEFT: *In ancient Egypt cats were worshipped in the form of the cat-headed goddess Bast, portrayed here in bronze.*

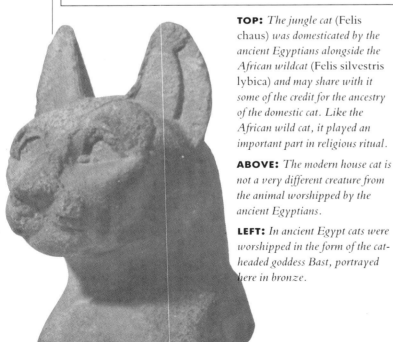

THE CAT AND MAN

The cat curled by the fireside is one of our favourite images of domesticity. Yet at the same time one of the greatest attractions of the cat is just how little we have truly domesticated it. Even whilst enjoying the comforts of civilisation to the full, it retains all the independence of spirit – even aloofness – that makes it unique amongst man's familiar animals.

Physically, the house cat has changed surprisingly little from the form of its wild ancestors. Whilst the basic model of the dog has given rise to breeds as diverse as the Great Dane and the Yorkshire Terrier, the cat remains much as nature designed it. In temperament, too, it remains little affected by domestication. Its natural instincts have been so little blunted that the pampered fireside pet can walk out of the house and take up a wild existence as successfully as if the centuries of domestication had never occurred: indeed, it is estimated that some 3 million feral cats are living wild in the United Kingdom today.

In fact the cat appears to have entered man's life later than other animals. While the dog has been domesticated for at least 12,000 years, the cat has probably been an inmate of man's house for only a third of that time.

THE BEGINNINGS

Domestication of the cat probably began in the Middle East at least 4,000 years ago. There are several species of small wild cat found around the world today that are so closely related to the domestic cat that they will interbreed with feral cats living on the boundaries of human habitation. However, it seems likely that the direct ancestor of our domestic cat is the African wildcat, or caffre cat *(Felis libyca)*, which looks like a slightly larger and heavier tabby house cat rather of the Abyssinian type, and which was tamed by the ancient Egyptians. The closely related jungle cat *(Felis chaus)* may also have been involved in the development of the domestic cat, for it too is depicted in Egyptian paintings and its mummified remains have been found in Egyptian cat graveyards.

The reasons for domesticating yet another species at this later period are lost in time, but it is likely that the importance of corn in the economy of ancient Egypt led the Egyptians to encourage wild cats to live beside them to keep down the numbers of mice and rats fattening themselves on their hard-earned harvest.

There was probably also a strong religious reason for domestication, as cat gods in various forms were recognized in many areas of the world and, from about 1580 BC, an Egyptian cat cult grew up around the cat-headed goddess Bast or Pasht, who symbolized maternity and fertility. Religious ceremonies were held annually when mummified cats were entombed at a temple of the cat goddess.

*Cats are frequently represented in Egyptian art. The bronze figure (**LEFT**) is typical, with the cat seated in an alert yet dignified pose and adorned with necklace and earrings.*

*The Egyptian cat-headed goddess Bast, portrayed here with many smaller cats at her feet (**ABOVE**), was worshipped as a fertility deity. The association of cats with fertility is widespread, perhaps because of the conspicuous nature of feline mating rituals. The Norse fertility goddess was said to ride in a chariot drawn by lynxes, the largest cats of the regions where she was worshipped.*

Even the household mouser shared the sacred status of all cats in Egypt. Killing a cat was sacrilege: a Roman soldier who killed one was executed despite the fact that he belonged to an occupying army. When a cat died, it was embalmed and the household went into mourning. Hundreds of thousands of mummified cats have been discovered – in the late nineteenth century some nineteen and a half tons of cat mummies were excavated at a single site.

The cult of Bast endured for nearly 2,000 years. Archaeologists have found a vast array of artefacts associated with the feline cult, ranging from jewellery and statues to lifelike murals.

When considering the reasons for domesticating the cat, we must not ignore man's simple liking for keeping pet animals of all kinds, not necessarily for any practical cause. Anyone who has watched a litter of kittens at play can instantly recognise one reason why cats found their way into people's homes as companion animals. There is no doubt that the cat played an important part in ancient Egyptian society as a controller of mice. A lifelike wildfowling scene painted at the tomb of Nebamun at Thebes depicts a tabby cat aiding the human fowler in much the same role as the modern gundog plays today, and it has been suggested that the Egyptians trained their pets to serve in this field as well.

THE SPREAD OF THE CAT

The export of cats from Egypt was banned, which delayed their spread to other countries, but it is likely that travelling merchants eventually took them to other parts of the Mediterranean region. The Greeks maintained the traditional link of cats with the moon, but never held these creatures in as high a regard as the Egyptians. Aesop, the teller of fables, linked them to the female form as exemplified in the goddess Venus, and this association has remained strong to the present day.

The hunting ability of the domestic cat was not of great significance to the Greeks because they already kept a form of weasel or marten for this purpose. The Romans also considered cats largely as pets, although they were regarded as having a guarding role at the fireside. Pliny the Elder included domestic cats in his work on natural history during the first century AD. Advancing Roman armies introduced the cat to regions of Europe.

In the East, where they were probably introduced by sailors, between 2000 BC and 400 AD, cats became prized for their ability to control vermin over-running agricultural areas. Ceramic figures showing cats in a seated position had to be displayed in the house to ward off poverty, as this also became associated with their ownership. Cats were similarly valued as protection against evil spirits at night. Buddhists appreciated the cat's apparent power of meditation, while in Hindu areas they were popular as pets. The Indian feline goddess Sasti, symbolizing maternity, maintained the traditional sexual or fertile power of the cat.

The cat kept its respected position in Asian societies throughout the Middle Ages up to modern times; it is considered sacred by many of the Eastern religions such as Buddhism. Unfortunately, attitudes in Western society have not always been so sympathetic. While there are many references in Medieval literature and art in appreciation of the cat, particularly in the late eleventh and early twelfth centuries, when Europe was invaded by hordes of black rats that had travelled from the East on boats with the Crusaders, the over-riding attitude of European Medieval society to the cat was one of suspicion and hostility. The Church linked the cat with pagan beliefs. The cat was often incriminated in cases of witchcraft, and indeed it was thought that witches could actually change into cats. In Tudor and Elizabethan England many cats were burned in public as symbols of heresy and agents of the Devil.

Even today superstitions about black cats, which were supposed to be witches' familiars, abound. The supposed effects of a black cat's presence vary from country to country. In the United States, Belgium, Spain and many other European countries, it is seen as an omen of ill fortune, while in South America it is though to bring bad luck, bad health and even death. In Britain, however, it is

RIGHT: *Leonardo da Vinci was one of many artists to be fascinated by the fluid form of the cat. These studies form part of a series of explorations of the cat's sinuous and curving lines.*

BELOW: *The association of cats with the occult dates back to the beginning of their relationship with man. They were frequently linked with witches, and this seventeenth century drawing shows three witches with their familiars – a dog, a mouse, an owl and, inevitably a kitten.*

FAR RIGHT, ABOVE: *Here Satan himself is depicted in the form of a sinister black cat tempting two feline angels.*

FAR RIGHT, BOTTOM: *These cats grandly dressed, illustrate a 19th century fable.*

more commonly seen as a sign of good fortune, particularly if it walks across one's path. In Yorkshire, for example, the wives of fishermen kept a black cat in their homes while the boats were out, believing that if the cat was kept safe, the safety of the men was likewise assured; if the cat escaped or was lost, the outcome could be fatal for the men. In Cornwall custom dictates that a person meeting a strange black cat should draw a cross on the front of his shoe with a wet finger.

Gradually, from the seventeenth century onwards, the sinister reputation of the cat as a beast of the occult world began to give way to the view more familiar today, of the cat as a household pet.

RIGHT: *The Ashanti lion, from Africa, is a hollow model of cast bronze which was used for weighing gold.*

FAR RIGHT: *Tippu's Tiger, from Mysore, India, is a mechanical toy made in 1790, which makes growling and screaming noises.*

BELOW: *Cats are well representd in the art and myth of the early civilizations of the New World. This stylized cat carved out of onyx comes from Teotihuacan, Mexico.*

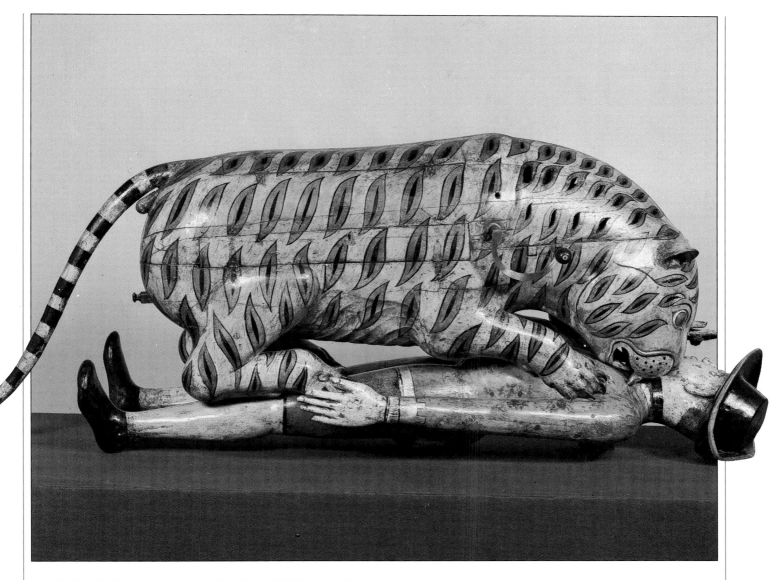

THE MANY ROLES OF THE CAT

Cats, large and small, appear to have played a significant role in the cultures of many different societies, judging from the number of objects which have been discovered portraying them.

The ancient Egyptian representations of the cat, connected with the cult of the cat-headed goddess Bast, are well-known, but many other cultures have given more than ordinary significance to various species of cat.

The big cats, naturally, have attracted their share of attention. The lion has symbolized royalty and power to many civilizations: long after the Assyrian kings with their royal lion hunts were no more than a memory, the East African Masai used the ritual of the lion hunt as the great test for their warriors, the *moran*. The lion and leopard both feature largely in medieval heraldry and heroes like Henry the Lion, Duke of Saxony, and Richard the Lionheart turned to the big cats for titles signifying their kingly powers. Indeed, in medieval iconography the lion is fre-

quently used to represent Christ, sometimes fighting the dragon Satan.

In Asia it was the tiger that symbolized majestic strength. In China the tiger was the symbol of supernatural power and of money, and gamblers burned incense to tiger images; tiger flesh is still eaten in China in the belief that it will improve both health and sexual potency.

In the early civilizations of the New World, the jaguar and the puma were worshipped by cults comparable to the Egyptian cult of Bast. The Mayan civilization developed a mighty jaguar cult with great stone temples with jaguar faces carved upon the walls; the Incas and the Aztecs worshipped the puma, known today by some Amerindian tribes as 'the Cat of God'. Stylized representations of these cats were modelled in clay or carved out of stone.

In the west, the Norse goddess Freya was represented riding in a chariot drawn by lynxes. Oddly enough, later on the lynx came to symbolize Christ, its piercing vision being connected with all-seeing divinity.

ABOVE: *Today the main role played by the cat is that of a pet — one which fully partakes in the comfort of the human lifestyle.*

THE MODERN CAT

By the nineteenth century, the domestic cat was beginning to take up its present role as a valued companion. Its rising status was assisted by the popularity of the cat with Queen Victoria, who owned two blue Persians. In the United Kingdom, the first National Cat Show was held at the Crystal Palace in 1871, and the National Cat Club was founded in 1887. The cat was first officially imported into the United States in 1749, and the first large American Cat Show was held in New York in 1895.

The changing pattern of Western society has gradually led to an increase in the popularity of the cat and a change in attitudes. While the majority of mixed breed cats used to be kept primarily as cheap and effective pest killers, today that function is largely fulfilled by modern rodenticides.

However, the cat has become increasingly valued as a companion animal, with its independent lifestyle posing less of a burden than the almost constant attention required by a dog. In 1985 there were 5.9 million pet cats compared to 6.1 million dogs in the United Kingdom, with 20 per cent of all households owning at least one cat. By comparison, the cat population in the United States has risen 5.7 per cent annually since 1972, while the dog population has held steady or declined slightly, according to a report by Business Trend Analysts. About 27 per cent of all households in the United States now keep cats; 40 per cent keep dogs. These figures mark a significant shift from 1983, when 46.3 million cats and 50.2 million dogs were kept.

As a companion animal, the cat continues to play an important part in our lives. It has been shown that pet ownership helps people to cope with the stresses of modern life. Pets can play an important part in the normal development of children, helping to develop the ability to give and to accept affection, and promoting a sense of responsibility in caring for their pets. Although the benefits of cat ownership are enjoyed by humans of all ages, companion animals such as the cat have another especially important role to play in providing company and affection for the elderly, particularly the housebound. It is often impossible for the elderly to give dogs the regular exercise they require, and cats are often therefore more suitable as companions.

Many elderly people living alone depend upon their pet cat, which becomes, in a very real sense, their family.

The role of the cat today is reflected in our art and literature as writers, poets and artists depict them as beloved pets which nonetheless retain an element of feline mystery. Lewis Carroll created the vanishing Cheshire cat – illustrated by Tenniel – for *Alice in Wonderland,* while Edward Lear gave the world the whimsical classic tale of *The Owl and the Pussycat.*

T. S. Eliot revealed himself as one of literature's great cat lovers with his *Old Possum's Book of Practical Cats,* while Paul Gallico has focused on cats in his charming best-sellers.

Cinema and television have been responsible for the creation of some famous cartoon cats. Felix the Cat was the original animated feline, followed by Tom with his mouse opponent Jerry, and the equally evil Sylvester.

The sinister image of cats gained a new interpretation in films such as *Diamonds are Forever*, while individual cats have found starring roles on television, from Jason of the BBC programme *Blue Peter* to Morris of the NVC *Today.* Cats have also been used to extol the virtues of many products through advertising. In 1981 they were even represented in their own stage musical, *Cats*, the highly successful adaptation of T. S. Eliot's verses by Andrew Lloyd-Webber.

Today the links between humans and cats have never been stronger. The huge numbers of cats kept as pets all over the world and their popularity in all aspects of art and culture reflects a bond which has strengthened in the face of a rapidly changing society.

ABOVE: *Two classic felines of modern times. Tenniel's famous depiction of Lewis Carrol's Cheshire Cat, was the forerunner of such stars of the cartoon movie culture as Felix, first of a long line of animated cartoon cats.*

CATS OF TODAY

Modern cats take many forms. Amongst the wild cats, the cheetah (**ABOVE**) is unique in its dog-like attributes, including non-retractile claws. The American puma or cougar (**RIGHT**) is an example of parallel development: although it is not one of the big cats, it has evolved a form sufficiently lion-like to earn it the name of 'mountain lion', although it is lighter in build and maneless. The Siamese (**LEFT**) is one of the most striking breeds of domestic cat, both in appearance and in personality.

23

PHYSICAL ATTRIBUTES

The domestic cat is not very different from the divine mouser of the Egyptians, nor from its wild relatives. All felines, from lions and tigers to the smaller species, including our household pet, are essentially similar in their construction as active and agile hunters, with a characteristic suppleness.

THE FRAMEWORK

The body is lithe, muscular and deep-chested, the limbs short and powerful, and the head short and rounded, with large wide-set eyes, small nose and well-developed sensory whiskers.

The cat's body has evolved over the centuries to allow the rapid movements that we know so well. The sudden spring, the pounce, the impressively athletic standing jump, the seemingly effortless climb and the devastatingly fast short springs are all outstanding characteristics of the cat family.

The skeleton of the cat is a magnificent example of physical engineering. Unlike the dog's skeleton, which has a wide range of variations, the cat's original shape has been retained with only slight changes.

The three functions of a skeleton are to dictate the shape, to protect the vital organs, and to provide a framework to which the body's other parts are attached.

Where the cat is concerned, there are about 230 bones, varying in size and shape. These are held together by more than 500 muscles. By far the strongest of these muscles are in the lumbar region and the hind legs, and in the neck and shoulders. The whole structure is covered by a skin which is designed to hang loose, thus giving the animal another aid to agility.

The cat's body is remarkably flexible. The elasticity and mobility of the spinal column allows them to contort their bodies to an apparently impossible degree. The point of

RIGHT: *The cat's climbing ability comes from the powerful muscles in the hind legs, the highly flexible forearms and the rectractile claws for gripping. The cat's frame is a natural masterpiece of elasticity, allowing it to run and jump with ease (**LEFT**), using the pads of its feet as shock-absorbers. This protects the bones on which its weight lands.*

UNDER THE SKIN

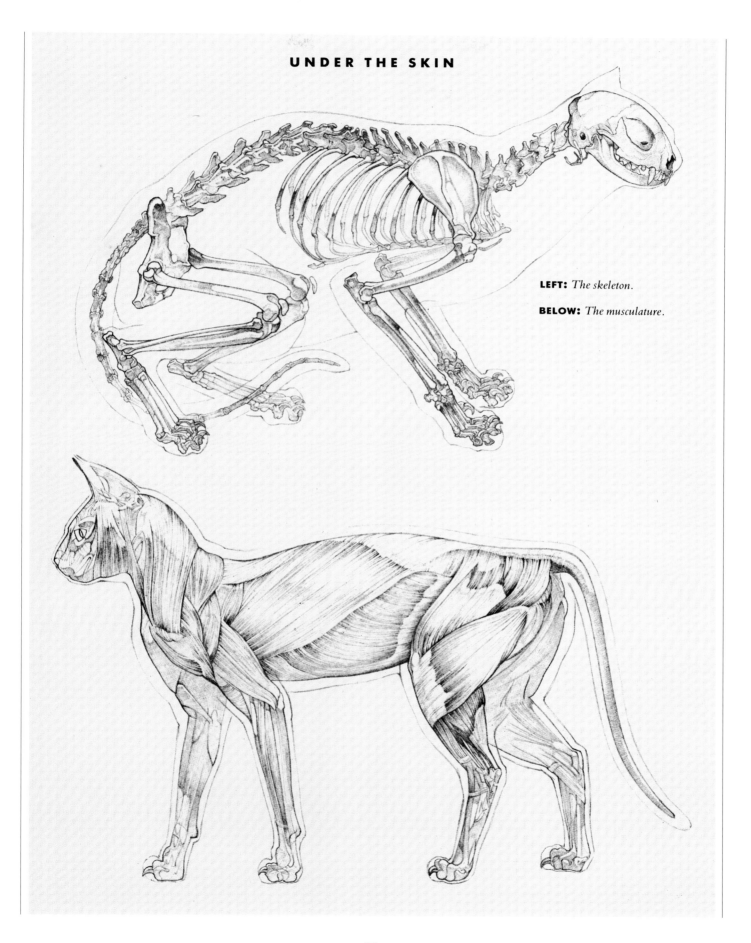

LEFT: *The skeleton.*

BELOW: *The musculature.*

the shoulder is open and free, which allows the animal to turn its foreleg in almost any direction without difficulty. In addition to this, the collar bone or clavicle is small or absent and not attached to the breast bone or shoulder blade, adding to the ease of movement.

The flexible skeleton and superbly supple muscles give cats the ability to twist and turn and to squeeze through the tiniest of gaps. They are able to move in many different ways – from sinuous stretching, or stealthy and almost unnoticeable creeping, to rapid powerfully controlled leaps and jumps.

The alert head is carried by a deceptively powerful neck: the strength and flexibility of the neck and shoulder muscles enable the cat to turn its head in all directions, like an owl.

The forelegs are well adapted to climbing, sprinting, holding or merely washing, because the radius, the long forearm bone, can move around its accompanying bone, the ulna, while the wristbones remain in a fixed position. The hindlegs can only move backward or forward, but are well-developed and propelled by very strong muscles enabling the cat to spring and pounce in a single swift movement.

*Whether a big cat like the lion (**RIGHT**) or a small cat like our own house cat (**ABOVE**), the feline streamlined body shape enables it to 'fly' through the air with the greatest of ease, and, combined with superb co-ordination, to pounce on its prey.*

WHAT MAKES A CAT

MAJOR ORGANS

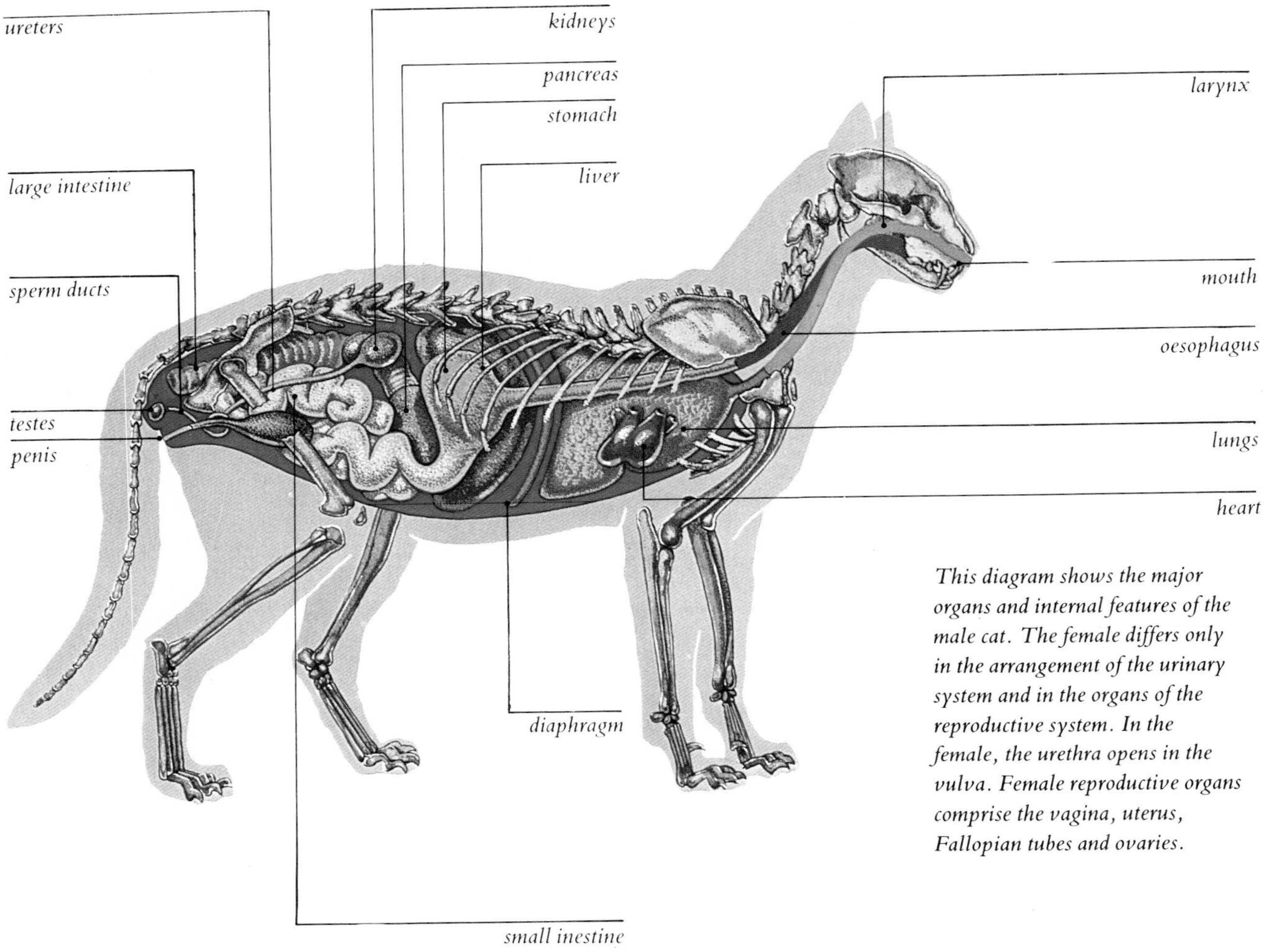

ureters

kidneys

pancreas

stomach

larynx

large intestine

liver

sperm ducts

mouth

oesophagus

testes

penis

lungs

heart

This diagram shows the major organs and internal features of the male cat. The female differs only in the arrangement of the urinary system and in the organs of the reproductive system. In the female, the urethra opens in the vulva. Female reproductive organs comprise the vagina, uterus, Fallopian tubes and ovaries.

diaphragm

small inestine

THE INTERNAL ORGANS

The internal organs of the cat, like its skeleton and musculature, follow the typical mammalian pattern with appropriate adaptations to fit the cat's way of life as a predator.

Its digestive system features the short simple gut characteristic of carnivores, the flesh diet requiring a shorter digestion period than vegetation. The food is swallowed in chunks, rather than being chewed up first, to be broken down in the stomach, and its high protein level means that a high proportion can be utilized, with a correspondingly small output of waste.

The desert origins of the cat's ancestors have led to the urinary system being adapted for water conservation. The kidneys, which filter out waste matter from the blood stream, reclaim most of the water filtered into them for minimal wastage of fluid, producing a more highly con-

centrated urine than most mammals – a feature characteristic of desert dwellers. This enables the cat to survive on a low water intake, and to live longer without water than most animals – cats have been known to survive up to 6 weeks deprived of liquid.

The disadvantage of this adaptation is that the kidneys have, as it were, little margin for error and have become the cat's weak point. Too dry a diet, or even laziness on the cat's part in putting off going outside to empty its bladder, can put too much strain on already hard-worked kidneys. Nephritis, or inflammation of the kidneys, is a common complaint in elderly cats.

The cat's circulatory system is markedly rapid and efficient, an adaptation to the hunting methods of a predator which spends long periods inactive and yet from time to time undertakes sudden bursts of violent activity.

TEETH AND CLAWS

The round head and short jaws characteristic of all cat species mean that space for teeth is limited, and as a hunter the cat has developed quality of teeth to compensate for lack of quantity – it has only 30 teeth, compared for example with 42 in the dog. The teeth are designed to grip and tear flesh: grinding and chewing teeth are absent, and the cat's digestion is consquently adapted to deal with chunks of meat swallowed whole. The canines are highly specialized, being better developed than in any other class of carnivores. This feature was taken to its greatest extreme by the prehistoric sabre-toothed tiger, familiar to us all from artists' reconstructions showing the tremendously elongated upper canines which were used to kill prey animals by stabbing through the tough hide.

The cat's tongue is also a specialized instrument. It is thickly coated with little horny projections (papillae), creating a rough surface to help hold the prey and even to rasp and file flesh off a carcass.

Like the teeth, the cat's claws have evolved to aid it as a hunter. They are long and razor-sharp, and are vital to the cat not only for killing prey but to assist in climbing; they are also used to scratch marking posts where the cat leaves its scent, aided by glands between the pads, to mark out its territory.

Unlike dogs, cats can retract their claws by means of elastic ligaments which attach the claw to the last joint of the toe, pulling it upwards. This protects their sharp points; it also means that these deadly weapons can be safely sheathed except when needed for use, when the tendons of the muscles pull the toe joint down and the claws are thrust out. The cheetah *(Acinonyx jubatus)* is unique as the only cat which lacks retractile claws. Cats' claws keep growing throughout life, like human fingernails, and the cat prevents them from becoming overgrown and keeps the points sharpened by scratching on trees or on the hard ground.

TEETH AND TONGUE

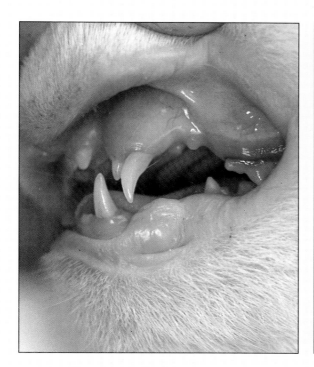

ABOVE: *The cat's canine 'eye' teeth are more highly developed than in any other carnivore. The adult teeth erupt at about five months of age, which helps in assessing the age of a cat.*

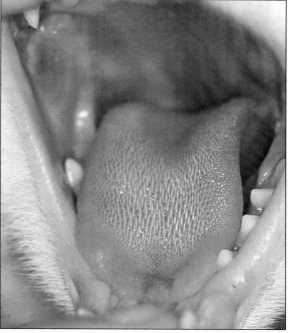

ABOVE: *The surface of a cat's tongue is covered with tiny projections which make the tongue into a natural rasp. In the big cats these are hard enough to strip the hair from a carcass and to file off layers of flesh. The rough tongue also acts as a natural comb when the cat licks itself, grooming the coat and removing any debris.*

TEETH AND CLAWS IN USE

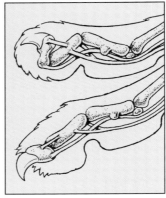

The powerful teeth and claws make the cat family deadly predators. They are highly effective hunting weapons, whether used by the lion (**TOP**), which depends upon its hunting skills for survival, or by the domestic cat, which, although its food is provided by man, retains the instinct to hunt as in the wild, stalking and killing mice and birds. Teeth and claws are also weapons for attack and defence between cats in territorial disputes (**ABOVE LEFT**). As the diagram (**ABOVE RIGHT**) shows, the claws of the cat's feet are attached to the bones of the toes, and can be retracted by means of ligaments, which are under muscular control. The muscles exert their effect through tendons, attached to the bones. Amongst all the species of cat, only the cheetah lacks this mechanism for retracting the claws, which serves to protect the sharp points from wear and also to sheathe the weapons during play.

LEFT: *The clouded leopard (Panthera nebulosa) is beautifully marked with cloudy blotches unevenly bordered in black on the body, and smaller spots on the face and paws. This apparently ornamental pattern serves to break up the body outline and help the hunter blend into its background when stalking prey.*

BELOW: *The leopard (Panthera pardus) is normally spotted, but a black form occurs not uncommonly. Melanism is also not infrequent in other species such as the jaguar and occasionally the cougar. When domesticating the cat, man may have encouraged the production of black individuals by selective breeding. For centuries the black cat was associated with witchcraft, perhaps because it played a ritual role in ancient religions.*

THE CAT'S FUR

The cat's fur and skin act as efficient insulating agents to keep the moisture in its body at the right level, and also to provide protection against bites, scratches and blows. They are sensory organs that can register pain, pleasure, heat and cold in instantaneous reflexes. The cat either sheds or grows fur to maintain a body temperature suitable for the climate.

The fur is also used to produce a threat display when necessary. The hairs are unconsciously controlled by the autonomic nervous system, and if the cat is angry or frightened the hormone adrenaline is activated, making each hair stand fully erect so that the animal appears as large as possible. With its fur standing on end and its tail fluffed out like a bottle brush, the small cat is metamorphosed into an alarming opponent to unnerve an opponent and deter a would-be attacker.

The cat's fur is also, of course, one of its great beauties. The wild cats may have a plain colour, usually a variation

LEFT: *Geoffroy's cat* (Felis tigrina), *a South American species, features the tabby-style markings found in many of the small wild cats. Numerous small spots and streaks break up the pattern of the coat to provide effective camouflage in undergrowth. Both grey and brown forms of this species occur. The earliest domesticated cats inherited tabby-marked coats from their wild ancestors. The original form was the mackerel-striped tabby, rather than the blotched tabby which is commoner amongst domestic cats today.*

upon the shades of tawny, but typically they are marked with stripes, spots or blotches. The purpose is essentially camouflage, to hide the cat both from its prey and from other predators, but the effect is often highly decorative. In some species the markings are dramatic, such as the tiger's vivid stripes, the leopard's spots and the jaguar's rosettes, whilst many of the smaller cats are subtly patterned much like the domestic tabby. Amongst the species which are apparently unmarked, such as the lion and cougar, the cubs are often spotted in infancy, which has led to speculation that this may reflect a spotted ancestor.

Colour mutations do occur in the wild, perhaps the best-known being the black (melanistic) leopard – Kipling's Bagheera. The wild cats from which our domestic cats are descended were tabbies, striped in the mackerel pattern which is more familiar today. The tabby pattern is created by dark bands of markings with 'agouti' markings in the light areas between the actual stripes, forming an effective camouflage. With domestication, man developed the basic tabby colouring to give a vast number of coat colours, variations on the original theme. However, the tabby remains the genetically dominant colour, and even appar-

ently self-coloured varieties often show 'ghost' tabby markings, which are notoriously hard to eradicate in such colours as the reds and creams.

Coat length also varies. Most wild cats have a short coat, but species which live in the colder zones, such as the lynx, have developed long dense coats. This feature is seen at its most extreme in Pallas's cat *(Felis manul)*, which has the longest fur of any wild feline species, and, despite its small size, its astonishingly shaggy appearance has made it one of the candidates for the role of the Abominable Snowman.

Amongst domestic cats, man has developed this capacity to vary the coat to produce some beautiful longhaired breeds, as well as two curly-coated varieties, a wirehair and even a hairless breed.

To keep the coat in prime condition, the hairs are regularly moulted and replaced by new growth. The wild cats tend to moult in spring and autumn, although, unlike some species, they rarely show much difference between the summer and winter coats. The protected environment of the domestic cat has led to a modification of this process, and most tend to shed a few hairs all the year round.

TABBY VARIATIONS

Man has developed the original brown tabby colouring of the ancestral wild cats into several distinct varieties. The black tabby markings may appear on the ground colour of silver (**BELOW**) or brown, or become themselves brown on a red ground. The markings themselves form standard recognized patterns, including the classic blotched tabby, with oyster-shaped rings on the sides, a butterfly pattern on the shoulders and one or more black necklaces. Variants are the mackerel tabby, whose black stripes run from a spinal line in a fishbone pattern, and the spotted tabby, now considered a separate variety.

Non-pedigree tabbies feature almost endless variations on the tabby theme, although they never quite match their pedigree cousins in richness of colour or evenness of markings. Their coats often show gleaming white 'shirt-fronts' and 'socks' (**LEFT**), frowned upon in pedigree specimens. Amongst pedigree varieties, one of the most difficult achievements of selective breeding has been the 'masking' of the tabby markings to produce the Red Self (**BELOW**), ideally a uniform red colour but genetically a tabby with greatly reduced markings. Nearly all specimens have traces of 'ghost' markings, particularly on the face, legs and tail, harking back to the dominant ancestral colour.

THE ACROBATIC CAT

Everything about the cat – its flexible skeleton, its supple muscles, its efficient breathing apparatus, its keen senses and instantaneous reflexes, its retractile claws – is designed to make this animal a natural gymnast of acrobatic grace.

Although the domestic cat is by nature a lazy animal, which spends more of its time dozing in a comfortable spot than in physical activity, when it wishes or needs to be active it has both speed and agility at its command.

Cats are digitigrade, which means that they walk on their toes, rather than the soles of their feet, making them very light of foot. The soft pads, on which the hunting cat can move so stealthily, are also on the toes; the heel-bone is well-developed but is set far back and never touches the ground. The pads of the feet form cushions, which act as shock-absorbers to protect the vital bones on which the cat's weight rests.

Cats are amongst nature's fastest movers over a short distance. They cover the ground in a series of giant leaps, and do not run in the same fashion as most mammals, such as the dog. They move the front and back legs on one side, and then the front and back legs on the other. The only

other mammals to do this are the giraffe and the camel, whose swaying gait does not resemble that of the cat at all.

The cat climbs by propelling itself with the powerful hind legs as far as possible and then by scrambling up, using the flexible forearms and strong, fully-controllable retractile claws to gain a firm foothold. If impelled by the need to flee from an enemy, this initial leap and scramble may carry the cat anything up to about 12 feet.

The sure-footedness of the cat is famous. Its well-developed sense of balance enables it to walk unconcernedly along a narrow fence like a circus performer on a tightrope. This aptitude has to be learned by kittens, who are very timid at first but gradually gain confidence.

The flexibility of the spin enables a cat halfway across a 'tightrope' to turn and retrace its steps without falling. It balances on its hind legs, then transfers the weight to one front leg, which is placed as far back between the hind ones as possible. The next step is to bring the other front leg around to carry the weight, while it shifts its hind quarters.

Cats can leap from a considerable height, but accidents do happen and they occasionally fall. It is proverbial that 'cats always land on their feet', and in fact this is almost

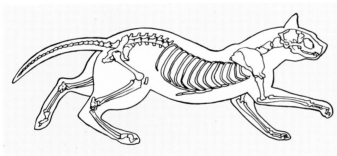

ABOVE: *The cat's skeleton is designed for maximum power and flexibility.*

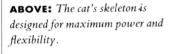

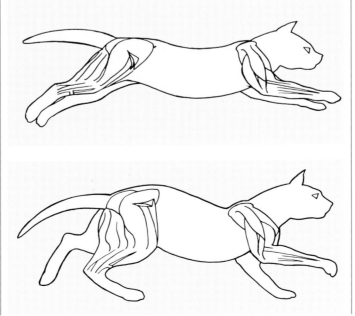

LEFT: *The musculature is equally significant in forming the perfectly adapted predator's build.*

THE FELINE GYMNAST

Cats are natural climbers, often finding security in heights. To climb, the cat leaps on to the trunk of a tree, holding on with extended claws, and moves up using its powerful forelimbs. To descend, it often prefers to turn and jump, rather than ease down backwards.

RIGHT: *Probably the most well-known feline attribute, in terms of movement, is the righting reflex – the ability to land on all fours from a fall. An automatic sequence of movements has been evolved by cats and is completed within a split second of a fall, guaranteeing a safe landing. The cat first adjusts its head to an upright position, then rotates and twists the body accordingly, prior to landing. Any other subtle readjustments to balance are perfected by the tail.*

always so, for a falling cat twists to right itself while still in mid-air, using its tail as a balance, in order to make the landing squarely on its feet, enabling its powerful legs to absorb the shock.

The cat's nervous system is perfectly adapted not only to co-ordinate the movements of the finely tuned muscles, bones and sinews that make up the locomotory system, but also to interpret the wide range of information received from the highly developed sense organs.

All the senses of the cat, as a hunter, need to be highly developed. Sight and hearing, taste, touch and smell all contribute to the cat's natural ability as a predator, the first two of these being the most important.

THE ANATOMY OF SIGHT

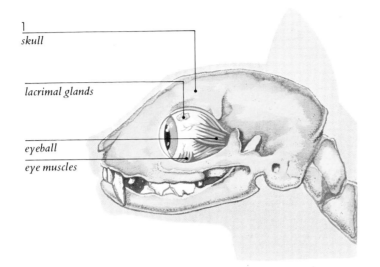

1

skull

lacrimal glands

eyeball

eye muscles

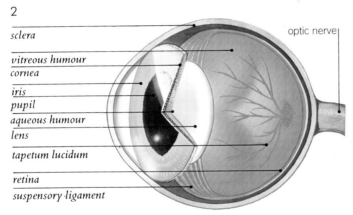

2

sclera

vitreous humour

cornea

iris

pupil

aqueous humour

lens

tapetum lucidum

retina

suspensory ligament

optic nerve

LEFT: *The eyes of the cat are set well forward in sockets in the skull, positioned to give efficient three-dimensional vision (1). The actual structure of the eye does not differ significantly from that of other mammals, except for the tapetum lucidum, a special feature designed to increase the intensity of light falling on the retina (2). The light-sensitive retina is the part of the eye where the image actually registers, and impulses from here are then conveyed along the optic nerve to the appropriate part of the brain. Because the eyes are set in slightly different positions, the cat's field of view is overlapping (3). This binocular vision enables the position of prey to be judged very accurately. Without such information, the cat would strike slightly off-target, allowing the prey to escape. By contrast, and befitting the cat's role as hunter rather than hunted, its peripheral vision is poor: the cat can only see in a fairly restricted field on either side of its head.*

3

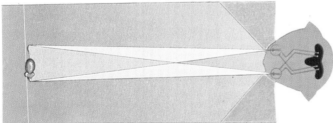

RIGHT: *The diameter of the cat's pupils changes according to the available light. In dim light the pupils are enlarged and circular, and in bright light they contract to slits. The pupils also reflect a cat's mood, dilating with fear or contracting with anger.*

SIGHT

Vision is perhaps the cat's most important sense and, not surprisingly, all cats have large well-developed eyes which like man's, are positioned at the front of the face to give the sharp focus of binocular vision. Most felines are at least partly nocturnal, and the cat's eye is adapted to see well in poor light. Cats cannot, as is sometimes thought, see in complete darkness, but they are equipped to utilize all available light.

The actual structure of the cat's eye does not differ significantly from the typical mammalian model. It is characterized by pupils which adapt their size according to the available light, narrowing to just a slit in bright conditions to make full use of such light as there is.

This ability to expand and contract the pupils is also used to signal mood, being a conspicuous feature. The pupils dilate under the influence of anger, fear, aggression or sexual excitement. A long slow blink signifies contentment and may be used as a greeting.

Because of the importance of this eye language, many species of cat have markings which accentuate the eyes – a sort of natural eyeliner – which are also often found in domestic tabbies.

The cat's ability to see at night is further enhanced by the presence at the back of the eye of a special reflective layer, the *tapetum lucidum*. This structure acts like a mirror, reflecting light rays back through the light-sensitive cells in the retina so that any light entering the eye passes through these cells and is then reflected back through them again. It is the reflection from the tapetum which makes the cat's eyes shine in the beam of a torch or car headlights at night. This eyeshine is so characteristic of cats that, although it occurs in other night-adapted animals, it has been called *chatoyance*, from the French word *chat* (cat).

In order to catch prey, cats have developed binocular vision. Most prey animals have the eyes positioned at the sides of the head, giving the widest possible field of vision to enable them to keep watch for predators, but limiting the field at the front where the images from the two eyes overlap, which is the area which has sharp focus. Predators which hunt largely by sight, such as cats and owls, have the eyes positioned towards the front of the face, giving a narrower overall field of vision but a much greater area of overlap. This overlapping field of vision enables prey to be located with pinpoint accuracy.

This ability is not as pronounced in some breeds of domestic cat, such as Siamese, and these may not prove such successful hunters as a result. Kittens, being born blind, have to grow to understand the sense of vision and are unlikely to be abe to use this faculty fully until they are at least 12 weeks old.

CATS' EYES

ABOVE: *Cats' eyes vary in colour as do humans', but the colour of the iris does not affect the efficiency of eyesight. The only eye colour that has any implication for the cat's senses is blue – blue-eyed cats are often deaf.*

HEARING

The ear of the cat is a very sensitive organ responsible for hearing and balance, both very highly developed senses in the cat. The ear consists of the ear flap, or *pinna*, the outer ear canal which leads down to the ear drum, the middle ear behind the ear drum which contains the three bones that transfer sound vibrations, and the inner ear, deep within the skull, which contains the organs responsible for hearing and balance.

The cat's hearing is very acute, another adaptation to its predatory role in life, although in most feline species the ears are quite small. The serval is one species with markedly large ears, and this cat appears to depend as much on the sense of hearing when hunting as upon sight.

The hearing is assisted by the cat's ability to turn its ears like homing devices in the direction of sound. The ears can be moved separately to assist the cat in focusing its hearing. This flexibility of the ears is also used to signal the cat's mood: they can be pricked forward in curiosity, exploration or friendliness, laid backward in aggression and flattened parallel to the head when fighting. They can also lie inwards or outwards in submission.

Cats can hear sound frequencies two octaves higher than humans can, as well as sounds of lower intensity. A cat investigating the undergrowth will often be seen to lift its head and turn its head alertly towards some sound which is quite inaudible to a human but which to the cat is clearly recognizable as the squeak of some small prey animal.

Structures in the ears also serve to maintain the cat's sense of balance, giving the cat an indication of its position relative to gravity. It is this faculty that enables a falling cat to right itself in mid-air in order to land on its feet.

THE ANATOMY OF THE EAR

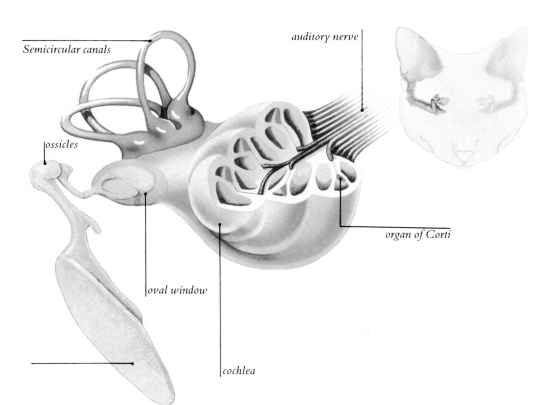

Semicircular canals

auditory nerve

ossicles

oval window

organ of Corti

cochlea

ABOVE: *Structures in the ears provide the cat with the means to hear and also serve to maintain a sense of balance. Sound waves are funnelled down through the external ear flap or pinna, down the external auditory canal, to the ear drum. In the concealed middle ear the ear ossicles convert weak vibrations of the ear drum into stronger vibrations of the oval window, part of the snail-like cochlea. The sound sensing organ of Corti, in which different pitched sounds cause vibrations in different parts of the organ, extends along the spirals of the cochlea. The vibrations in the organ of Corti cause nerve signals to be sent along the auditory nerve to the brain. The semi-circular canals comprise the balance organ, which helps to give the cat an indication of its position relative to gravity.*

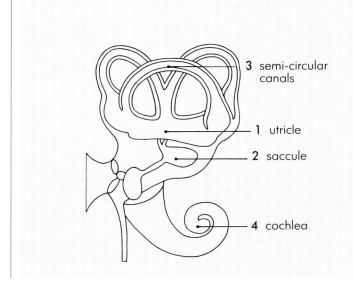

3 semi-circular canals

1 utricle

2 saccule

4 cochlea

LEFT: *The vestibule apparatus is the cat's balance and orientation monitor, located in the inner ear, informing the cat which way up it is. In the chambers of the utricle (1) and saccule (2), tiny crystals of calcium carbonate press down on minute hairs, if there is any change in up or down orientation. Fluid in semi-circular canals (3) moves in response to any movement in direction or acceleration. All these changes are immediately signalled to the brain. The cochlea (4) is the hearing organ.*

ABOVE: *Blue-eyed White cats sometimes suffer from deafness. This may be the result of a congenital lack of the organ of Corti in the inner ear, an inherited abnormality which appears to be linked with the lack of pigmentation. Interestingly, in the case of Odd-eyed Whites, which have one blue and one orange eye, this disability is likely to be confined to the ear on the blue-eyed side of the face. Orange-eyed Whites generally do not have any impairment of hearing.*

SMELL AND TASTE

Although sight and hearing are important to the cat, the sense of smell is less so. The nose is much less prominent in domestic cats than in many other species and, as this suggests, cats are much less dependent on their sense of smell to chase their prey than are many other predators. This sense is used primarily in feeding, social and sexual activities. The nasal passages are lined with the turbinate bones – delicate scroll-like passages.

The cat's nose is not well protected, relying on the sensitive whiskers around it to help it to avoid knocks. It is easily injured, therefore, and a chastening tap on the nose may cause a lifetime of trouble.

The senses of taste and smell are closely associated, since the nasal passage opens into the mouth, with impulses registering in the olfactory lobe of the brain. Although taste-buds are present on the tongue, the cat does not appear to respond to sweet items, unlike other mammals.

In the roof of the cat's mouth lies an additional and highly specialized sense organ which is not found in humans. This is known as Jacobsen's organ and enables the cat to respond to scent particles in the air. Molecules of a scent are picked up from the air on the tongue, which is then pressed against Jacobsen's organ. A connection is made with the hypothalmic region of the brain, which triggers an appropriate response.

The mouth itself is of great importance. A cat may lose limbs, sight and hearing and still survive. But if its mouth is disabled it can neither feed nor fight. The teeth are formed to permit the cat to carry delicate kittens at one moment and mercilessly tear its prey apart at another. From the mouth come those varying sounds which man interprets as

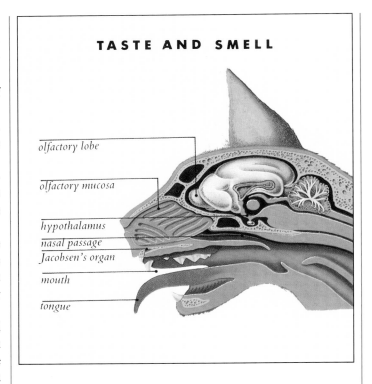

TASTE AND SMELL

olfactory lobe

olfactory mucosa

hypothalamus
nasal passage
Jacobsen's organ

mouth

tongue

seduction, satisfaction, begging, warning, and an expression of pain. The tongue tastes, is used for lapping, and its rough, sandpaper-like surface is used as a comb in grooming and in shows of affection for human companions.

TOUCH

Finally, we must consider the sense of touch, which is important to all animals. The whole skin of course is a sensory organ which can register pain, pleasure, heat and cold in instantaneous reflexes. In addition, however, the

RIGHT: *All species of cat have well developed whiskers. Those species which live in dense cover, such as Temminck's cat (Felis temmincki), shown here, have the longest whiskers, to help them find their way through the gaps in the undergrowth.*

FAR RIGHT: *The pads of the paws are extremely sensitive. An inquisitive kitten explores the world with eyes, ears, nose, whiskers and paws.*

cat has certain specialized sensory aids, most notably the long and sensitive whiskers, or vibrissae, which are actually specially modified hairs.

Any small movement or touch at the tip of the whiskers is transmitted to a net of fine nerves at their base. This sensitivity to the immediate environment aids the cat to make its way through dense thickets, avoiding damage to itself. Most breeds have 12 whiskers below the nose on each side of the face, with additional ones above the eyes and on the sides of the head.

The pads of the feet are also highly sensitive to pressure. They are pliant, soft and supple and can grip and feel. They are essential for the instantaneous movements characteristic of the cat. Combined with the retractile claws, they make the paws as a whole into highly developed tools for grooming, digging, burying, playing, hunting and exploring.

Chapter Two

BREEDS OF CAT

THE DEVELOPMENT OF BREEDS

From the ancestral wild cat man has developed domestic cats with a range of colours, body types, head shapes and general conformation. It is not known when the various divergences from the original type first occurred, although breeds such as the Siamese claim considerable antiquity.

The wild cat's tabby coloration with its characteristic mackerel-striped pattern gave rise to variants such as the blotched tabby, in which the black patterning is broken down into spirals or whorls, and the spotted tabby, where the stripes break down further to give spots. The basic brown tabby yielded other tabby colour variations, and gave way altogether to create self-coloured varieties. A number of breeds show the so-called Himalayan pattern, a light body colour but with dark extremities, best-known in the Siamese.

The original short coat has produced three variations, the Longhair, the Rex, which has short wavy hairs, and the Wirehair, with hairs of normal length but with a rough wiry texture.

Variations in body type also arose, with a range from the very compact, cobby animal to the slender, long-legged rangy form, the latter characteristically found amongst the Oriental breeds. A more dramatic mutation gave rise to the Manx cat, in which an inherited malformation of the lower part of the vertebral column has produced a tail-less breed.

Many breeds have arisen through some spontaneous mutation which was perpetuated by man because he found it attractive. A recent example is the Rex cat, the Cornish form deriving from a kitten born in 1950 and the Devon form from an unrelated kitten born in 1960. Other breeds have been created deliberately by crossing existing forms in an attempt to combine attractive characteristics from each. One of the most attractive of these is the Colourpoint, which was artificially created from Siamese and Longhairs to have the colour pattern of the former and the body type of the latter.

BASIC GENETICS

An understanding of the laws that govern the inheritance of characteristics will enhance one's understanding of the relationships between the different breeds of cat, and is essential for the serious breeder aiming to produce a true-breeding strain.

In order to learn how characteristics are passed on from generation to generation it is necessary to understand a little about the principles of inheritance. In the latter half of

THE MANX

This cat is said to originate from the Isle of Man, but cats without tails occur in other parts of the world, such as China and Russia.

THE REX

This breed was first discovered in 1950 on a farm on Bodmin Moor, Cornwall, England.

NORTH AMERICA

THE CHINCHILLA

The original breed is credited to a Mrs Vallence who in the 1880's mated a smoke-coloured cat to a silver tabby, to produce the first Chinchilla.

THE RUSSIAN BLUE

Prior to 1900, this cat was known as the Archangel Blue and may have been introduced into Britain by sailors trading from the Baltic port of Archangel in 1860.

SOME POINTS OF DEPARTURE

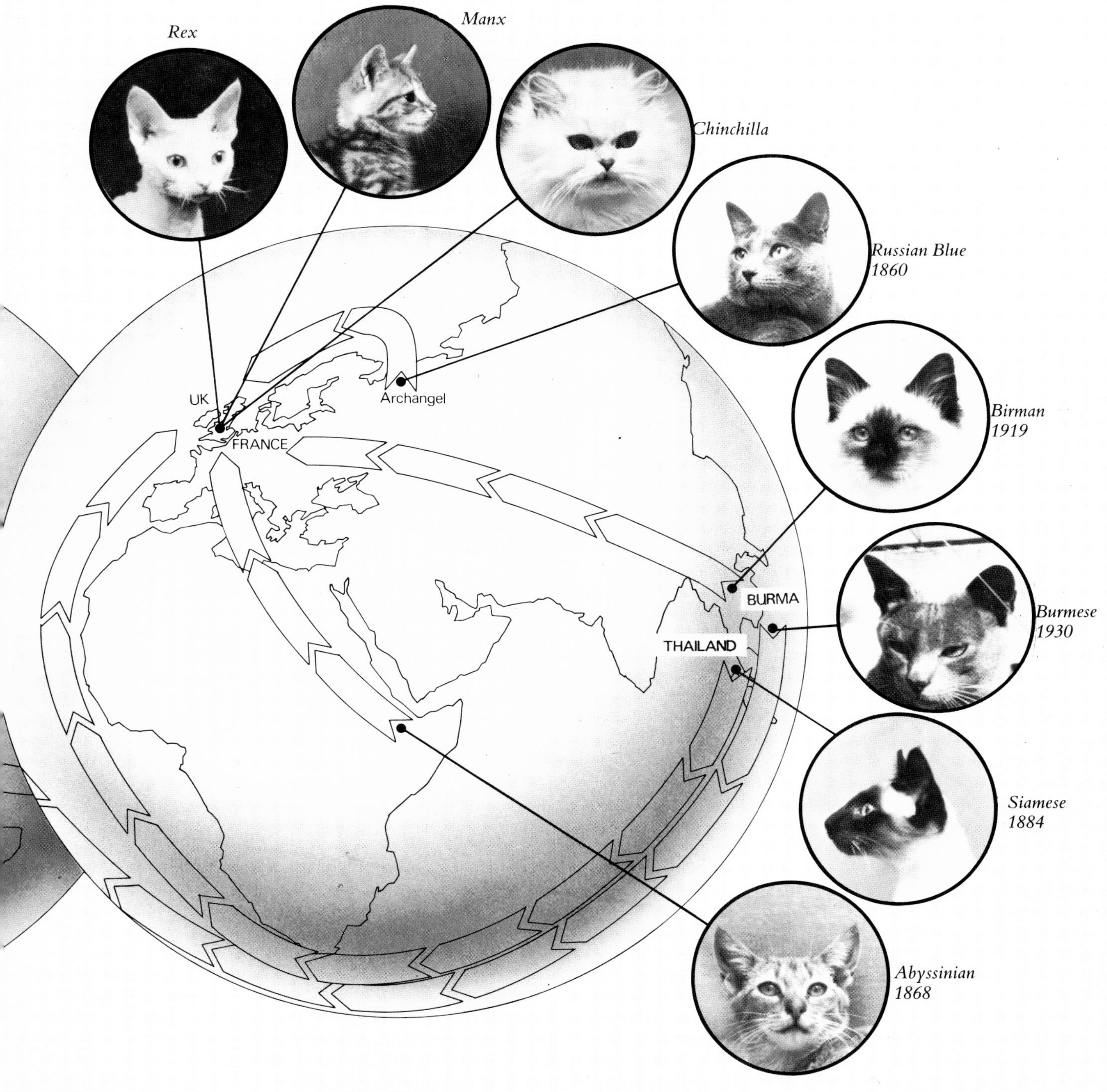

Rex

Manx

Chinchilla

Russian Blue
1860

Birman
1919

Burmese
1930

Siamese
1884

Abyssinian
1868

UK

FRANCE

Archangel

BURMA

THAILAND

THE BURMESE

Burmese cats may be traced back to a single brown female named Wong Mau which was introduced into the United States of America from Burma in 1930.

THE BIRMAN

The Sacred Cat of Burma first appeared in France in 1919 when a pair of cats were sent to two soldiers who had come to the assistance of the priests of a Burmese temple.

THE SIAMESE

The first recorded pair of Siamese cats were introduced into Britain by the English Consul General for Bangkok in 1884.

THE ABYSSINIAN

The first reliable reference to the breed was in 1868 when Lord Robert Napier returned to Britain from Abyssinia (Ethiopia) after a military expedition, bringing one of the cats with him.

SYMBOLIZING GENES

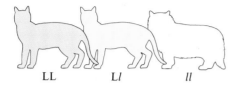

LL   Ll   ll

For convenience when discussing genetics, the genes are abbreviated to a single letter, written in the upper case if dominant (L), and lower case for recessive (l). For example, since short hair, (L) is dominant over long hair, (l), a cat has to possess two recessive longhair genes, (ll), to have long hair. The genes interact at random, and the expected ratios of genotypes will only be seen if the average of a large number of matings is taken. For example, it is unlikely, but possible, that two heterozygote short-haired cats could produce a litter of three long-haired kittens. It is much more likely that they would produce three short-haired or two short-haired and one long-haired kitten.

the nineteenth century, an Austrian monk by the name of Gregor Mendel studied the inheritance of characteristics of garden pea plants. This led to the branch of biology known as *genetics* – the study of heredity. He found that the basic unit of heredity was the *gene*. Genes match in pairs, and each pair of genes determines a different trait such as eye colour, hair length and so on – although some traits such as body shape may be *multi-factorial* and controlled by several different genes. The cells responsible for reproduction, the sperm in the male and the ova in the female, each carry only one of the pair of genes for each trait so that when the two reproductive cells unite at the time of fertilization, the new cell formed has inherited half its genes from its male parent and half from its female parent. This cell then multiplies many times to form all the cells of the new kitten. Each cell contains the identical genetic code passed on from the parents to that first cell. The genetic code controls the shape and function of all the various tissues in the body.

Certain genes are said to be *dominant* over others. For example, in cats the genes for short hair are dominant over

those for long hair. This can be illustrated by taking a closer look at how the laws of inheritance work for the genes controlling hair length.

The genes for hair length are denoted by the symbols 'L' for short hair and 'l' for long hair. A capital letter is always used to indicate the dominant gene of a pair, and lower case for the other, the *recessive*, which will have no effect on the cat's external appearance if the dominant gene is also present. This means that if the pair of genes in the genetic material of a cat are both L, or short-hair genes, then the cat will have short hair. If both genes are l, or long-hair genes, then the cat will have long hair. However, if the cat has one short-hair gene, L, and one long-hair gene, l, it will have short hair because the short-hair gene is dominant and suppresses the long-hair gene.

However, that short-haired cat will be *heterozygous* for that particular trait, and can pass on the long-hair gene to future generations. If it mates with another heterozygous short-haired cat, it can produce a long-haired kitten – quite a surprise for the owner! If, however, both genes are the same – LL or ll – then the cat is homozygous for that trait. Therefore, it follows that if a cat is long-haired, it must have homozygous long-hair genes, *ll*, but if a cat is short-haired it may be heterozygous, *Ll*, or homozygous short-hair LL. There is no way to tell by looking at a short-haired cat, or in genetic terms a cat with a short-haired *phenotype*, whether it is homozygous or heterozygous for that trait – only an analysis of the offspring of that cat will reveal its hidden genetic make-up, or *genotype*.

In the case of some traits, however, neither gene is fully dominant and the condition known as *incomplete dominance* is the result. An example is seen when Siamese and Burmese cats are paired together. The ensuing litter is likely to contain some kittens of Siamese and some of Burmese appearance, but also some kittens known as Tonkinese, which have an intermediate appearance showing characteristics of both parents.

New colours and even varieties can arise within a species because the genetic material is not immutably fixed. The nature of a gene may suddenly change in an individual cat by mutation, a random mistake in the order of the chemical code within the genes. These mutations occur very infrequently when embryos are developing and sometimes cause harmful disorders in the development of the animal – sometimes so harmful that the affected embryo dies or is born with congenital defects. However, on occasions, these mutations are not harmful and may result in the production of a new characteristic, such as the recessive 'dilute' mutation, d, of the normal gene, D, that controls the density of hair pigmentation. For example a cat with two of these recessive genes will have a blue coat colour as opposed to a black coat colour for a cat with either two D genes or one of each. The dilute gene will also lighten the coat of a

INHERITANCE

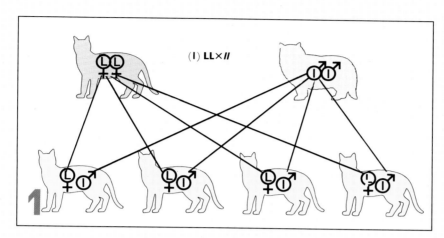

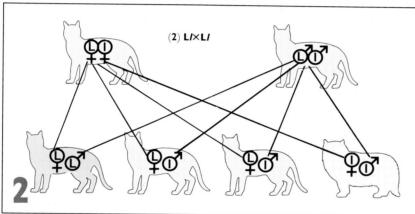

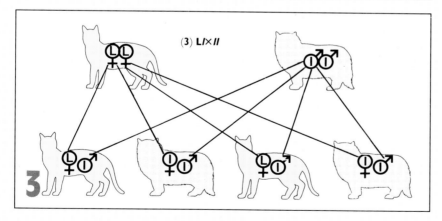

How specific traits are passed on.

If a homozygous long-haired cat (ll) is crossed with a homozygous short-haired cat (LL), the resultant kittens will be dominantly short-haired, but will be heterozygous carriers of the long-haired gene (1). If two heterozygote cats (Ll) are crossed, they will produce kittens in the ratio of three short-haired to one long-haired kind (2). But, if a heterozygote short-haired cat (Ll) is crossed with a homozygote short-haired cat (LL), only short-haired kittens are produced. However one in four of the kittens will be heterozygous and carry the long-hair gene. If a heterozygote short-haired cat (Ll) is crossed with a homozygot long-haired cat (ll), the cross will produce homozygote long-haired kittens and heterozygote short-haired kittens in equal proportions (3). If homozygotes are crossed (either LL×LL or ll×ll), they will 'breed true' and produce offspring with the same trait.

In reality, if two short-haired cats are mated and produce a long-haired kitten, it becomes apparent that they must both be carriers of the long-haired recessive gene l – a long answer to a short question. However, understanding the theory does answer the question of how traits are passed on from generation to generation.

cat, that would otherwise be brown to a lilac colour. Therefore, the colour and characteristics of a newborn kitten depend on its genetic background.

New mutations can arise spontaneously at any time. As we have seen, the curly-coated Rexes first appeared in the early 1950s. Similarly, in 1961 a mutation of ear shape occurred in a kitten born on a farm in Scotland and this gave rise to the breed known as the Scottish Fold, which has uniquely folded, flat ears.

Similar mutations may crop up at different times in quite unrelated populations of cats. The mutation for a curly-coat arose twice, in Cornwall and in Devon, but in fact proved to be two quite separate mutations when the two strains were crossed: Cornish and Devon Rex mated together produce normal short-haired kittens instead of ones with curly-coats. The gene for a wirehaired coat arose in New York in 1966, and was subsequently selectively bred to create the American Wirehair breed. However, a similar gene had also occurred in London after the Second World War, although in this instance cat breeders did not seek to perpetuate the mutation.

Not only colour and hair length are genetically controlled, but also the sex of offspring. The genetic material that determines the genes is present in strands called *chromosomes*. The cells of the cat have 38 chromosomes arranged in 19 matching pairs. However, one pair of chromosomes, known as the sex chromosomes, may consist either of a matching pair of large X chromosomes if the cat is female, or a large X chromosome and a smaller Y chromosome if the cat is male. Ova from the mother always contain one X chromosome, whereas semen contains an equal number of sperm with one X and one Y chromosome, so there is an even chance of the new offspring being either XX, and thus female, or XY, and thus male. The chance is completely random.

Certain characteristics are said to be *sex linked*, that is, they only occur in one sex. This happens when the controlling gene is located on the sex chromosome. The classic example is the Tortoiseshell cat, which is always female – or at least never a normal male.

The most common tortoiseshell colouring is a mixture of black, yellow and orange, with the addition of orange controlled by the dominant O gene. This gene is found only on the X chromosome and is therefore sex-linked. The tortoiseshell colour is an expression of a combination of a dominant O gene for orange coloration and a recessive o gene for normal coloration (the precise colour depending on other genes present). Therefore, an OO female cat will be orange (normally called red by breeders), an oo female will not have any red coloration, and an Oo female will be

SEX DETERMINATION

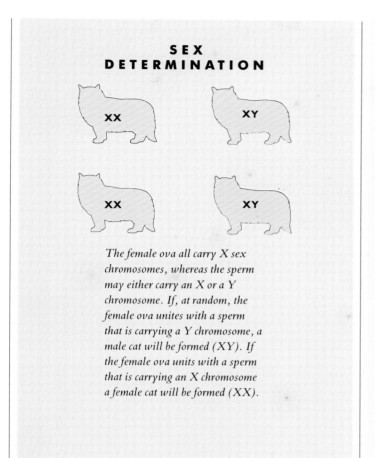

The female ova all carry X sex chromosomes, whereas the sperm may either carry an X or a Y chromosome. If, at random, the female ova unites with a sperm that is carrying a Y chromosome, a male cat will be formed (XY). If the female ova units with a sperm that is carrying an X chromosome a female cat will be formed (XX).

TORTOISESHELL GENETICS

The black and orange patterning on a 'tortie' typically occurs in female cats with one orange (O) and one non-orange (o) gene. It is linked to sex because the genetic message associated with this trait is normally only found on the female, X, chromosome.

Males normally only possess either the orange (O) genes or the non-orange (o) gene. But very rarely a genetic mistake occurs and a male with two X chromosomes, plus one Y chromosome, crops up (XXY). If one of these X chromosomes carries the orange (O) gene and the extra X chromosome carries the non-orange (o) gene, a tortoiseshell male is produced. However, the abnormality of his sex chromosomes means that he will not be a true male and will be sterile.

tortoiseshell colour. Since a male cat has only one X chromosome, he can only be O – in which case he will have a red coat colouring, or o, in which case he will not have a red coat. There are a few reported cases of apparently male cats that actually have a disorder of the sex chromosomes. For example, they may have two X chromosomes and one Y chromosome. Such a cat may appear to be a male Tortoiseshell, but is in fact a masculinized female, and will invariably prove sterile because of this chromosomal abnormality.

Genes which control an obvious characteristic such as colour are termed *major genes*. However, there are other genes whose effect is comparatively minor. These are termed *polygenes* because a number of them act together ('poly' meaning 'many') to bring about an effect such as controlling the actual shade of a colour. It is the polygenes which are responsible for the richness of colour in the selectively bred pedigree Tabby cat, as opposed to the duller hue of the mongrel Tabby.

Certain genes produce abnormalities leading to death or severe deformity, and are termed *lethal genes*, whilst *semi-lethal genes* produce less severe but still undesirable deformities. In breeds of livestock man has occasionally perpetuated a recessive lethal gene where the heterozygote form is felt to be attractive, as in the case of the Manx cat.

The lack of tail in the Manx is due to a dominant Manx gene, M. All Manx cats are heterozygous for this gene because homozygous MM cats invariably die before birth due to severe spinal deformities, the M gene proving lethal in the homozygote. The heterozygote shows the effects of the semi-lethal gene in some degree of spinal abnormality. In a good specimen of Manx this produces the short back and absence of tail, but some specimens are more seriously affected by spina bifida and an abnormal anal region.

The official bodies that govern the breeding and exhibition of pedigree cats review any new variety that arises and, if it is considered that a new mutation carries an undesirable semi-lethal factor, may refuse to recognize that variety. This means that kittens cannot be registered with the governing body as pedigree and cannot be exhibited. It is thereby hoped to prevent the perpetuation of harmful characteristics. If the Manx mutation were not long-established, it would probably not have been accepted by the cat fancy's governing bodies because of its semi-lethal nature. Recently, the Governing Council of the Cat Fancy in Great Britain has refused to recognize the Scottish Fold, with its mutation for ear shape which it is considered could lead to ear infections or deafness, and the Peke-faced Persian, which has a flat, compressed face like a Pekingese dog.

BREED CLASSIFICATION

Cat breeds are not as clearly distinct from each other as are dog breeds, the range of variation in shape and size being far less significant. Indeed, it was not until the late nineteenth century, when the cat fancy first became established on an official basis, that British fanciers first made a serious attempt to classify the breeds.

Initially colour was regarded as the significant factor in classification, but later a more consistent scheme was evolved on the basis of body type and origin (or supposed origin).

The stockily-built, broad-headed cats were designated 'British' in type, and the long-bodied, wedge-headed cats were classed as 'Foreign' or 'Exotic'. Modern classifications of cat breeds, although differing in detail from country to country, are essentially founded upon this distinction between types.

In Britain today all breeds are categorized into four groups. Coat length is one dividing factor: Longhairs (including the semi-longhaired varieties) form a group on their own. The Shorthairs are then divided into British and Foreign by body type, and amongst cats of Foreign type the Siamese varieties are considered so distinctive as to be separated out into a group of their own.

In the United States, the 'British' type is known as 'Domestic', certain breeds are considered to fall outside the British/Domestic and Foreign categories, and all Longhair breeds apart from the Angora, Balinese, Birman, Himalayan, Maine Coon and Turkish Van are classified as 'Persian', a term no longer officially recognized in Britain. Details within the standard for any one breed differ in many cases from those of the British cat fancy, often so much so that the same cat could not win its breed class in both countries.

RIGHT: *The Colourpoint is a Longhair with Siamese colouring. Like the Siamese, it comes in several colour schemes: this specimen is a Blue-cream. Longhairs are characterized by a cobby body, round head with small neat ears and large round eyes, and by a long silky coat.*

TOP: *Blue-eyed White Shorthair. The British Shorthair is a sturdy animal, with strong bones and a thick body set on short but well-proportioned legs. The head is apple-shaped, with small, slightly rounded ears and big round eyes.*

ABOVE: *The Burmese is a Foreign Shorthair, with the typical slim body, long legs and slender tail. The head is wedge-shaped, with large pricked ears and slanting eyes. Most Foreign Shorthair breeds have a particular predisposition for human company.*

Some varieties recognized by the Americans are not accepted in Britain, in some cases because a new variety is not considered to have established itself properly, and in some cases for health reasons, the variety being considered to carry a congenital undesirable weakness. Less frequently, varieties recognized in Britain are not accepted in the United States.

The official standards for each breed are controlled by a governing organization which seeks to promote consistency of standards as well as looking after the cat fancy as a whole. In Britain this is the Governing Council of the Cat Fancy (GCCF). In the United States there are nine associations, of which the Cat Fanciers' Association (CFA) is the most prominent.

Each breed is allotted a breed number: when a new breed is recognized a new number is provided for it. Different colours within a breed are usually referred to as varieties and take the same breed number followed by a distinguishing letter. For example, the original colour variety of the Burmese is Brown, which takes the number 27. Other colours were developed later, and so we now have such varieties as the Blue Burmese (27a) and Chocolate Burmese (27b), right down to the Lilac Tortie Burmese (27j).

BREED NUMBERS

LONGHAIRS

1	Black
2	White (Blue eyes)
2a	White (Orange eyes)
2b	White (Odd eyes)
3	Blue
4	Red Self
5	Cream
6	Smoke
6a	Blue Smoke
7	Silver Tabby
8	Brown Tabby
9	Red Tabby
10	Chinchilla
11	Tortoiseshell
12	Tortoiseshell-and-White
12a	Bi-coloured
13	Blue Cream
13a	Any Other Colour
13b	(1) Seal Colourpoint
	(2) Blue Colourpoint
	(3) Chocolate Colourpoint
	(4) Lilac Colourpoint
	(5) Red Colourpoint
	(6) Tortie Colourpoint
	(7) Cream Colourpoint
	(8) Blue-Cream Colourpoint
	(9) Chocolate-Cream Colourpoint
	(10) Lilac-Cream Colourpoint
	(11) Tabby Colourpoint
13c	Birman
13d	Turkish
50b	Self Chocolate
50c	Self Lilac
51	(1) Red Shell Cameo
	(2) Red Shaded Cameo
	(3) Red Smoke Cameo
	(4) Red Tortie Cameo
52	(1) Cream Shell Cameo
	(2) Cream Shaded Cameo
	(3) Cream Smoke Cameo
	(4) Blue-Cream Cameo
53	Pewter

SIAMESE

24	Seal Point Siamese
24a	Blue Point Siamese
24b	Chocolate Point Siamese
24c	Lilac Point Siamese
32	Tabby Point Siamese
32a	Red Point Siamese
32b	Tortie Point Siamese
32c	Cream Point Siamese
32x	A.O.C. Siamese

SHORTHAIRS

14	White (Blue eyes)
14a	White (Orange eyes)
14b	White (Odd eyes)
15	Black
16	British Blue
17	Cream
18	Silver Tabby
19	Red Tabby
20	Brown Tabby
21	Tortoiseshell
22	Tortoiseshell-and-White
25	Manx
25a	Stumpie Manx
25b	Tailed Manx
26	Any Other Variety
28	Blue-Cream
30	Spotted
31	Bi-Coloured
36	Smoke
39	British Shorthair Tipped

FOREIGN SHORTHAIRS

16a	Russian Blue
23	Abyssinian
23a	Sorrel Abyssinian
23c	Blue Abyssinian
27	Burmese (Brown)
27a	Blue Burmese
27b	Chocolate Burmese
27c	Lilac Burmese
27d	Red Burmese
27e	Tortie Burmese
27f	Cream Burmese
27g	Blue Tortie Burmese
27h	Chocolate Tortie Burmese
27j	Lilac Tortie Burmese
29	Havana
29c	Foreign Lilac
33	Cornish Rex
34	Devon Rex
35	Korat
37	Foreign White
37a	Foreign Black
38	Oriental Spotted Tabby
38a	Blue Oriental Spotted Tabby
38b	Chocolate Oriental Spotted Tabby
38c	Lilac Oriental Spotted Tabby
38d	Red Oriental Spotted Tabby
38f	Cream Oriental Spotted Tabby

BRITISH (DOMESTIC) SHORTHAIRS

These Western breeds originated from working non-pedigreed cats of Europe and North America. While these cats may at a first glance appear somewhat similar to a crossbreed cat, over the years the body shape and coat have been developed to a peak of perfection. The European Shorthairs are bred for a stocky, powerful body, with a broad chest, well-built legs and a thick, well-set tail. The head is round and broad with good width between the ears, full cheeks, a short, broad nose, good muzzle, with neat small ears, rounded at the top.

They are very tough and sturdy cats, with a calm and affectionate temperament that makes them ideal as family pets. They love to be a part of the family and are usually more than willing to share their home with other animal inmates.

These delightful creatures are active and graceful and show great interest in everything going on in the house and garden. Definitely on the credit side, they are not so destructive to furniture and curtains as some other breeds. They tend to sharpen their claws outside, often reserving a favourite tree for this purpose. They are also great believers in exercise and this keeps them in top condition.

The short coat requires only simple care from the human owner to keep it healthy and shining.

The fur is short, fine and close lying, and is found in any of the possible coat colours and patterns, although only a limited number are officially recognized by the governing bodies.

Self (plain) colours include Blue, Black, White and Cream, but there are also subtly shaded colours such as Smoke and Blue-cream. There are the various Tabby colours and patterns, and there are cats with a mixture of colours, the Bicolours and the Tortoiseshells.

The **BRITISH BLUE** and the **BLACK** are among the most popular short-haired breeds. The Blue should be level in colour with no tabby markings, shading, or white of any sort. Its large, full eyes should be copper, yellow or orange. The Black's coat should not show rusty tinges or any trace of white. Its eyes can be of deep copper or orange. Any trace of green is regarded as a fault.

The **WHITE** is an eye-catching variety, with its dazzling coat which must be free from any hint of yellow. It may be orange-eyed, blue-eyed or 'odd-eyed', with one eye of each colour. Unfortunately, congenital deafness often occurs in Blue-eyed Whites, due to a degeneration of the hearing apparatus deep within the ear that develops between four and six days after birth and can affect one or both ears.

LEFT: *The British Blue Shorthair is now considered to be indistinguishable from the Chartreuse, which originated at the monastery of La Grande Chartreuse in France during the Middle Ages. Once thought to be a distinct species, the breed is now amalgamated with the British Blue. Coat colour must be pure blue; eye colour must be orange. Quiet, calm and affectionate by nature, Blues make excellent pets.*

ABOVE: The Silver is one of the three short-haired Tabby varieties, the others being Red and Brown. In the Silver form the coat must be silver, with black tabby markings on top. As a general rule, all Tabbies have affectionate natures and make good pets, but the Silver Tabby is considered especially friendly.

RIGHT: Orange-eyed White Shorthair. Whites may have eyes that are blue, orange or odd – one of each.

*American breed standards differ from those of the British cat fancy. These are American Shorthairs: **LEFT**, a Blue Tabby, one of six tabby varieties recognized in the United States, and **ABOVE**, the American version of the Blue-cream, with the colours divided into patches.*

Odd-eyed Whites may be deaf on the side of the head which corresponds to the blue eye.

In spite of their appearance, Whites do not need a lot of extra attention to keep their coats clean – most are very fastidious, spending long periods licking and cleaning their fur.

CREAM Shorthairs are notoriously difficult to breed and because of this, are still comparatively rare. Occasionally, a natural Cream is born, but it is more usual for them to be striped or barred. There is, however, very little contrast in colour and few really good specimens are seen at today's shows.

The Cream is presumed to be a development of the Red Tabby because, genetically, cream is a dilute of red. The shade aimed at is a true, even cream colour, with no markings or paler fur, although lighter shades are given preference. Any signs of red at all along the back or elsewhere are penalized, while eye colour must be either copper or orange, as hazel is not now considered acceptable.

The **TABBY** Shorthair occurs in three recognized forms, and it is important for exhibition purposes that the tabby markings are clearly discernible. The standard tabby pattern is strictly laid down, and is not possessed by all those pet cats commonly called tabbies. The markings should be three dark stripes down the back, with an oyster shape on the sides and a butterfly mark on the back of the neck.

Clear markings should encircle the neck, throat and legs, while the tail is ringed all the way down to the tip, which should be of the darker colour. This form of patterning is termed the Blotched Tabby.

A modification of the classical tabby pattern is seen in the so-called Mackerel Tabbies. The markings in this case are reminiscent of a fish skeleton. A dark line runs along the back from head to tail, and bands run off from this down either side of the body. These need to be thin, yet complete and numerous.

Tabby cats probably received their name from the fact that their coat patterns recalled the markings on the watered silk – 'tabby' – made at Attabiy in ancient Baghdad.

Tabbies of both Blotched and Mackerel pattern occur in different colours. The Brown Tabby type is quite common among the mongrels, but the pedigree variety, which is of a much richer hue, is the least common of all tabbies. The ground colour is coppery brown, and there should be no trace of white fur or brindling, such as is commonly found in mongrel tabbies. Permitted eye colours are hazel, deep yellow or orange, while green is also acceptable under the CFA ruling.

Red Tabbies are red in colour, with a darker pattern of markings on their coat, and copper eyes. The familiar mongrel version is the 'ginger' or 'marmalade' cat, but the pedigree Red Tabby is definitely neither ginger nor orange,

LEFT: *The Manx cat is bred in the full spectrum of colours. This red tabby and white shows a vestigial bump where the tail should be in a normal breed.*

BELOW: *The Tortoiseshell carries three colours, black, red and cream. The colour is sex-linked and only occurs in females – the rare male is always sterile.*

and perhaps the most beautiful of the tabby types.

Finally, the Silver Tabby has a silver ground colour and black markings, with green or hazel eyes. Of all tabby varieties, the Silver is by far the most popular.

Akin to the Tabby is the **SPOTTED CAT**, an old short-haired breed portrayed in Egyptian myth as the killer of the serpent which represented evil. Originally this breed was classed as the Spotted Tabby, but tabby markings are no longer permitted apart from stripes on the head and face. The spots must be clearly defined and not over-lapping. The British standard is more rigorous than the American, specifying head markings to match those of a Tabby, and either broken rings or spots on the tail. Colours recognized are Brown, Red and Silver.

A quite different colouring type is found in the delicately shaded **BLUE-CREAM**. This colour is defined quite diffe-rently in different countries. In Britain, it is required to have blue and cream hairs evenly intermingled throughout the coat to create a unique soft pastel shading, a cream blaze on the face being favoured to set it off to advantage. In America, quite another effect is achieved by requiring the blue and cream to be separated in patches in the coat to form clearly delineated markings.

This discrepancy arose because the early Blue-creams sent to America had these markings, which the British were trying to breed out in favour of intermingling the colours, and this became the accepted pattern in the United States.

The **TORTOISESHELL** has a coat of three colours – black, red and cream. The markings should be distinct and bright, ideally with a red blaze on the head. As we have seen, this colour variety is genetically sex-linked, and only occurs in female cats. The rare male Tortoiseshell cat is invariably sterile. Tortoiseshell females must therefore be mated to other colours, usually Blacks or Creams, and produce a colourful mixture of kittens.

Add white to the attractive mix of colours and we have the ever-popular **TORTOISESHELL-AND-WHITE**. The deco-rative markings earned this variety the nickname of the 'Chintz cat' in Britain, and the 'Calico cat' in the United States. Like the Tortoiseshell, this colour is restricted to females. The amount of white present varies; for exhibi-tion purposes white should not appear to dominate, with predominantly coloured individuals being preferred.

The **BICOLOUR**, as its name suggests, is a two-tone cat, with a coat of any solid colour broken by white. Black and white ('Magpie') has always been the most popular colour combination; other acceptable shades include blue, cream and red. The patches of colour should be clearly marked and evenly distributed, with not more than two-thirds of the coat being coloured, and not more than half being white. The face is patched, ideally with a white blaze, and the eyes are orange or copper. Any tabby markings are frowned upon.

An unusual breed which may be found in any of the recognized Shorthair colours is the **MANX**, instantly identifiable by its lack of tail. The Manx has been called the 'Rabbit cat', from its rabbit-like hopping gait, derived from the combination of a shortened spine and long hindlegs; its coat, too, resembles a rabbit's, with a soft dense undercoat and rather long thick topcoat.

In fact, the length of the Manx tail is variable. The ideal, the 'rumpy', has no sign of a tail but just a dimple at the end of the vertebral column, but many individuals have

more than a vestige of tail. Some have a stub of a tail, usually with the vertebrae fused and immovable, and are called 'rumpy-risers'. Those with a stump significant enough to be moved, though often deformed and bent, are described as 'stubbies' or 'stumpies', while some, the 'longies', have a tail of nearly normal length.

As we have seen, the gene causing the Manx cat's absence or reduction of tail carries a lethal factor. Because kittens inheriting the Manx gene from both parents are so severely affected by spinal deformity as to die in the womb, it is necessary to mate the Manx with tailed individuals. Even so, some kittens are born with serious congenital abnormalities. Indeed, some cat fanciers are opposed to the breeding of Manx altogether for this reason.

Nevertheless, the Manx cat has been in existence for at least 500 years and has gained a special place in folklore. Apart from the Siamese, it is the most instantly recognizable breed, and has featured on the coinage of its native island. In spite of their genetic problems, Manx cats are delightful characters, and often live to an advanced age.

*The Manx is often considered to be a tailless cat, but the remnants of a tail are often present and these cats are described accordingly, depending on the actual tail length. The origins of the breed remain obscure, although its development was initially centred on the Isle of Man, off the west coast of England. Manx are bred in a variety of colours and markings, including white (**FAR LEFT**) and black and white patterns (**LEFT**)*

ABOVE: *The Spotted Cat is reputed to be an old breed—cats showing a similar pattern of markings were known in Ancient Egypt. The British standard is more specific over the precise pattern of markings than its American counterpart. Colours include the Silver Spotted (shown here), Red Spotted and Brown Spotted.*

SIAMESE AND FOREIGN SHORTHAIRS

The term foreign is not meant to indicate exotic lands of origin, although some of the ancestors of these animals probably came from far away places. The group includes types developed in North America, Europe and Britain. In general, the term can be said to indicate the appearance of the cat, with its slim sophisticated shape, long tail and slender legs. The heads of these beauties are wedge-shaped with large pricked ears and oriental slanted eyes. Most of them dislike the cat's usual solitary way of life and insist upon the company of humans, or of another cat if there are no available people.

The **SIAMESE** must be the best-known and certainly the most popular of the Foreign Shorthair type, although the cat fancy actually classifies them as a breed on their own distinct from the general Foreign Shorthair category. The characteristics of the Foreign type are taken to extremes in the Siamese, with its elongated, svelte body and long wedge-shaped head; in disposition, too, this breed takes the Foreign Shorthair's characteristic liking for human company to great lengths. The Siamese is probably the most demanding of all breeds, and yet in return must rate as the most responsive.

The evolution of Siamese is shrouded in mystery. Some authorities suggest the breed originated from temple cats kept in Burma. Another theory is that Siamese are descended from the sacred cats of Egypt. Some support for this idea comes from the resemblance of the Siamese to the cat goddess variously called Bast, Bubastis and Pasht. What is known for certain is that the breed was kept for centuries in Siam (Thailand) before it was brought to Britain. Ownership of the Siamese in its native land was a privilege confined to the royal family; only after protracted discussions lasting years was a Miss Walker permitted to take one pair plus a single queen to England. Siamese cats were first exhibited at a British show in 1871, where reaction to them was less than favourable. One contemporary report described them as 'unnatural'.

These early Siamese proved extremely delicate. Long before the era of antibiotics or vaccinations, they frequently succumbed to enteritis and respiratory diseases. Nevertheless, the breed was established in Britain and by 1880, Siamese were also seen in the United States. Many individuals suffered from squints and kinked tails. Such deformities were accepted by breeders at first and elaborate tales were told to justify their continued presence in the breed.

According to one story, Siamese were left to guard a highly prized temple vase and such was their devotion to the task that they never took their eyes away from the vase, which caused them to develop a squint. Their kinked tails supposedly resulted from holding the precious vessel.

In fact both these defects have a genetic origin. Both still sometimes occur in the breed, although to a much lesser degree than previously, and nowadays they merit disqualification when such cats are exhibited in shows.

The colouring of the Siamese is distinctive, with its light body colour and darker points – that is, ears, mask, paws and tail – and sapphire blue eyes. The original and still the most popular variety is the Seal Point, whose points are dark (seal) brown, but there are several 'colour schemes' to choose from: Blue Point, Chocolate Point, Lilac (or Frost) Point, Red Point, Tortoiseshell Point, Cream Point and Tabby (or Lynx) Point.

The Chocolate Point may have arisen as long ago as 1900, but this is not clear because the term 'chocolate' was also used for solid-coloured cats. It was certainly known by 1931, but was at first regarded as a poorly coloured Seal Point, although it was eventually recognized as a colour in its own right. The points are darker than in the Seal, and

*The Siamese is the best known of the Foreign Shorthair type cats. Its attractive colouring, piercing blue eyes and extrovert personality make it a cat hard to ignore. The range of colours is increasing all the time. The Seal Point (**LEFT**) is the original Siamese variety, and more recent developments include the Red Point (**ABOVE**) and Chocolate Point (**FAR LEFT**).*

to breed this colour were made over 80 years ago, but only since 1955 has there been a concerted effort to breed them. In the United States this variety bears the attractive and descriptive name of Frost Point.

Seal, Chocolate, Blue and Lilac Points are the four traditional breed colours, and the British cat fancy classifies these as one variety, grouping more recent colours such as Red under a separate heading although still under the classification of Siamese. Americans make a more significant distinction between these two categories, classing the latter colours as Colourpoint Shorthairs.

Since the Second World War a range of new colours of Siamese have been created, although such developments are not favoured by all breeders. This is because it proved necessary to use other breeds, such as the Abyssinian, to introduce the desired shading, and then to restore type by back-crossing to Siamese. Purists argue that some of the essential Siamese character must be lost by the introduction of non-Siamese blood.

The Red Point, with deep red points and a clear white body, and the Tortie Point, with points of red or cream or a combination of both, were among the first of the new colours to be bred. Tabby Points, known as Lynx Points in the United States, were recorded as long ago as 1902, when a Swedish geneticist deliberately created this form, but were not taken up as a colour variety until 1940 and remained scarce until the 1960s. Cream Points were also developed.

There have been problems over classification of these new forms. It proved impossible to distinguish between Red Points and Red Tabby Points by sight, although they are genetically distinct, and a similar problem arose with Tortie Points and Tortie Tabby Points.

Amongst the scarcer colours are the Silver Point, only currently recognized in New Zealand, the Shadow Point or Smoke Point, the Cinnamon Point and the Lavender Point. Perhaps the most striking of this group is the Albino, a pure white form with blue eyes rather than the red eyes of the true albino and described in Britain as the Recessive White. American breeders classify such cats as Oriental Shorthairs.

Irrespective of colour, the beauty, personality and sheer exoticism of the Siamese have made it a popular pet, ideal for owners who want to relate closely to their cat – in many ways the Siamese temperament is more like that of a dog. However, it is not for those who feel that cats should be seen and not heard! It is probably the most demanding of breeds and yet in return must rate amongst the most reponsive.

The lively nature and acrobatic disposition of the Siamese can prove overwhelming on occasions, especially if the cat is housed permanently indoors; many owners find that the solution is to take their pet out for walks using a harness

the body colour is ivory rather than the creamy shade of the older variety.

The Blue Point could have been bred as early as 1896 and was certainly known before 1900. This variety may have been bred earlier in Siam, where solid blue cats were known and, crossed with Seal Points, would have yielded Blue Points. They are a most striking form, with a frosty, glacial white body colour blending into blue along the back and with somewhat darker blue points. Early specimens were of a rather poor type and were crossed with Seals to improve the head shape, possible at the expense of ideal coloration.

The Lilac Point is a difficult variety to produce. The points should be a delicate shade of pinkish-grey, with faded lilac pads and nose offset against a milky body coloration. All too often the points tend towards blue on the nose and towards chocolate on the tail. The first attempts

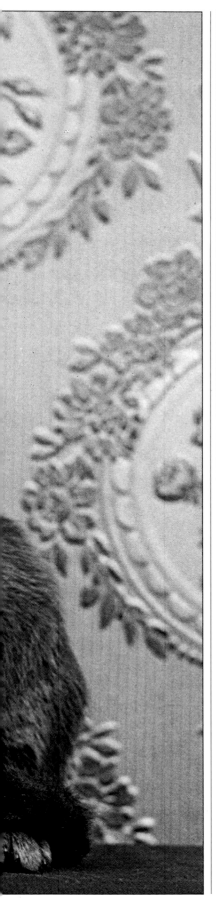

One of the most popular pedigree breeds, the Burmese is now being produced in different colour varieties, not all of them officially recognized. **LEFT:** *the Chocolate, or Champagne, Burmese.* **BELOW:** *the Lilac, or Platinum, Burmese.*

LEFT: *Until 1963 the original Brown Burmese (shown here) was the only colour recognized, and many breeders today still maintain that this is the only acceptable form of the breed.*

RIGHT: *The Blue Point Siamese was first recognized officially in the 1930s and continues to be a popular variety.*

RIGHT: *The Foreign Black (Ebony Oriental Shorthair in the United States) has a long body, giving it a svelte and elegant appearance. Its close relationship with the Siamese is further emphasized by the occasional existence of a squint and a kinked tail, two faults inherited from that breed. In Britain the Foreign Black is not officially recognized as a separate breed: only Foreign Whites and Lilacs are accepted. In the United States, a much wider range of colours is accepted, ranging from selfs, shaded colours, smokes and tabbies to parti-colours.*

BELOW: *The Cornish Rex is a cat of fairly normal build with a poodle-like curly coat. It has a long thin tail, long legs, a straight nose and a moderately dense coat.*

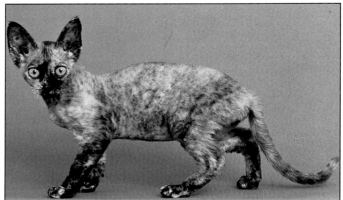

ABOVE: *The Devon Rex is an odder-looking variety than its Cornish cousin. Its much wider ears and shorter nose create a face quite unlike that of any other breed.*

RIGHT: *The Tabby Point Siamese is known as the Lynx Point in the United States.*

and lead. Siamese are almost uniquely noisy, using their raucous voices to inform and demand. They can also be extremely affectionate but, if roused, are likely to be difficult to handle. The sexual side of their nature is highly developed, and neutering is essential if the cat is not to be bred from, the queens maturing very early and tending to be particularly loud and demanding when in season.

A breed on its own, the Siamese is the perfect pet for some owners and definitely a cat to be avoided for others.

There are several breeds deriving from the Siamese, generally retaining its type and temperament but varying in colour. Amongst these are the varieties known as Foreign Colours in Britain and as Oriental Shorthairs in the United States, which might be described as a self-coloured version of the Siamese, which they resemble in type and character. The British cat fancy recognizes only two colours for championship purposes, the **FOREIGN LILAC**, a frosty grey with a pinkish tinge, and the **FOREIGN WHITE**, a distinctive blue-eyed pure white variety. In America a wider range of colours is recognized.

Another self-coloured breed is the **HAVANA**, a rich brown coloured cat with green eyes, developed again from the Siamese, in the 1950s. British and American Havanas diverge in appearance and temperament, the British form having a more foreign appearance and livelier nature than its American counterpart, the result of British breeders' preference for developing the breed on the lines of the Siamese.

A most distinctive variety which owes some of its ancestry to the Siamese is the **BURMESE**. Like the Siamese, the Burmese has a shaded coat, with the points darker than the body colour, but the contrast is far less extreme. The traditional Brown variety is a rich seal colour with darker sepia points, but other colour forms are not being bred, some recognized by the governing bodies of the cat fancy and some not.

In the same way as the Blue Point Siamese was produced as a dilution of the Seal Point, a Blue Burmese has been established. This is a relatively pale blue, really a silver-grey, and at present has a poorer quality coat than the Brown. The Chocolate (termed Champagne in the United States), which is a creamy brown with darker points, and the Lilac (Platinum in the United States), which is greyish with a pinkish tinge, were largely developed in the 1970s. Further variations include Creams, Reds, Blue-creams and Tortoiseshells. The British cat fancy recognizes more of these colour varieties than the North American fancy. In the United States a longhaired form, described as the Tiffany, has been developed, but has not yet achieved official acceptance.

The Burmese has a definite Siamese look, with a long, lithe body, pointed head and slanted eyes. The demanding personality of the Siamese is tempered, however, to create an equally friendly and self-confident but less demanding and highly-strung animal which makes a delightful pet.

Diverging from the Siamese-descended breeds, we come to the **RUSSIAN BLUE**, a most attractive cat of a distinctive medium blue shade with a sparkling sheen given by silver-tipped hairs. Despite its name, the true origin of this breed is unknown, although it is said to have been brought to Britain in 1860 by sailors trading from the Baltic port of Archangel, and was once known as the Archangel Blue.

Another blue-grey breed with a silvery sheen is the **KORAT**, which is relatively rare in Britain, although more popular in North America. It is highly prized in its native Thailand, where it has existed for centuries and is regarded as a symbol of good fortune. The Korat is not very hardy, lacking an undercoat, and can suffer from chills and respiratory infections in cooler climates.

Different again is the **ABYSSINIAN**, a variety similar in appearance to the sacred cats portrayed in Ancient Egyptian art, although it is probably not a direct descendant but a manufactured breed created in Britain at the turn of the century by the skilful breeding of Tabbies. Like the cats depicted in Egyptian wall paintings, it is lithe and slender in build (although less elongated in shape than the Siamese) with a long tapering tail, wedge-shaped head, large pointed ears and large eyes.

The coat of the Abyssinian is unusual; ticked with black or dark brown, it resembles rabbit fur in its soft and un-catlike shading. The usual colour is a ruddy golden-brown the underparts lacking ticking to appear an orangish-brown shade. There is also a red mutation, known as the Sorrel Abyssinian, with a rich copper colouring; and a Blue variety is being developed.

The lively and affectionate personality of the Abyssinian makes it a popular pet. Less demanding than the Siamese, it shares the breed's responsiveness to its human family.

New breeds are continually being developed or imported, and one such which resembles the Abyssinian in type is the **EGYPTIAN MAU**, which has been kept in its homeland for many generations, but was first brought to the United States in the 1950s and did not reach Britain until 1978. This breed bears a close resemblance to the spotted tabbies depicted in Egyptian art as long ago as 1400 BC and may be the only modern breed to be naturally spotted. Its markings follow a prescribed pattern; the forehead bears a characteristic 'M' pattern, with frown marks extending back and separating into individual spots along the spine. These coalesce again over the hips, to form a solid line. The tail is banded with thick stripes and ends in a dark tip. Two 'mascara' lines are recognized around each of the eyes, extending to the sides of the face. Barring is seen on the legs, with distinct matching spots being preferred on the body itself. On the underparts, spotting should contrast against the relatively light coat colour. These markings are far more important in exhibition terms than the body colour. Three colours are recognized: Bronze (with brown markings), Silver (with charcoal markings) and Smoke (with pure black markings). Green eyes are preferred, but amber is also permitted. In character, this is an active but relatively quiet cat, affectionate towards its own circle, but reserved with strangers.

Until recently there were only two types of coat in cats, the longhair and the shorthair, but then a genetic mutation gave rise to perhaps the most unusual breed to come under the Foreign category, the curly-coated **REX**. In fact there

ABOVE: *Burmese resemble the Siamese in shape but have a more civilised personality. The Brown variety is the oldest colour form.*

LEFT: *The Brown Tortie Burmese is one of the more unusual recent developments.*

BELOW: *The Somali is a longhaired form of the Abyssinian, first developed in the 1960s.*

RIGHT: *The Russian Blue has a very soft, short fur, a medium blue in colour with a silvery tinge.*

were two mutations, one in 1950 in Cornwall and one in 1960 in the neighbouring county of Devon, giving rise to two varieties, the Cornish and the Devon Rex. Both have the characteristic curly coat, rather thinner in the Devon variety, but type is quite different. The two mutations are genetically distinct and if mated together give birth only to straight-coated kittens.

The **CORNISH REX** is the less exaggerated of the two varieties. With its slender medium-length body, long legs and medium wedge-shaped head, it may be described as a cat of more or less normal type with a 'poodle' coat.

The very different **DEVON REX**, on the other hand, is so unusual in appearance that it has been called 'the cat from outer space'. Certainly it is a strange, pixie-like creature. The short wedge head, little pointed face with full cheeks and short nose, the large low-set batwing ears and enormous wide-spaced eyes give it a permanently startled appearance. The body is smaller and more broad-chested than in the Cornish variety, and the hindlegs are longer than the forelegs.

The Devon Rex is a unique breed which people tend to fine either very appealing indeed or quite off-putting in appearance.

Both Rex varieties are now bred in a wide variety of colours. They make good pets, with their lively, affectionate and inquisitive personalities. The curly coat has the advantage of shedding less than normal fur, requiring little grooming and making them ideal pets for anyone with an allergy to cat hair who does not wish to let this prevent them from owning a cat. Some special care is needed to keep them warm, as the thin coat (especially in the Devon variety) does not provide much insulation. The large, open ears may be vulnerable to dust and should be checked and cleaned regularly.

RIGHT: *'The cat from outer space', the Devon Rex. This study clearly shows the unusual appearance created by the imposing batwing ears, startled-looking round eyes and crinkled whiskers.*

BELOW: *The Cornish Rex is the 'poodle cat', with its curly or wavy, rippling coat.*

LONGHAIRS

Longhairs are of course distinguished by their long, soft and silky fur, but also typically by their physical conformation, which is massive and cobby with short thick legs.

The head should be round and broad with full cheeks and a short, snub nose. The ears should be small, neat and spaced well apart, and the eyes should be large and round. The cat's tail should be short and thick, and the coat long and silky, with no woolliness.

The longhaired breeds probably arose as a simple mutation of the gene for coat length. It has been suggested that the longhaired wild species Pallas's cat (see page 13) may have been interbred with domestic cats to introduce this factor. Pallas's cat has been reported to be kept in semi-domestication in Central Asia, but modern zoologists tend to believe that it is unlikely to have contributed to the development of our modern Longhairs.

As far as is known the first Longhairs appeared in the East. The earliest record of their appearance in Europe is that of a seventeenth-century Italian traveller who brought back a pair from Persia. Longhaired cats were generally known as Persians until quite recently, and are still given this name in the United States.

It is not known when Longhairs first appeared in Great Britain. Certainly by the nineteenth century they were occasionally advertised for sale, at very high prices, and some were exhibited at the first cat show held in Britain in 1871, although their rise to popularity did not begin until later in the century.

Longhairs are renowned for their placid and gentle temperaments, usually making excellent pets and probably able to adapt to a life indoors better than most cats. The long coat makes daily attention from an early age essential, and a Longhair is not for you if you are looking for a cat that will not take up much of your time.

Most of the colours found in the British Shorthair have their Longhair counterparts with a similar colour standard – Black, White, Bicolour, Red, Cream, Blue-cream, Tabby, Tortoiseshell, Tortoiseshell-and-White and Smoke. There are also some colours specific to Longhairs.

The **BLUE** is perhaps the most popular and occurs in various shades from a deep true blue through grey to almost lavender. The early specimens often showed tabby features as well as white markings, which are not permitted today. Kittens are often hard to assess for colour, as they not infrequently display tabby markings which may disappear with the baby coat to be replaced by the correct self-colouring. The eyes are brilliant orange, set off against the delicately coloured fur.

BLACKS are one of the oldest varieties. Ideally they should be as black as coal, with deep orange or copper eyes. Like blues, they are hard to evaluate as kittens, when a potentially correctly coloured animal may appear greyish or brindled. The adult coat will easily become rusty-coloured if the cat spends much time sun-bathing, so pets which are allowed full freedom are very rarely perfectly coloured.

WHITES, like their Shorthair counterparts, may have blue, orange or odd-coloured eyes, and the Blue-eyed variety may suffer from deafness. This is a particularly glamorous colour variety, and it is important for exhibition purposes that the white be as pure as possible, without any rusty tinge or yellowing. Whites are believed to be the very oldest of the longhaired breeds.

The **RED** is one of the most difficult varieties to breed successfully for exhibition because the standard's require-

The Cameo is a breed typified by contrasting colours, with a white underocat and the tips of the hairs coloured. The actual intensity of the colour varies, but should be deepest around the head, on the feet and legs, and along the back. Varieties include the Cream Shaded (RIGHT). Cameos are popular in the United States and are currently on the increase in Britain.

ABOVE: *The Shaded Silver is somewhat similar in appearance to the Chinchilla, though darker in colour. At one time the breeds were amalgamated in Britain, although outside the country the distinction has always remained. In Britain today, the Shaded Silver is re-emerging as a breed in its own right.*

ABOVE: *Highly popular during the last century, the Brown Tabby Longhair is now relatively obscure. The problem of finding suitable outcrosses may have contributed to the Brown Tabby's fall from popularity, and pairing these cats together over several generations results in a loss of type. It is also not easy to produce the desired sable coloration.*

RIGHT: *The Bicolour Longhair has been bred in a variety of colour combinations, set against white. The original form was black and white but blue, cream or red are now acceptable. For exhibtion purposes, the areas of colour must be clearly delineated and a good contrast between the coloured areas and the white is significant,. The long coats of these cats need regular grooming to keep them in the best possible condition.*

RIGHT: *The Black Longhair is a striking cat. The colour takes some time to develop, however, and is likely to be fairly poor until the cat is about six months old. Individuals which seem unpromising at an early age may well develop into adults with jet black coats. The coat will easily fade in sunlight, however.*

BELOW: *Cameos are a more recent creation, first bred in the United States in 1954. Five basic colours are recognized, including the Red Shaded (***BELOW LEFT***) and the Red Tortie (***BELOW RIGHT***).*

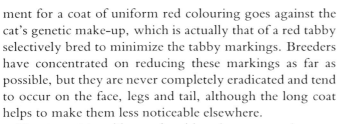

ment for a coat of uniform red colouring goes against the cat's genetic make-up, which is actually that of a red tabby selectively bred to minimize the tabby markings. Breeders have concentrated on reducing these markings as far as possible, but they are never completely eradicated and tend to occur on the face, legs and tail, although the long coat helps to make them less noticeable elsewhere.

The **CREAM** is a dilute red and has the same tendency to produce tabby markings, which are a fault. The early Creams were Fawns, and later it was stipulated that the desired shade was that of Devonshire cream. This has been modified further to require a shade classed as 'pale to medium' under British rules, whereas American breeders aim for an even buff colour. Various shades are produced today, the important feature being evenness of colour, and the avoidance of 'hot' reddish fur.

The earliest Creams were of a different type to that regarded as typical Longhair conformation today. They had bigger ears and noses, longish heads, and a rather long body shape. They were crossed with Blues to improve their type, and this gave rise to the beautiful Blue-cream

As with the Shorthair variety, the **BLUE-CREAM** standard differs significantly between Britain and the United States, the former country aiming for an intermingling of the blue and cream hairs while the latter requires them to be separated into distinct patches. The British version when applied to a long coat achieves a wonderful shot-silk pastel effect.

TABBY Longhairs occur in Brown, Red and Silver, with the United States also recognizing Cream and Blue varieties The Brown Tabby Longhair is the oldest colour variety, but, although very popular during the last century, it is now relatively rare, as is the Silver Tabby. The tabby

ABOVE: *The Blue Longhair has been popular ever since 1889 when Queen Victoria bought one, thus setting an instant trend. This colour tends to be of particularly strong type, males in particular being very large, stocky cats.*

LEFT: *One of the most admired of the long-haired breeds is the Chinchilla. Despite its delicate and almost fairy-like appearance, this is a sturdy animal which does not require coddling.*

markings are softened by the long coat, which tends to break up the clarity of the pattern.

TORTOISESHELLS and **TORTOISESHELL-AND-WHITES** remain popular, with their combination of bold colouring and decoratively long fur, as do the **BICOLOURS**.

The **SMOKE** is another spectacular Longhair variety, although it is not easy to produce a good specimen and this colour has always been rare. Two colour varieties are recognized, the Black and the Blue. In both, the undercoat is white and the topcoat coloured, so that when the cat moves the contrast of colour is most pronounced, although considerable grooming is needed to show this feature to best advantage. One of the most prominent features is the silvery ruff around the neck, contrasting with the black or blue head. The tiny coloured ears have silvery tufts, and the legs and paws are solidly coloured.

In the United States, where this variety has always been popular, new colour varieties are being developed, including the Cameo Smoke and Tortoiseshell Smoke.

Smokes are often outcrossed to Blues or Blacks to maintain type, and it is often hard to identify the Smoke kittens out of a litter as they are born almost black and it may take several months before the colour becomes apparent. Breeders of Smokes will often retain kittens until about six months because of the difficulty of identifying a good specimen in the early stages. Even when a potential show winner has been picked out, this is one of the hardest varieties to produce in top exhibition condition: indeed, the coat may only be at its peak for about two months every year.

Shading is also a feature of the **CHINCHILLA**, which at a casual glance could be taken for a white cat with emerald or blue-green eyes. On closer inspection, however, the fur proves to comprise a white undercoat and delicately black-tipped top coat which creates a sparkling silvered effect. This black tipping occurs on the back, flanks, head, tail and sometimes lightly on the legs, the chin, chest and stomach being pure white. In the early days of this variety's appearance some confusion arose with a slightly darker version known as the **SHADED SILVER**, and in Britain the two were amalgamated in 1902. In the United States, however, the Shaded Silver continued to be recognized as a variety in its own right, and now it is beginning to re-emerge in Britain.

A recent development amongst the shaded varieties is the **CAMEO**, another two-toned cat with a white or silver undercoat and red tips to the hairs of the topcoat. Genetically it is either an orange chinchilla or a red smoke. Variation in the amount of top colour has created five colour varieties. The Shell Cameo is the lightest of these, with a very white undercoat topped with pale orange shading. The Red

ABOVE: *The Birman is said to have had an illustrious history and is sometimes known as the Sacred Cat of Burma. Many breeders believe, however, that the breed was created in recent times from Siamese/Longhair crosses. The typical areas of white on the paws are referred to as gloves, whereas the white areas extending up the hindlegs are known a gauntlets, terminating at points called the laces.*

LEFT: *The Colourpoint combines Siamese markings with Longhair coat and body type. This specimen demonstrates the original Seal Point colouring, but Blue, Chocolate, Red, Lilac and Tortie Points are also recognized, with further shades acceptable in some countries.*

TOP: *The ever-popular Tortoiseshell-and-White.*

ABOVE: *The Blue Longhair with its brilliant orange eye colouring.*

LEFT: *The Maine Coon is a hardy North American breed, developed in New England during the latter part of the nineteenth century.*

Shaded or Shaded Cameo shows noticeably darker shading and has a white-cream belly with red or cream on the sides, according to the American standard. The Smoke Cameo or Red Smoke shows considerably more shading and has red bands on the body, referred to as 'ticking'. The two other variants are the Shaded and Shell Tortoiseshell varieties, which like other Tortoiseshell are exclusively female. In addition, Cream Cameos have been bred, but are excluded under current standards.

Copper eyes are favoured, although the use of Chinchilla blood in the creation of this variety has left its mark in a tendency towards green eye colouring.

The breed has grown rapidly in popularity in the United States and is now recognized in Britain.

A delightful combination of the Siamese with the Longhair gave us the **COLOURPOINT**, a cat with Siamese markings imposed upon the coat and cobby body type of the Longhair.

In the United States the breed is known as the Himalayan because the coat patterning is similar to that of the Himalayan rabbit. Further confusion over nomenclature arose when

the description 'Khmer' was used on mainland Europe for a brief period. These cats are also classified differently within the longhaired category on opposing sides of the Atlantic. British breeders class them as a colour variety of the Longhair, whereas they are considered a distinct breed in the United States.

The colours recognized are generally as for the Siamese: Seal-point, Blue-point, Chocolate-point, Red- (Flame-) point, Lilac-point and Tortie-point are accepted in both Britain and the United States, while the former also acknowledges Cream varieties and American fanciers extend the list to include Tabby- (Lynx-)point and Blue-cream-point, as well as solid-coloured Chocolates and Lilacs produced by permitted cross-breeding with Longhairs to improve type.

Colour contrast is less intense than in the Siamese, as the points darken in response to local environmental temperature, the effect of which is reduced by the insulating properties of the long coat.

In character the Colourpoint falls midway between its parent breeds, being bolder and more inquisitive than a

NORWEGIAN FOREST CAT

The Norwegian Forest Cat is a very hardy breed, somewhat reminiscent of the Maine Coon in appearance, although the two breeds are totally unrelated. The Norwegian Forest Cat has a long, weather-proof coat in two layers, the woolly undercoat providing warmth, the glossy outer coat keeping out rain and snow. Despite the length of the coat, these cats are not difficult to groom and the coat does not mat or tangle easily. The hindlegs are longer than the forelegs, making the rump higher than the shoulders. Still rare outside Scandinavia – only 16 were registered in the United States in 1982, Norwegian Forest Cats are particularly noted for their disposition. They have a reputation for making affectionate and intelligent pets.

Longhair, but less so than a Siamese. they are truly beautiful cats when well kept, but require every bit as much attention as any other Longhair.

Two slightly less long-haired cats recognized in Britain are the Birman and the Turkish Van.

The **BIRMAN** is a shaded cat with dark points, differing from the Colourpoint in its shorter hair, more oriental type and characteristic white paws.

The history of this Longhair is obscure, although its alternative name, Sacred Cat of Burma, suggests that it originated in the East. These cats, according to legend, were kept at the Temple of Lao-Tsun, which housed an image of a golden goddess, Tsuyn Kyan-Kse. One of the cats there, called Sinh, formed a close attachment to the head priest, Mun-Ha. During a raid on the temple centuries ago, Mun-Ha was killed while praying and as he lay dying, he was touched by Sinh who was suddenly transformed. The cat's yellow eyes changed to blue, like those of the goddess, and the fur of the body became golden. His face, tail and legs took on a brown hue, but where his paws were in contact with the priest, the fur was pure white, which symbolized goodness.

Sinh himself died shortly afterwards, but the dramatic change in his appearance encouraged the remaining priests to fight off the attack. When they met to choose a successor to Mun-Ha, the priests were amazed to observe that all the temple cats had changed like Sinh. When the cats surrounded one of the priests, called Lioa, this was taken as a sign of divine choice, and Lioa became the new head priest.

As with all legends of origin, the individual is at liberty to believe that his cat is descended directly from the temple cats of the East, or, as some breeders consider, that it is another recent creation derived like the Colourpoint from selected Longhairs and Siamese.

Birmans are not usually temperamental cats, and this, coupled with their striking appearance, has made them increasingly popular.

The **TURKISH VAN** is also spectacularly marked, its chalk white coat setting off brilliant auburn markings on head and tail. This variety has sometimes been called the 'Swimming Cat' from its unique penchant for water.

The Van cat is generally accepted to be a colour variety of the Turkish breed known as the Angora, recognized in the United States but merged with the basic Longhair form in Britain. A British 'Angora' has been recreated from judicious crossing of Oriental Shorthairs carrying Longhair genes; although this form physically resembles the original variety, traces of Siamese blood remain in voice and character which distinguish it from the American Angora.

A North American Longhair which is beginning to appear in Britain is the large and handsome **MAINE COON CAT**. This takes its unusual name from the fancy that its large size and bold coat patterning in the brown tabby form derived from hybridization between a cat and a raccoon. Originally a working cat, catching vermin on farms, its striking appearance (toms can weigh up to 15½lb (7kg)), physical hardiness and companionable nature make it an attractive pet. There is a similar though unrelated European breed in the form of the **NORWEGIAN FOREST CAT**.

LEFT: *The Turkish Van Cat is closely related to the Angora and originated from the area around Lake Van in Turkey. An unusual breed, one of the most striking peculiarities of these cats is the fact that they appear to enjoy water and will even choose to bathe. They have white coats with auburn markings on the face and tail. Like Angoras, they do not have a thick undercoat.*

ABOVE: *The Blue-Cream Longhair achieves a shot-silk pastel effect with its mingled colours.*

ABOVE: *The Tortoiseshell Longhair has a coat of three colours – black, red and cream.*

LEFT: *The desired orange eye colour of the Blue Longhair took time to establish, at first occurring only in darker-coloured specimens but today selective breeding has produced light Blues with good eye colour.*

SOME ODDITIES

New cat varieties are developing all the time, sometimes from deliberate cross-breeding of existing forms and sometimes arising as a spontaneous genetic mutation.

Deliberate cross-breeding is undertaken to create a new variety mingling the virtues of the parent breeds, as we have already seen in the Colourpoint (see page 74). Other examples currently being developed include the **TONKINESE**, a pretty Siamese-Burmese hybrid which arose in Canada, the **BURMILLA**, another Burmese cross, and the **BOMBAY**, a North American black cat developed from sable brown Burmese and black American Shorthairs.

Genetic mutations may be more dramatic and can be used to create a completely new breed such as the Rex (see page 64), with its unique curly-coat. Probably the best-known example is the tailless Manx (see page 56). Many of the lesser-known varieties have not been granted universal recognition by the cat fancy, because it is felt that they carry some genetic weakness which ought not to be perpetuated.

A mutation of coat type comparable to that of the Rex arose in 1960 in New York, when a kitten was born with a unique wiry coat and became the ancestor of the **AMERICAN WIREHAIR**. This mutation had also occurred in Britain a few years earlier, but no decision was made in that case to establish the variety. In the United States, however, when study of the hair of the mutant had revealed that its structure was unlike that of other similar cats, such as Rexes, a deliberate policy of line breeding was undertaken to establish the Wirehair on the same lines as the American Shorthair. The breeders' quest has been helped by the fact that wiry hair is a dominant feature, so cats with such coats can be bred in the first generation following the mating of a Wirehair to a Shorthair of good conformation. The use of longhaired breeds has been avoided in order to maintain the distinctive appearance of the coat. This must not be patchy, although on some parts of the body, typically the underparts, it is not quite so wiry. The Wirehair has a similar temperament to the American Shorthair.

A more controversial mutation gave rise to the **SPHYNX**, or Hairless Cat, which first appeared in Canada in 1966 and was subsequently established by crossing with American Shorthairs. Apparently naked at first glance, the Sphynx does possess a thin, down-like coat, notably on the extremities of the body.

There is considerable opposition to the breeding of this bizarre variety, and neither the CFA nor the GCCF recognize the Sphynx, although some smaller American associations accept them. Despite their rather grotesque appearance, however, if thise cats are kept warm, they do not appear to present any significant problems with regard to care.

Another controversial variety, again not recognized in Britain on the grounds of health problems, is the **PEKE-FACE PERSIAN**, a variant of the Red and Red Tabby Longhairs, in which facial appearance has been developed to resemble that of a Pekingese dog. As a result the nose appears abnormally compressed into the face, and there are excessive skin folds in the facial area.

Given their reduced and distorted facial characteristics, it is not surprising that these cats can suffer from respiratory difficulties, as well as overcrowding of teeth in the mouth. Tear-staining of the fur, because of deviation and constriction of the ducts draining the eyes, has also been reported. In order to try to maintain some normality of function in the facial region, breeders typically pair Peke-faces with the appropriate form of the Red Longhair, rather than to each other.

The **SCOTTISH FOLD** arose in 1961 in Scotland. This variety differs from all other breeds in having folded, flat ears. Like the wirehair gene, the folded-ear gene proved

LEFT: *Amongst recently created breeds, the Bombay is one of the more attractive varieties. This sleek black cat is derived from Burmese crossed with black American Shorthairs. The coat should resemble satin in texture and should lie close to the body. The body is reminiscent of the Burmese; a strong, intense copper is the preferred eye colour. The breed was given a standard in the United States in 1976, but has not yet received one in Britain.*

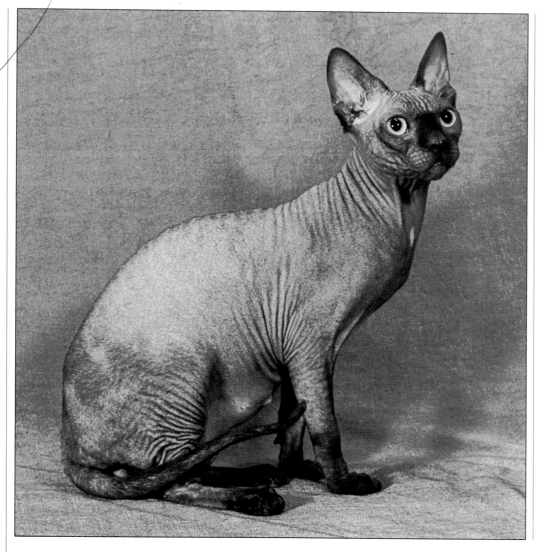

LEFT: *The Sphynx is sometimes referred to as the Hairless Cat, although this breed does possess a thin covering of hair, notably on the extremities of the body. The first hairless cat appeared in Canada in 1966 and the breed was subsequently established using American Shorthairs as out-crosses. Refused recognition by most official associations, the Sphynx remains a controversial breed.*

dominant and the variety was therefore easily established. However, in the 1970s the Governing Council of the Cat Fancy of Great Britain decided to stop permitting regis-tration of the breed, partly because it was felt that the unusual ear shape might give rise to infections, and partly because the folded-ear gene can also produce a thickening of the tail and hindlegs, interfering with normal movement. The breed is nonetheless popular in the United States, where attempts are being made to minimize the latter prob-lem and a wide range of colours has been bred.

A happier and longer-established mutation is that which gives rise to the **JAPANESE BOBTAIL**, known in its native country for centuries. The distinctively bobbed tail may prove to be as long as 5in (12.5cm) at its maximum length, but only appears to be about half this size under normal conditions when it is held in an upright position.

The mutation concerned is quite different from that which gave rise to the Manx. Manx taillessness arises from a dominant gene causing some degree of deformity to the whole spine, whereas the Bobtail condition is recessive and does not carry the risk of spina bifida.

In Japan, these cats are regarded as providing good fortune for their owners. The variety most in demand is the *Mi-ke* or three-furred type, which corresponds to the tortoiseshell-and-white form of other breeds. The coat is comprised of a combination of red, white and black fur.

The Bobtail was introduced into the United States in the 1960s, but remains scarce elsewhere. With its introduction to the West, emphasis was placed on colours which cor-respond to the original Japanese form. Tricolours are there-fore favoured, along with composite colours such as Whites, Blacks and Reds. Bicolours, being black or red and white are also recognized, along with a tortoiseshell form. The development of the breed in the United States has given rise to other colours as well, so that now only Siamese markings and the agouti appearance of the Abyssinian are expressly forbidden.

With its engaging appearance, highly sociable and affec-tionate nature and exotic origin, it will be surprising if the Bobtail's popularity does not spread further afield.

ABOVE: *New breeds are continually being developed. One such is the Burmilla, derived from the Burmese. Recognition of new breeds and varieties depends on the organization and country concerned.*

ABOVE AND LEFT: *The characteristic tail of the Japanese Bobtail resembles that of a rabbit. The breed has been introduced to the United States from Japan, but remains scarce elsewhere. Colours include black and white (**LEFT**) and red tabby-and-white (**ABOVE**).*

RIGHT AND BELOW: *The Scottish Fold is instantly recognized by its folded flat ears. Now banned from exhibition in Britain, because of fears that the unusual ears might give rise to infections or deafness, the breed is nevertheless popular in North America, where it has been bred in a wide range of colours. Folded- and normal-eared kittens are identical at birth, folding beginning to show at four weeks.*

BELOW: *The Peke-face resembles the Red forms of the Longhair in all respects except its face, which is compressed in the manner of the Pekingese dog. This characteristic may give rise to certain health problems, and, while popular in some areas of the United States, the breed is not recognized in Britain.*

ABOVE: *The Tonkinese is a Siamese/Burmese hybrid.*
ABOVE RIGHT: *Scottish Fold.*
RIGHT: *American Wirehair.*

RIGHT: *The steward lifts each cat out of its pen and holds it for examination by the judge. The show cat needs to be confident when handled by strangers. If it is nervous in its pen and tries to hide, or if it tries to escape while being held and examined, then it is obviously not going to display itself to best advantage. A cat's temperament is important if it is to be exhibited: proud, quiet cats will create a more favourable impression than those which are wriggling and anxious.*

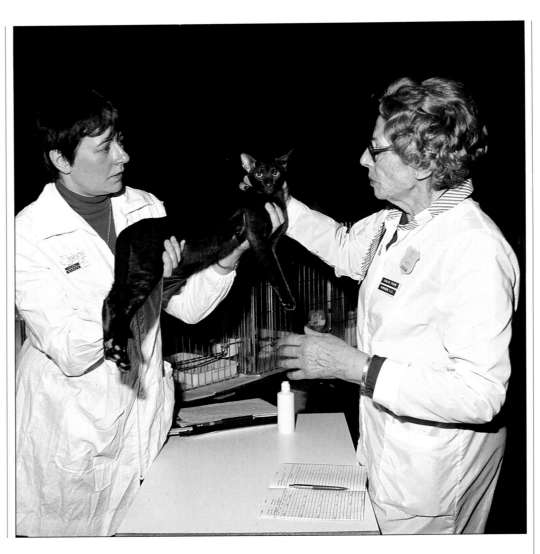

THE CAT SHOW

The public showing of cats can be traced back to 1598, when a number were exhibited as part of the St Giles's Fair, held at Winchester in Hampshire, England. During subsequent years, occasional shows were held in association with such events, but only towards the end of the nineteenth century did serious competitons involving cats begin in earnest. Harrison Weir conceived the idea of selectively breeding and then exhibiting cats, and established the first standards, described as Points of Exhibition, to which exhibits are still judged today.

The first major show was staged at Crystal Palace on 13 July 1871, and attracted 160 entrants. Shorthairs were very much in evidence at these early shows, although at the 1875 exhibition there was a class for wild or wild hybrid cats, which was won by an ocelot. The trend towards exhibiting received a significant boost with the attendance of royalty at some of the major events during the latter years of the century.

The increasing popularity of cat shows led to a greater interest in the establishment and development of new breeds and varieties. From the original predominance of Shorthairs, Longhairs began to attract attention, with their beautiful coats requiring loving preparation for exhibition, and in 1896 there were no fewer than 204 Longhairs entered for the National Cat Club's show. Breeders sought to produce new colours. One of the most famous developments occurred in 1889, when a London breeder mated a smoke-coloured cat to a Silver Tabby and from one of the females of the resulting litter produced the first Chinchilla. Silver Lambkin, as he was called, took the cat world by storm with his unusual silvery coat, and his stuffed body may be seen today at London's Natural History Museum.

It was inevitable that a body to oversee the development of both shows and breeds should come into existence, and the National Cat Club was established in 1887. Harrison Weir was the first president, and a studbook and registry of breeds was begun. Cat shows in North America began in 1895, when a show was held at Madison Square Garden in New York. Cat breeders in other countries soon followed suit, and there are now a vast number of cat shows held throughout Europe, North America and elsewhere in the world.

All shows are held under the supervision of the national governing bodies, with the actual organization of the particular show being undertaken by individual clubs. Pedigree cats, to be eligible for exhibition at these shows, must be registered with the governing body. It is also a good idea to join a local club, where help and advice can be gained from experienced breeders. All shows are publicized in the various cat magazines, and the first step is to obtain a show schedule listing all classes, and an entry form.

The entry form should be completed with care and returned, with the entry fee, before the closing date. The structure of the show varies according to the country concerned. Exemption shows give the novice exhibitor a sound introduction. Championship shows provide the fiercest competition, with breeders seeking challenge certificates in the adult open classes. A cat winning three challenge certificates under three different judges at separate championship shows qualifies for the title of Champion, which entitles it to enter the Champion of Champions class at subsequent shows and, with a further three wins in this category, to the title of Grand Champion. In the case of neutered cats a similar system operates, but winners are referred to as Premiers rather than Champions.

Although cat shows are associated with pedigree cats, there are also classes for non-pedigree pets at most shows, which are well supported.

The cat show is a beauty show, so it is important to present your cat in top physical condition with healthy coat, clean, sound teeth and claws which are not overgrown. It will be judged not only on its show points but on its presentation, which depends upon impeccable grooming but also upon good food, fresh air and exercise long before the show entry. Many exhibitors like to bath their cats before a show to ensure that the coat appears at its best, although this is not essential and in many cases regular careful grooming may suffice. The grooming of light coloured breeds often includes the use of powder on the coat: this is a useful aid but all traces must be brushed out thoroughly the day before the show, or the cat will be disqualified.

The cat's temperament and behaviour are also relevant. It is essential that the cat be accustomed to handling at an early age so that it is confident when the judge or stewards approach it. At the show it will be benched in a small wire pen and surrounded by the visiting public; it if has not had experience both of confinement and of crowds it is likely to be terrified and will not show itself to advantage. Indeed, a truly frightened cat will be impossible for the judge to examine and may be disqualified for nervousness. Making sure that your cat is prepared for this experience is not only a question of fairness to the animal, but also vital if you wish to achieve anything with your entry.

The ideal show cat appears to enjoy the experience, seeming to revel in the admiration it receives, and will even purr while the judge is going over its points. Some less extrovert cats endure the business patiently, but other cats never seem to become accustomed to the show atmosphere and are better kept at home.

At a British show, cats are normally first inspected by a veterinarian to reduce the risk of diseases being contracted or transmitted, always a risk when many cats are brought together in one place. They are then placed in their pens, where a white blanket, a feeding bowl and a litter tray are provided. After exhibitors have carried out the final grooming they are asked to leave the hall while judging is carried out. The judge examines all the entries, assisted by stewards who take the cats out of their pens in sequence. In the United States the system differs in that judging is carried out in public.

Rosettes and sometimes trophies are awarded to the winners, although money prizes are small. Membership of the appropriate breed club brings eligibility for special club trophies. The principal reward of showing, however, irrespective of winning, is the social aspect of meeting people with similar interests and expanding one's own knowledge. This should never be overlooked in the pursuit of rosettes. First and foremost, however, is the well-being of the cat which provides these outings. Loving training to ensure that the cat is confident and happy in the show environment, and scrupulous attention to its health and hygiene to avoid spreading infections, will bring the best rewards.

ABOVE: *Cat shows are advertised in the cat fancy magazines, which also print the judges' reports from the shows.*

Chapter Three

CHOOSING YOUR CAT

The cat has retained and even increased its popularity as a pet over the centuries, despite the fact that today we no longer keep it for reasons of religious significance nor, with the development of modern rodenticides, do we rely on it as a vermin controller. The contemporary cat is owned simply for pleasure. The fact is that the cat's graceful beauty, mystique and playfulness, coupled with its innate cleanliness and comparatively small demands upon its owners, make it an appealing companion in its own right.

In many ways the cat is the ideal pet for modern life. It requires less attention than a dog with regard to regular exercise, and an older cat that is going outdoors will not need the same amount of human company as a pet dog. Despite their reputation for being aloof, cats often seek out their owners and respond well to affection and attention. Unlike dogs, they can also be kept indoors on a permanent basis: this will be essential, in fact, in areas where the traffic is an ever present hazard, or in the case of a valuable stud animal. Cats are reasonably clean and straightforward to care for; they retain a degree of self-sufficiency that makes it acceptable for someone who goes out to work all day to keep a cat, whereas a dog kept in such circumstances would suffer from loneliness and boredom.

The first thing to be taken into consideration is how suitable your home is for a cat. If you live in a flat or in any type of rented accommodation, it is wise to ensure that you are permitted to keep pets under the terms of your lease. It is surprising how many people discover that they are not permitted to keep pets in their household after they have gone out and bought their new pet!

Secondly, unless you are prepared to keep your cat indoors, do you have the facilities to allow your cat outdoors safely? This may be impossible in a flat, or in a house adjacent to a busy main road without access to a garden. If this is the case you will need to think about your attitude to living with a litter tray, which will need continual changing and disinfecting.

Within the house, you need to think about the possible need for some reorganization to minimize the risk of accidental damage by the cat – or to it! A kitten may well choose the best chairs to exercise its claws on – some breeds, and some individuals, are more prone to furniture-wrecking than others – and you should also consider what your attitude will be to cat-hairs in the house. Although cats are famous for their ability to pick their way along a shelf without knocking off any ornaments, this is a skill which

ABOVE: *Cats need to exercise their claws, and a cat kept indoors will need a scratching post provided to save your furniture.*

LEFT: *If your work takes you out of the house most of the day, the answer may be to have two kittens to keep each other company.*

ABOVE RIGHT: *If your choice is a long-haired breed, the beautiful coat will require regular grooming to remain attractive and healthy.*

RIGHT: *The pet cat is dependent on its owner for its meals and should not be expected to forage for itself.*

has to be learned by kittens, who may smash your china, and which even some adult cats never learn.

If you go out to work, it is not fair to leave a kitten alone in the house all day, although older cats can be allowed to enter and leave the house at will while the owner is out. Under these circumstances, it would be better to obtain two kittens to keep each other company, although you will still need to make arrangements for someone to call in to give them their midday meals during the first months.

Then there is the question of expense. While cats are far from being the most expensive of pets to keep, some costs are unavoidable. Regular outlays will include food - allow for the cost of a standard can of good quality cat food per day. You may decide to feed fresh food, or supplement the diet with table scraps, but this should serve as a guideline.

Cat litter will almost certainly be needed initially and may continue to be a regular purchase. Surprisingly enough market research has shown that expenditure on cat litter by the cat-owning public exceeds expenditure on all veterinary services several times over! Include this in your calculations, especially if your cat is to be kept indoors.

Initially, and thereafter annually, you will have the cost of vaccinations against contagious diseases. It is a false economy to skimp on these, since apart from the distress and inconvenience caused if your cat should pick up one of the diseases that can be prevented by vaccination, the costs of treatment would be likely to far outweigh any savings you might make.

Unless you take on an adult animal which has already been neutered, you will also have to pay the cost of castration or spaying. This is practically unavoidable for the pet animal, as the entire tomcat does not make an acceptable pet, whilst the female cat cannot be guarded against unwanted pregnancies as easily as, for example, a female dog, and, however appealing may be the idea of kittens, they may be hard to find homes for and the population of unwanted cats is already far too large.

Whilst thinking about finance, there is also the possibility that, during the cat's lifetime, an accident or illness may lead to further veterinary fees, which can be very high. It is possible to take out insurance against this risk: your veterinary surgeon will usually be able to provide details.

Finally, remember that you will need to make arrangements for the cat's welfare every time you go away on holiday. Unless you are able to arrange for a friend or neighbour to look after your cat while you are away, the cost of boarding can add considerably to the cost of your vacation.

All these factors should be borne in mind before you decide to obtain a cat but none of them should pose insuperable problems if you are prepared for the degree of commitment that any pet needs, and without which you cannot expect the many rewards of responsible pet-keeping.

RIGHT: *The appearance and temperament of one of the pedigree breeds may appeal to you enough to make the purchase of a pedigree kitten worthwhile. For example, if the elegant Russian Blue, with its silvery colouring and quiet affectionate character, attracts you, you will not find quite these qualities in a non-pedigree kitten.*

PEDIGREE OR MONGREL?

More than 94 per cent of all pet cats in the United Kingdom are not pedigreed. Breeds of domestic cat are less distinctive than their canine counterparts, and there is not such a difference between pedigree and non-pedigree. Whereas with a puppy there is always a risk that the small mongrel puppy you purchase may become a large dog, such as a cross between a Great Dane and an Irish Wolfhound, cats are a fairly standard size and shape, and you will therefore have a pretty fair idea of what you are taking on with a non-pedigreed cat.

However, each of the pedigree varieties has been deliberately bred to intensify certain traits of appearance and temperament. If you are attracted by a particular characteristic, and can afford the extra expenditure, you may decide that you have a distinct preference for a pedigree animal.

Those who fancy a cat with distinctive characteristics may be attracted by the curly coat of the Rex or the taillessness of the Manx, features most unlikely to be found in the non-pedigree population of cats. Longhaired cats occur amongst non-pedigrees as well as pedigrees, but the fur will be less long and silky, just as certain colours which do occur in the mongrels are never quite as vivid as when selected for over generations of careful breeding. The pedigree varieties have characteristic temperaments, noticeably different from breed to breed, which may particularly attract you when deciding on the cat you want to live with.

To summarize, Longhairs require more grooming than Shorthairs, and tend to leave more hair around the home, so they may not be the best choice for people with limited time. On the other hand they have a unique beauty and tend to have a gentle and affectionate nature. British Shorthairs are hardy and companionable; their coats require little care and they are generally easy cats to live with. The Foreign Shorthair breeds tend to have more forceful personalities, particularly the extrovert Siamese, which either appeals strongly or appals potential owners. More delicate breeds, such as the Rex, need fairly warm surroundings, which could be a drawback if you prefer a cool house or live in a cold climate.

In some quarters there is a prejudice against pedigree animals, as opposed to crossbreds, based on the fear that breeders concentrating on fixing show points in their animals have inadvertently bred in a predisposition towards some weakness. This is regrettably the case with some breeds of dog but is far less a cause for concern with cats.

The shape and form of the pedigreed cat remains much closer to the original wild form of cat than that of many breeds of dog. One would like to think that this is due to sensible restraint on the part of cat breeders, but it must also be said that, pedigreed cats have been selectively bred for a much shorter time than dogs and there has been less time to produce the more extreme variations. Certainly, any highly inbred animal is likely to be less resistant to disease than one with a very wide mix of genes, and some of the effects of selective breeding may mean that the pedi-

greed cat will need closer attention than a mixed breed cat. For example, the long coat that has been carefully nurtured in many pedigreed Longhairs will often cause severe problems if the cat is left to its own devices to keep its own coat in order. Similarly, the 'pushed-in' face of many long-haired cats tends to make the eyes run due to interference with the mechanism for draining tears from the eyes, although this can usually be kept under control with regular cleaning of the eyes.

A conscientious cat breeder will be conscious of any problems to which his or her breed may be prone, and will endeavour to produce sound and healthy animals. If a pedigree cat is what you want, there is no need to reject the idea on health grounds: it makes sense, however, to look for a caring breeder rather than someone producing kittens as fast as possible as a source of money.

On the other hand, the continuing popularity of the non-pedigree cat attests to the fact that a mongrel makes just as good a pet as a pedigree.

While it is easier to predict what the temperament of pedigree cats is likely to be, crossbreds are certainly not lacking in either colour or character. They can become just as devoted to their owners and, contrary to some stories, are neither more nor less susceptible to illness than pedigree cats. The amount of grooming they require is obviously dependent on the appearance of their coats; those with relatively long fur will need to be combed and brushed more regularly.

Just as when seeking a pedigree cat, you will be doing yourself a favour if you are reasonably selective about the source of your 'moggy'. A cuddly-looking farm kitten may have had very little human contact in its formative days and grow up less human-oriented than one which has been brought up in the heart of a family.

RIGHT: *The unspayed female cat may produce three litters a year. She may mate for the first time when she is as young as three months of age, and may be receptive to the male again as early as ten days after giving birth. Unless you can take the reponsibility for a steady stream of kittens, spaying is the best answer to avoid adding to the large population of unwanted strays.*

MALE OR FEMALE?

The choice between a male (tom) or female (queen) is only of any real consequence if you wish to breed from your cat. If you want to keep the cat purely as a pet, you will certainly wish to have it neutered, for its own sake as well as for your own. Such surgery is not only carried out to prevent the birth of unwanted kittens, but also serves to facilitate the integration of a cat kept solely as a pet into domestic life.

The entire tomcat, once it reaches sexual maturity at around seven months, is not a desirable creature with which to share your home. It will spray the furnishings with pungent urine, will prefer wandering after females to your company, and will need regular patching up after fights with the other cats of the neighbourhood. It is also likely to make you highly unpopular with your human neighbours!

Similarly, it is not desirable to keep an unspayed female. Whilst she will not become unpleasant in the home like the male, without constant monitoring she will become pregnant at such regular intervals as to become a kitten-producing machine rather than a companion, and you will have the responsibility for finding homes for kittens in a world where rescue societies are already inundated with unwanted cats and kittens. It is possible to shut the female indoors when she is in season, but since she may cycle every three weeks this means that she will need to be shut up for a great deal of her life. During her season her behaviour is likely to be both disturbed and disturbing, with noisy cries and even spraying of urine about the house.

The female cat which is left unspayed but not allowed to breed is likely to have a shorter lifespan than the spayed female. If she is prevented from mating she will usually call repeatedly until irritable and exhausted; there is also a strong possibility of her developing a womb infection. Spaying will remove the risk of such troubles as ovarian cysts and pyometra in later life.

Neutering is usually a safe and routine operation (see page 122). It costs more for females since the operation is more complex.

After neutering, there is no real difference in personality between the sexes, although some people consider that the neutered female is the more affectionate.

If, on the other hand, you wish to breed from your cat, you will be thinking in terms of obtaining a female. Keeping a male cat as a stud is practically a specialist job. The anti-social habits of the entire tomcat mean that he must be housed in his own quarters, where his owner needs to spend time with him every day to keep him used to handling. He will need regular opportunities to serve an adequate number of queens, and only the very largest catteries will house enough queens to keep a stud cat contented, while other breeders will only bring their queens to him if he is a top show winner. For breeding purposes, therefore, you should stick to the female, and take her to the best outside stud you can find.

The choice to keep an unspayed female and breed from her should not be made lightly, however. For the ordinary owner, there is rarely any financial benefit to be gained from keeping and breeding from a pedigree queen – blood-lines are only established over a period of years, with considerable work and effort.

As well as the responsibility for the kittens, you will have additional work in terms of caring for the queen through the periods when she comes into season but you do not wish to have her mated - she will need a rest in between litters, but she is unlikely to agree with you on the subject. However, you may choose to have one litter and have the queen spayed afterwards: the operation can be carried out safely at any age.

MALE, FEMALE OR NEUTER?

LEFT: *The entire tomcat makes an undesirable housemate, with his drive to spray his strong-smelling urine even indoors. Neutered, he will not only become fit to live with but will lead a contented life as a pet, a well as expecting a longer lifespan than if he were exposed to the stressful and violent life of the active tom.*

ABOVE: *After neutering, there is no significant personality difference between the sexes and either sex will fit into the household well.*

KITTEN OR ADULT?

BELOW: *Kittens need more care than cats but may be a better choice for first-time pet owners. You will be able to enjoy the fun of the youngster's playful discoveries of its brave new world, and it will quickly familiarize itself with your lifestyle to grow up as one of the family. A kitten is likely to adapt better to the noise and boisterousness of children than an adult cat, and to become a playmate to them, although children should always be supervised with animals.*

Kittens, although initially more demanding, will generally settle better in a new environment than older cats. They are often more responsive to their new owners and are less likely to wander or get lost although, by way of compensation, an adult cat will probably be housetrained already. The age and history of a kitten will be familiar, whereas with an older cat, details such as its past vaccination record, if any, may not be known. This may not necessarily be important, but it will be virtually impossible to age the cat with any degree of certainty.

If you have young children, a kitten is likely to be the better choice as it will be able to join in the children's play where an older, more dignified animal might simply find their noise and energy irritating. Obviously, young children should never be allowed to play unsupervised with any animal: the risk of injury to the kitten or to the child is too great to take.

There are often plenty of homes available for kittens, but giving a home to an adult cat will often save that cat from having to be put to sleep. Since cats are very much creatures of habit, an adult cat will probably take time to settle into a new environment and will probably be fairly set in its ways. There is always a chance that the cat has been re-homed either due to ill health or behavioural problems, so a veterinary check-up is a good idea.

RIGHT: *An adult cat will usually adapt well to a new home. Cats never seem to outgrow their playfulness so, once it has settled in, the adult will give you much of the entertainment to be expected from a kitten, while normally not needing to be taught the rudiments of civilized behaviour such as house-training. Problems may arise if the cat has been unfortunate in its earlier experiences of people, but kindness and patience will settle most behavioural difficulties.*

SOURCES

If you have decided on a pedigree cat or kitten, the best source is the breeder. Addresses of breeders can be obtained through the various cat magazines or by visiting shows, as well as by studying advertisements in local papers or asking your veterinarian.

Most breeders will give every assistance to a customer. If possible, it is well worth travelling to the breeder's premises to pick out your kitten in person and also to see for yourself the surroundings in which it has been raised. As a rule, kittens reared in a home environment where they have received plenty of human attention at an early age are like to settle better as pets. Those which have lived in a cattery since birth are likely to be shyer when transferred to a domestic environment, and older individuals will generally take longer to adapt to such a move.

Pedigree kittens are occasionally sold in pet stores, but this implies a breeder who is not particularly caring about where the kittens end up, and this lack of care may have been reflected in the rearing of the kittens. A responsible breeder will have gone to a lot of trouble to ensure that the kittens have had a good start in life, with the correct diet and plenty of handling, which is vital if they are to grow up to be healthy and well-adjusted adults.

Again, kittens sold from a petshop will have been exposed to more stress and more risk of infection than those which go directly from the breeder to their new home.

It is occasionally possible to obtain a pedigree cat from an animal shelter or rescue society, as they do occasionally receive pedigree animals which have strayed, lost favour with an uncaring owner or perhaps become homeless through the death of the owner. Such animals are likely to be adults rather than kittens and are very unlikely to possess registration papers, but some very beautiful cats do pass through the hands of these animal charities.

If you would like a non-pedigreed cat, again it is best to try to find a private home with a litter of kittens that need new owners.

Crossbred kittens are always available, often advertised as 'free to good homes'. It is important to visit the home. Some will be the progeny of queens whose owners do not care enough about them to have them neutered and allow casual litters to be born regularly. The queen will have had little extra care during her pregnancy, too frequent pregnancies may have left her in poor condition and unable to care for the kittens as well as she should, and the litter may show permanent effects from lack of care and human handling.

Other litters will have been born into caring homes where scrupulous attention is paid to hygiene, worming and good food, and the kittens will have grown up accustomed to being handled and played with. This is the sort of home you should be looking for when seeking a kitten. A good start in life is the best guarantee of a cat that will be a pleasure rather than a liability in your household.

Kittens sold in a petshop are again not recommended because of the greater stress and risk of infection to which they will have been exposed.

Animal welfare organizations often have a large number of kittens and cats in need of permanent, caring homes. The work of such groups in the vast majority of cases is entirely voluntary; whenever adopting a pet from such a charity, a donation should be made to their funds to enable them to continue their work. Many animal rescue schemes prefer to 'vet' potential owners to make sure that they are suitable, and often provide a follow-up advisory service. They will usually not permit an animal to leave their care unless they are sure that it is in good health, and in cases of genuine hardship many of these charities will help with the cost of neutering.

Whether your choice is a pedigree kitten or a 'moggy', and whatever source you decided to obtain your new pet from, it is always worthwhile to select the animal personally. Some kittens will be more forward and friendly than others, or it may simply be that a particular colour appeals more strongly to you; visiting the home environment from which it comes will give you the best opportunity to pick a healthy, confident animal which attracts you as an individual.

*The most significant factor when considering the source of your cat or kitten is the interaction with humans which the animal has experienced. A rescued stray (**ABOVE**) may have had some very negative experiences causing it to lose its trust in people and requiring great patience on the part of its new owner to overcome. Farm kittens (**RIGHT**) may not have been handled much during their formative early weeks, and may remain less human-oriented than kittens reared in the house.*

SPOILT FOR CHOICE

Although there is not the wide range of sizes and shapes amongst cat breeds that we find in the dog, nonetheless there is a considerable variety of both style and temperament, from the cuddly, placid and baby-faced Longhairs to the svelte and raucous Siamese. Crossbred cats are available in a delightful range of colours and will prove just as attractive and affectionate pets as the pedigrees.

LEFT: *Seal Point Siamese.*

LEFT: *Non-pedigree cats come in almost all the colours of the rainbow.*

LEFT: *Smoke Devon Rex.*
RIGHT: *Silver Tabby Longhair.*

SPOILT FOR CHOICE
CHOOSING A KITTEN

The usual age for sending kittens on to their new homes is eight weeks, although some breeders may prefer to keep them until they have completed their vaccination course at about twelve weeks. It is possible to move the kittens from five or six weeks of age, especially if two kittens are being homed together. Although kittens sent to new homes at such a young age need more care and attention, they often grow up to become particularly affectionate cats. Older kittens will often settle well into a new home but should have plenty of human contact while still with their mother.

Aside from more personal preferences, the two most important considerations when selecting a particular cat or kitten are its disposition and general health. Before beginning a specific health check, it is a good idea to simply observe the litter to establish differences in temperament. Avoid kittens which are over-aggressive as well as those who hang back or do not seem particularly lively – passivity may indicate a cowed nature or be a sign of ill health. Kittens should be gregarious, playful and inquisitive.

The degree to which a cat is disposed towards the domesticated life is partly inherited as well as partly established from its early environment, so it is worth considering how friendly the mother of the kitten is. An amiable or a nervous temperament may well have been passed on to the litter.

The amount of handling both mother and kittens have been accustomed to is also crucial in deciding how human-oriented the youngsters will be. The more people who handle the kittens during their vital formative weeks, the more predisposed towards human company they will be.

The alley cats which abound in the cities do not take to human handling at all. Some are difficult, but most are downright dangerous. If they were not, they would hardly be able to survive. Many well-intentioned people have learned this the hard way. They rescue a kitten or litter, which has become separated from the mother, but no matter how patient or kind the humans are, these cats will rarely respond in anything other than a hostile fashion. The basic character seldom changes. If they come from wild, or semi-wild, stock that is the way they will remain.

Once you have established which kitten you would like spend some time checking its overall appearance for any sign of illness. The eyes should be bright and clear, the nose clean without any sign of discharge, and the ears also clean, without the tell-tale build-up of dark wax that indicates an infestation of ear mites.

Check the coat for any traces of flea dirt or scurf, and make sure that the anal area is clean, with no soreness or staining indicating diarrhoea or tiny white deposits resembling rice grains, indicating tapeworm infestation. Watch

the kitten walking, and look for any signs of lameness or lack of co-ordination. If such disabilities are noticed, the whole litter should be viewed with suspicion, as they may be infected with feline panleucopaenia or suffering from a dietary deficiency.

When you lift the kitten up, it should feel comfortably rounded, neither fat nor thin. The underside of the abdomen should be felt gently; if this is very rounded in a kitten, it is a likely sign of roundworms. Moving forward in the direction of the chest, a small swelling may be felt. This is likely to indicate a hernia of the umbilicus (or 'belly-button'), with tissue protruding through a small hole in the body wall. It is not a serious problem and can be corrected surgically if necessary, but will detract from the cat's value. Some breeders believe hernias of this type may be inherited.

You will want to be sure that the kitten is ready to leave its mother. Watch it lap and eat some food to be sure that it is truly weaned and able to feed itself. Some kittens are more forward than others. To check the age, open the mouth gently and make sure the kitten has a full set of teeth. If not, it may still be too young.

Sexing a kitten is harder than sexing an adult cat; although an experienced breeder is unlikely to make an error in this respect, a staff member in a pet store may not be so competent. It is worth checking to be quite sure. The distinction between the sexes is made largely on the basis of the relative distances between the openings below the base of the tail. In female kittens, the two openings – the anus with the vulva beneath – are virtually in contact with each other and the vulva appears as a distinct slit. The slit opening of the vulva of the mature female cat is more distant from the anus than in a kitten, but it is impossible to distinguish between neutered and intact females by this means. Male kittens do not have an external penis. The organ is contained in a circular opening, spaced a short distance below the anus. This gap is filled by the scrotum, although the testicles will not be prominent in a young kitten. Intact males have a distinct swelling in this region.

A responsible breeder will provide a diet sheet setting out the feeding regimen to which the kitten has been accustomed. This should be closely followed for the first weeks to reduce the risk of any digestive upset following the move.

In the case of a pedigree kitten, the breeder should also provide a fully completed pedigree certificate showing that the kitten has been registered with the appropriate registration authority such as the Cat Fanciers' Association (CFA) or the Governing Council of the Cat Fancy (GCCF). A transfer certificate to register the change of ownership must be filled in and sent to the appropriate authority once the sale is completed. It is always best to take along to the breeder someone with experience of the breed you are interested in to advise on your selection. You will find that the vast majority of cat breeders are highly reputable, and anxious to ensure that their kittens are going to good homes. However, as in any business, you will find the occasional charlatan out to make a quick fortune – so beware!

SEX DIFFERENTIATION

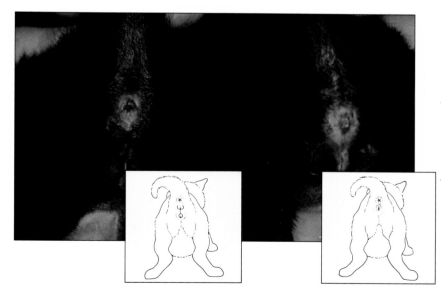

The easiest way to sex a litter of very young kittens is by comparing one sex with another – provided there is an example of each sex in the same litter. The vulva in a female kitten is a small slit-like opening just below the anus (**LEFT**). In the male (**FAR LEFT**) the small round opening that hides the penis is separated from the anus by the two slightly raised scrotal sacs.

CHOOSING AN INDIVIDUAL

Kittens vary in temperament, even within the same litter, but, in general, litters vary more than kittens do in any one litter. It is important to pick a kitten from a good home, where the entire litter should be healthy and alert. Aside from basic health considerations, colour and overall conformation will be factors for those seeking a pedigree cat, while those looking for a pet will probably be interested in general behavioural traits. Most people, however, will find that they respond more to one kitten than to the others: this type of appeal is, more often than not, purely subjective. The best advice is to spend as much time as possible observing the litter in order to make the right decision. While a few guidelines can be suggested, it is important to bear in mind that on another occasion, the kittens may behave quite differently.

THE AGGRESSIVE KITTEN *A kitten that bullies its littermates, scratches, hisses or snarls unnecessarily when handled gently may be overly aggressive. Such reactions may just be a reflection of the circumstances but a kitten that displays persistent bad temper will not make a good pet and may even be suffering from illness.*

THE OUTSIDER
A shy and retiring kitten may not have received the same amount of attention from its dam as have its littermates. It is often the smallest of the litter, the 'runt' which has not attracted its dam's maternal feelings as much as the stronger kittens. The smallest kitten will not necessarily make a poor pet, but avoid picking a very shy youngster as it is likely to grow up to be a timid and antisocial adult.

THE LIVELY KITTEN

A forward disposition is a good indication of intelligence and adaptability, and probably reflects frequent handling as well as a naturally bright and curious nature. This is the one to look out for as a pet as it has the right temperamental foundation for you to build on.

THE NERVOUS KITTEN

Nervousness may reflect a naturally wild nature or merely a lack of proper handling at a crucial age. Either way, it will be hard to overcome. If one kitten in a litter shows excessive nervousness, some of the others are likely to show similar tendencies, since it is to a large extent a reflection of their environment.

SIGNS OF GOOD HEALTH

Look for clean, clear eyes, nose and ears, and a clean glossy coat with no signs of fleas. Watch the kitten move: there should be no signs of lameness or lack of co-ordination. The belly should be comfortably rounded – a distended abdomen probably indicates an infestation of roundworms.

CHOOSING AN ADULT

Just as with a kitten, temperament and physical health should be investigated when you choose an adult cat.

The older cat will be less playful than a kitten, but it should not be over-timid or aggressive at the approach of strangers. It should be willing to be handled by humans: a cat which resents being touched will take a great deal of patience to turn it into a pet, and may, if it comes from feral stock, even prove untamable.

Check the cat's physical condition as with a kitten. The eyes must be free from any signs of discharge, and not obscured by the 'third eyelid', more correctly known as the nictitating membrane. When the pad of fat behind the eyes shrinks due to illness or poor condition, the eyes sink back into their sockets, causing the nictitating membrane or 'haw' to become prominent. it will be evident at the corner of the ear, nearest the nose. The nose itself should be clean, with the nostrils unblocked, while the ears must not show any excessive accumulation of wax, or appear dirty.

Stroking the cat will give an indication of its overall condition. Note any trace of flea dirt, scurf or soreness in the coat. The anal region should not show signs of staining, which could be an indication of diarrhoea. Deposits resembling rice grains around the anus itself indicate a tapeworm infection. The cat then must be encouraged to walk a short distance, so that any signs of lameness or lack of coordination will become evident.

Next, ask the owner's permission to carry out a closer examination. It may be necessary to have assistance to look in the mouth. With one person restraining the cat by grasping round its shoulders at the top of the forelegs, the task

RIGHT: *A cat which has to fend for itself may be hard to cure of the habit of scavenging for food, even when you are supplying regular meals.*

ABOVE: *ASSESSING AGE It is difficult to assess the age of the adult cat with accuracy. The adolescent cat (1) has a triangular body shape, all muscle above and a tiny abdomen below. When it reaches adulthood (2), the body shape becomes rectangular. Old age (3) brings a complete reversal of youth as the triangular shape is inverted, the muscles at the top tending to diminish and the abdomen to sag.*

THE HEALTH CHECK

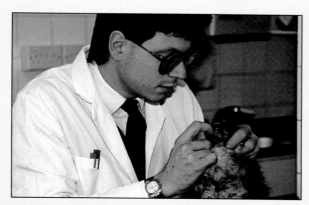

(1) *The mouth is a good indication of the cat's overall health. Look for clean pink gums and white teeth, although an older cat's teeth may be slightly yellowed. Bad breath may be a symptom of dental problems or of a more serious illness.*

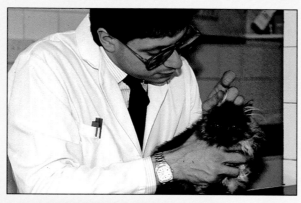

(2) *The eyes should be bright and clear, without discharge. Dull sunken eyes, weeping or a raised third eyelid are all warning signals.*

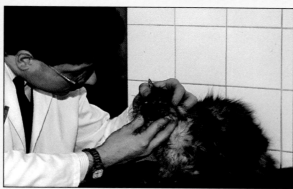

(3) *The ears must be clean. An accumulation of dark wax indicates the presence of ear mites, often also shown by an acrid smell.*

(4) *The coat should be glossy and free of mats. Check for bald patches, scurf or sore and irritated areas. Fleas are easily identifiable by their dark droppings amongst the fur.*

SIGNS OF GOOD HEALTH

(1) *Bright, clean eyes*

(2) *Clean ears*

(3) *A clean nose with no discharge*

(4) *Pink gums, white teeth, no sores or bad breath*

(5) *Elastic skin and clean, glossy fur*

(6) *Clean anus with no tell-tale soiling or soreness*

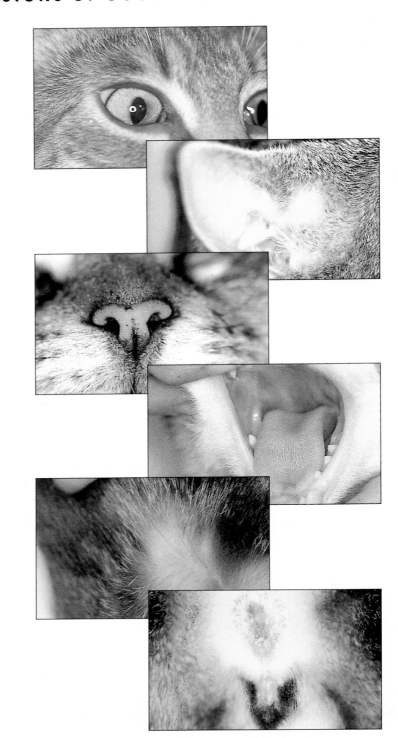

will be relatively simple. The left hand should be placed around the upper jaw, over the nasal region, while the lower mandible can be gently prised down with the other hand. Lefthanded people may find it easier to do this the other way round.

A final check on the cat can be made by picking it up. An arm should be gently placed round the chest just behind the front legs, while the other arm is used to support the rear. If there is no support given to its hindquarters, the cat will be very likely to struggle and may scratch, for fear of falling.

Stray or feral cats are much harder to handle, resenting all attempts to lift them up. Under these circumstances, a slightly different approach is ncessary, which entails holding the cat firmly by the loose area of skin over its shoulders known as the scruff, while again supporting the hindquarters. This will restrain the cat more effectively, preventing it from biting and scratching. However, if such restraint is required you should consider carefully whether the cat will make a suitable pet. It may relax with gentle handling, but if it fails to respond it may be incurably wild.

If the cat's history is unknown, it will be hard to assess how old it is. It may be possible for your veterinarian to make a guess at the age of a cat by its general bodily condition and the state of its teeth, but it is very difficult to judge the age of adult cats accurately in this manner. However, a young cat with deciduous (milk) teeth will be under seven months of age. The permanent canine teeth

erupt at around five months, allowing accurate assessment of the cat's age to be made at that time.

Sex differentiation is easier than with kittens, but you may not be able to tell whether a cat of unknown origin has been neutered or not.

This is not too difficult with a male cat unless you happen to be presented with a cat who is an entire male but has undescended testicles, known as a *cryptorchid*. Such a cat would not have any testicles present in the scrotum and would be infertile, but would have all the behavioural characteristics of an entire tom. Fortunately, cryptorchidism is fairly rare, but bear it in mind if you have an apparently neutered male of unknown origin behaving like an entire tom.

Determining whether a female is entire can be almost impossible once the hair has regrown over the operation site after spaying. Some cat owners who take on a female cat without knowing whether or not she is neutered are happy to let her roam freely and take a chance on her becoming pregnant, or are able to keep her indoors to see if she begins to call. If, however, you do not wish to keep your new cat indoors and do not wish to enlarge your cat family any further, your veterinarian may have to carry out a spaying operation to see if the womb is present. It is possible that he may find an obvious scar in the normal operation site once the hair has been shaved, but he may have to go the whole way and operate.

LEFT: *Taking on an adult cat from a rescue home may well prevent it from being put to sleep as one of the unwanted surplus cat population. The animal charities that seek to house strays will ensure that all cats for re-homing are in good health and usually neutered before passing them on. Such cats often seem to appreciate a loving home all the more for their previous insecurity, and generally become real members of their new families.*

Colonies of cats living wild in derelict areas of towns and cities, or on the fringe of human life in rural districts, are known as feral cats. Despite efforts by animal welfare organizations and concerned individuals, the increased risk of disease and injury, the effects of an inadequate diet and simple exposure to the elements will all make these cats' lives shorter as well as less comfortable than that of the well-cared-for pet. Feral cats are rarely suitable for adoption as pets, however: generations of wild living and lack of human socialization at a crucial period have adapted them for their wild lifestyle.

EAR TIPPING

Some feral cats have had the tip of the left ear removed. This is a simple method of identification used by some animal welfare organizations to mark cats which have been neutered and then returned to the colony. It is carried out painlessly under anaesthetic, does not handicap the individual in any way, and prevents the same cat from being re-captured for neutering at a later date.

FERAL CATS

In many big cities there are well-established colonies of feral cats, that is, cats which have reverted to living in the wild, generally on the fringes of human habitation. It has been estimated that there are some 3 million feral cats in the United Kingdom.

There are a number of animal welfare organizations and also concerned individuals who attempt to monitor these feral populations to some extent. It is practically impossible to eradicate feral colonies because of the sheer numbers involved and because the pool is constantly augmented by cats abandoned or left to fend for themselves by uncaring owners. However, some attempts are being made to control the population by trapping individuals and neutering them before their release.

Although a genuine stray which has known the comfort of life in a human home can easily be rehabilitated and will become a pet again, feral cats have often lived wild for some generations and have a genetic predisposition towards wildness as well as lacking human socialization during the impressionable period of kittenhood. It is therefore very difficult to domesticate a feral cat as a pet.

Cats that live on rough ground away from humans are likely to prove intractable; individuals from populations living near houses, which may have become accustomed to being fed by cat-loving individuals, may gradually allow themselves to be approached. A young feral cat can, with much patience, be conditioned to tolerate and even enjoy human attention. On the whole, however, feral cats are adapted to a wild existence and will never achieve the truly comfortable relationship with man of cats which have been bred and reared to become pets.

Chapter Four

THE NEW ARRIVAL

EQUIPMENT

You can buy a great deal of equipment for your cat's comfort from the vast array of products marketed through pet stores, but only a few are actually essential.

Before you bring your new cat or kitten home, you will need to obtain a litter box and cat litter, bowls and a bed. Other items can be obtained later, grooming implements and a carrying basket being among those most likely to be needed.

LITTER TRAY

One of the reasons why cats are popular as pets is that they are fastidious and clean in their personal toilet habits, habitually burying their excrement. The cat that has the freedom to do so will do this in the garden; the indoor cat will require a litter tray.

Even a cat that will normally have access to the garden will have to be kept shut in at first until it has learned to consider your house as home – and also, in the case of a kitten, until it has been vaccinated against contagious diseases – so you will have to provide a litter tray in the early days in any case.

Litter trays can be bought in various sizes; those made of sturdy plastic are relatively cheap and easy to disinfect. A tray for a kitten needs to have fairly low sides so that he can climb in – not more than 3in (7.5cm) in height. Adult cats prefer deeper litter and will therefore require a litter tray with higher sides. It is possible to buy litter trays with covers to prevent the cat from spreading litter around the house and to help control odours. If you intend to allow the cat outdoors after its settling-in period, you may not wish to buy a litter tray for short-term use, in which case an old seed tray or vegetable box with low sides and a solid base should prove adequate; plastic is preferable, because the wood will soon start to smell, even if used in conjunction with a deodorant cat litter.

The litter itself is sold in both pet stores and many supermarkets; a variety of brands are now on the market. Those containing fuller's earth are often preferred, since this absorbs well and also acts as a deodorant. Cat litter also comes in a range of colours. Fuller's earth brands are grey, whereas there are white 'lightweight' litters and a pink type which is claimed to be both absorbent and dust-free. There should be sufficient litter to give a reasonable pile on the bottom of the litter tray. To facilitate cleaning, it is a good idea to line the tray with a plastic sack held in place with the lid. The litter is poured onto the plastic and once soiled can be lifted out on the sack for disposal.

Cat litter is relatively expensive and heavy to carry in any quantity. Peat or fresh soil can be used as an alternative,

Basic equipment for any cat includes a litter tray, bed, bowls and some type of travelling container. These should be acquired before the new kitten is brought home. A scratching post is a useful extra, particularly if the cat is to be kept indoors. Toys for cats may be bought at pet stores, but your pet will probably obtain just as much pleasure playing with cotton reels, scraps of paper or a ping-pong ball. If you want your cat to wear a collar, make sure that it is an elasticated or easy-release type to avoid the risk of accidents.

faces, which may prove a disadvantage.

All such products must be used as indicated on the container, and made up using hot water. Soiled objects should always be washed with a detergent and rinsed to remove as much organic matter as possible, because this will otherwise handicap the action of the disinfectant. Maximum benefit will be obtained from a disinfectant if the object concerned can be immersed in the solution for several minutes. Another thorough rinse will then be necessary to remove any remaining traces of the disinfectant.

BOWLS

Saucers make adequate feeding receptacles in an emergency, but it is inadvisable to use them again for domestic purposes once the cat has licked them. The bacterial flora present in a cat's mouth is generally unpleasant.

It is sensible therefore to buy bowls specifically for the cat's use. They should be sturdy enough not to tip over easily. This can be a disadvantage of stainless steel containers although they are easy to keep scrupulously clean. Plastic feeding bowls can be scratched or chewed and may harbour germs. Glazed bowls are probably the best choice, as they are both heavy and simply to wash thoroughly, although they break readily if dropped. Three bowls will be needed – one each for food, water and milk. A fork or knife should be set aside for the cat's food. All bowls and feeding implements should be kept separate from normal household dishes and washed regularly in hot soapy water. Alternatively, disposable foil or waxed cardboard dishes can be used.

BEDS

The independent nature of most cats means that they will probably choose their own sleeping place in the end (or share yours), but it is a good idea to provide the new arrival with a bed of its own to give it a sense of security.

A cardboard box of suitable size with its top removed and one of the sides cut away to form an entrance will suffice as a bed, and can be discarded once the cat has decided on some other sleeping place. At a more sophisticated level, you can buy cat beds in a variety of designs ranging from the traditional wicker designs to plastic beds and even 'bean bags'. Plastic baskets are much easier to keep clean. They can be lined with newspaper and bedding placed on top. Cats do, however, enjoy bean bags, which contain polystyrene foam in the form of granules rather than real beans. Such bags must have removable, washable covers. If they are thought to be harbouring fleas, regular spraying with a suitable preparation coupled with repeated washing of the covers should keep these parasites at bay. Depending on the environment, it may be worth considering the purchase of either a fibreglass bed with a fitted electrical heater or a removable heating pad.

but are likely to be messier than a commercial product, and tend to spoil the coats of paler longhaired breeds. Sand may prove abrasive; sawdust may contain toxic chemicals used for wood preservation and could prove poisonous if consumed by a kitten. Fine particles may also enter the eyes, causing severe irritation.

To economize on litter, a special scoop can be bought to remove faeces along with soiled litter from the litter tray. This is not a pleasant task, however, and should not be undertaken by pregnant women because of the slight risk of contracting toxoplasmosis.

The scoop and tray should be washed with a suitable disinfectant after use. Many of the disinfectants regularly used around the home are, however, potentially toxic to cats. A reliable pharmacist will know the type of disinfectant required, if it is not clear from the container. Bleach can also be used under certain circumstances, for example for washing out cat pens or catteries, but can whiten sur-

CAT CARRIERS

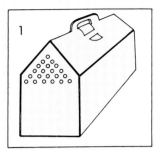

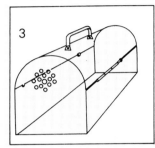

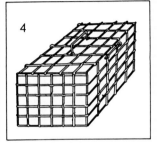

Cat baskets come in various designs, cardboard (1), wickerwork (2), fibreglass (3) or plastic-coated mesh (4) amongst them. All carriers should be completely secure. Cardboard carriers in particular should be checked before use as they have a short lifespan before developing weak spots. A top-opening basket (5) is recommended for ease of getting the cat in and out; a basket opening at one end may mean a battle, pushing the cat in and having to drag rather than lift it out.

CAT CARRIERS

At some stage in your cat's life you are likely to need to move it from one place to another. Show cats are likely to travel a good deal during their lives, and all cats will need to be taken to a veterinary surgeon or boarding cattery at some stage. You may move house; you may even decide to take your cat on holiday with you.

Whatever the circumstances, there is only one safe way to move a cat, and that is to transport it inside a secure basket. Neither conversation nor tranquillizers are effective substitutes. Admittedly there are some cats that travel the world perched like parrots on the shoulders of their owners. But the overwhelming majority leap off at the first opportunity and are never seen again. No matter how well-behaved your cat is, it is never acceptable to transport it loose in a car. It is simply not fair to run the risk of a crash should the animal startle the driver by a sudden movement or even by being unexpectedly sick.

A travelling basket is therefore a sensible investment. In an emergency you can use a cardboard box tied up with string, but this will be far from secure: wooden orange boxes, which can be closed firmly by means of wire loops, are preferable. But it is well worth buying a specially made carrier rather than relying on makeshift containers which often prove inadequate.

Cardboard boxes tied up with string fall into this latter category, as cats can escape without difficulty, simply by pulling a flap down with a paw and then squeezing out. In an emergency, wooden orange boxes, which can be closed firmly by means of wire loops, are preferable. It is far more satisfactory to have a purpose-made container at hand when required.

Special cardboard carriers for cats (1) can be purchased from larger pet stores and are cheap yet relatively safe. They are sold flat with ventilation holes already punched out, and once folded into shape have no loose flaps to give a possible exit. Particular attention should be given to the base though which will collapse if the folding is incorrectly carried out or if the cat is heavy. There should be a cardboard liner to fit inside the carrier, and it is a good idea to add paper on top of this because if the base becomes wet the cardboard will rapidly disintegrate. As an additional precaution, string can be tied around the box, passing through the handle, once the cat is inside. These carriers are not suitable for repeated use, as they may be scratched and weakened by the cat.

Wicker baskets (2) prove a much safer alternative, although straps on the doors can wear and break especially if the ties are plastic rather than leather. Designs with metal rods for holding the door shut are preferable for this reason. The door may be located either at the front or at the top of the basket. The latter are easier to use because the cat can be simply lifted into the basket and the lid swiftly closed,

112

whereas it may need to be bundled, sometimes with difficulty, into a basket with a door at the front. As with all carrying containers, these baskets should be lined with a thick layer of paper, because the cat may well urinate or defecate during the journey if it is upset.

Best of all, although more expensive, are the plastic or fibreglass carriers (3), which are durable, secure and can always be cleaned more easily than the wicker type, using a hose if necessary. This factor may be particularly important when moving cats to and from shows or a veterinary surgery, where diseases can be picked up and brought home to other cats.

Some people favour the all-wire baskets (4). The cat can see out of these so that it does not feel trapped. Others favour closed boxes on the grounds that they offer the cat a greater sense of security. It is a matter of choice, and you should consider the nature of your individual cat, whether it is bold and curious and will enjoy peering out, or whether it is a timid character which would prefer to hide in a secure closed-off container.

Whatever your choice, remember that cat baskets should be light enough to carry easily. They should close and lock securely. They should contain no spaces through which a cat can push its limbs or its head. The inside surfaces should be smooth. Frightened or angry cats will hurl themselves about. The basket should be large enough to easily contain the adult cat but not so large that it gets thrown from corner to corner. The materials from which it is made should be durable, light and washable.

GROOMING IMPLEMENTS

A long-haired cat is dependent on its owner's help to keep its fur in good condition. A short-haired cat is equipped to look after its own coat on a day-to-day basis, but will still benefit from your assistance, particularly when it is moulting and also if it has trouble with fleas. It makes sense, therefore, to equip yourself with the necessary grooming aids and accustom your cat to being groomed from an early age.

There are hundreds of grooming aids on the market, many of them indistinguishable from those used on dogs. The majority of the aids are combs, brushes or gloves.

You will need a suitable comb. Combs may be wide-toothed, fine-toothed, or combination wide- and fine-toothed. The comb is used to work right through the coat, teasing out tangles and removing dead hair and dirt.

Finely-spaced combs – known in the trade as flea-combs – may be useful in grooming short-coated or silky-coated cats. However, their use is limited on cats with more luxurious coverings, for they tend to glide over the surface without ever penetrating to the layer below. Although they are called flea-combs, it is important to remember that they do not automatically eradicate the target. Unless the

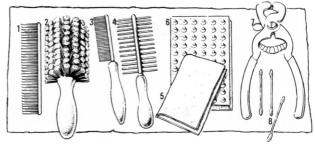

GROOMING EQUIPMENT

The grooming implements you will need depend to some extent on your cat's coat. A wide-toothed comb (1) and a fine-toothed flea comb (3), or a combination comb (4), together with a natural bristle brush (2) will serve for all types of fur. For a Shorthair, a chamois leather (5) and rubber brush (6) are useful. Cotton buds (8) may be used for cleaning ears, but take care not to probe deeper than you can see. Nail clippers (7) should also be used with care, and only be really necessary in the case of an ageing cat which is unable to keep its own claws in good condition.

flea is trapped and killed, the comb's only function may be to give the parasite a free ride to another part of the body.

One of the most useful combs is the one shaped like a garden rake, but with two rows of parallel teeth fairly widely spaced. This tool is so under-rated on the market that many good pet departments and shops do not even bother to stock it. However, it is well worth the effort involved in looking around for one. This invaluable aid can easily and efficiently penetrate and remove dead hairs from the thickest-coated animal.

A brush is needed to finish off the grooming. For a long-haired cat, a natural bristle brush is recommended as nylon can damage the hair and create additional static electricity in the coat. A crescent-shaped brush is ideal for this purpose, while an old toothbrush can be used around the face. For a short-haired cat, a rubber brush is suitable, and a chamois leather pad is useful to finish off the coat.

Other grooming aids you may consider acquiring include cotton buds for cleaning ears, dry shampoo for removing excess grease from the coat, and nail clippers, which are only required if the nails are definitely overgrown and whose use may be better left to the vet.

COLLARS

You may decide that you wish your cat to wear a collar with an address tag, to reduce the risk of losing your pet. The advantage of the cat carrying a tag becomes evident if it should get lost or become involved in an accident; the major drawback is that the collar may catch on something and prevent the cat from struggling free. It may also slightly damage the fur, particularly on a Longhair.

To minimize the risk of the cat being caught up by its collar, be sure to buy either the quick-release variety or an elasticated one which will stretch if caught, enabling the cat to wriggle free.

Special flea collars impregnated with toxic compounds are available for cats, but should not be regarded as an alternative to an ordinary cat collar. These flea collars need to be used with the utmost caution, and preferably only under veterinary advice: they can produce local skin irritation around the neck itself, and have been linked with the recently diagnosed nervous disease known as the Key-Gaskell syndrome (see page 223). Furthermore, these collars are usually not elasticated and therefore not safe for outdoor wear. Impregnated medallions, which can be attached to standard collars, are marketed in various parts of the world, but are not widely sold in Britain. These are safer than flea collars, but may not prove as effective.

SCRATCHING POSTS

To preserve your furniture and carpets, it is a good idea to provide your kitten with a scratching post on which it can legitimately exercise its claws.

Several types are available, but one can easily be made by fixing a piece of carpet to a flat piece of wood. The post must then be firmly attached to a wall so that the cat can scratch and pull on it.

The cat which is free to go outdoors will probably make use of natural objects such as trees, but all indoor cats will need some approved scratching area.

TOYS

Although important for kittens and enjoyed by adult cats, toys do not need to be elaborate. Just as a child will often disregard the expensive birthday present and play with the box in which it came, a ping-pong ball or an empty thread spool can give hours of fun to a kitten. Commercially produced toys such as rubber mice can be bought in pet stores, and those which are impregnated with catnip are often popular.

Not all toys sold for cats are safe or suitable for them, and it is important to check that there are no easily detached pieces which might be accidentally swallowed. The more elaborate cat toys sold by some pet stores, such as clockwork mice, may also be dangerous, as the cat may catch its tongue or a claw in the mechanism.

Do not encourage your kitten to play with yarn – they do find it very attractive, but if swallowed it may cause an obstruction.

CAT FLAPS

If the cat is to be allowed outdoors, it is well worth installing a cat flap to allow the animal to come and go at will.

There are various types of flap, but all work on the same principle of allowing the cat to push through a swinging flap. Some are fitted with a latch, allowing them to be secured at night, or whenever you want for some reason to keep your cat indoors. Some are simply operated by the cat's paw, the most popular type having a light spring or magnet which automatically closes the door after exit or entry and so prevents draughts.

However, you might find that you have a problem with unwanted feline friends entering via the flap. It is possible to purchase cat flaps that are activated by a magnetic collar on your cat and will therefore not allow any other cats to enter. Or you can lie in wait for an unwanted intruder, armed with a water pistol. A spraying with water will not harm a cat, but will probably convey the message that it is not welcome!

Once the cat can be allowed out of doors safely, it should be introduced to the cat flap and taught to use it. Persuading a cat to use a swing door of this type will require patience, because the animal will be frightened of being caught going through the flap itself. At first the hinged unit must be fixed back firmly, leaving just an entrance hole visible. The cat should be encouraged to enter and leave its home via this route. The next stage is to lower the flap partially, holding it in position by means of a stick. The cat inside should then be called through the hatch by placing a plate of milk, for example, on the ground just outside the flap as a lure. With the house door closed, it should not be too difficult to persuade the cat to venture forth through the flap. This procedure will then have to be repeated in the reverse direction, so the cat feels confident about returning back into the home through the flap. It will soon use its paw to push a cat door which hinges outwards, if this is propped open at first. Cats must always be encouraged to come in at night if they are allowed out during the day, so the flap can be closed.

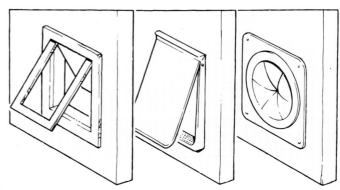

RIGHT: *A collar with an address tag reduces the risk of losing your pet if it should stray or be involved in an accident.*

LEFT: *Cats are easily house-trained, but, unless you intend to keep a litter-tray in the house at all times, ready access to the outdoors must be ensured. A cat flap is the easiest solution. All models consist essentially of a swinging flap through which the cat pushes its way. More elaborate models are adapted so that temporary one-way access can be arranged if you want to keep the cat in or out for some reason. Some will only permit your own cat to enter and will bar strays, being activated by a small magnet affixed to your cat's collar.*

SETTLING IN THE NEW KITTEN

There are a number of potential dangers facing the kitten in a new home, and it is advisable to restrict its domain at first. A kitten should only be obtained when there is someone who will be in close attendance for much of the day. Left alone to its own devices, the young cat may become tangled up in curtains, start to scratch a cherished piece of furniture or knock ornaments over. The kitten cannot be let out safely until its course of vaccinations is completed, and if allowed total freedom in the home, there is always a risk that it will slip outside undetected should a door or window be left open accidentally.

The necessary preparations should have been made for the newcomer in advance. A quiet corner of a room, out of direct sunlight, makes an ideal location for the kitten's sleeping basket and dirt tray, and it will soon come to recognize this area as its own territory. It is sensible to place a thick sheet of clean polythene over the floor in this area to avoid unnecessary soiling. Although cats are not really messy eaters, a certain amount of food or drink may be spilt on occasions, and the polythene will make it much easier to clear up. The feeding surface should always be wiped over daily, in any case, to ensure that it remains clean. Apart from presenting a direct health hazard to the kitten, meat residues attract flies in hot weather. A further advantage of the polythene is that any accidents close to the litter tray can also be cleaned up and disposed of more thoroughly.

When the new kitten first arrives home, open the travelling box as soon as the room is prepared and all doors and windows are shut. Other cats or dogs should be excluded at this stage. The kitten is likely to be upset after its journey and will need to be left quietly to settle down without unnecessary interference. Some kittens will venture out from their basket immediately, whereas others will be reluctant to leave and should be lifted out firmly.

The kitten will investigate the room cautiously, stopping to sniff around at intervals. After perhaps 15 minutes, if it has ignored the dirt box, it should be gently placed on the tray. Scooping the litter in front of the kitten for a brief period and using a restraining hand should encourage the animal to remain and use the box when it is freed. Cats are naturally clean animals. Once the kitten has adopted the tray, it should return of its own accord to perform its natural functions. After feeding and waking are usually the times for such activity; the tray must then be emptied as soon as possible after use because some kittens will ignore a soiled box.

After a drink of tepid milk and some food, the kitten can be placed in its basket and stroked to encourage it to sleep. Bedding must be provided in the basket; an old thick blanket is ideal for this purpose. It will help to keep the kitten snug, and cannot be ripped apart or accidentally consumed. Bedding must be washed regularly, particularly during the warmer months, because it will also prove a secure refuge for fleas.

In cold conditions, especially for the thinner-coated breeds, it is a good idea to put a heater right in the basket. There are heaters specially designed for this function, which operate on a low wattage and can therefore be run around the clock, if necessary, at very low cost. Such heaters are made in the form of a metal pad, generally about $10 \times 6in$ ($25 \times 15cm$), although certain manufacturers will make larger sizes to order if required, with the element underneath. Heat spreads evenly over the plate when weight is applied to its surface. These units are extremely durable and safe, and can be easily wiped clean if soiled. It is also possible to protect the pad by enclosing it in a plastic bag, although more mischievous kittens may get their heads inside, unless it is adequately sealed.

ABOVE: *Cats will investigate any small enclosed space. The interiors of washing machines, tumble driers and even ovens have a particular attraction because of the warmth, so make it your practice to check inside for sleeping cats before switching machines on.*

HOME HAZARDS

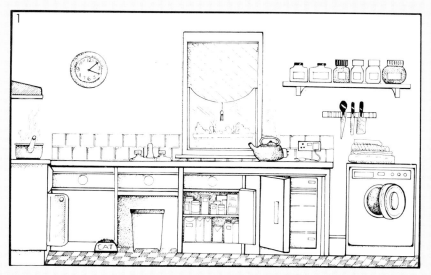

Homes may be dangerous places for a cat who is naturally curious and inquisitive and often, initially, through lack of experience, unaware of potential hazards. In a typical kitchen (1) accidents may be caused by pans of boiling water or hot fat that a cat is capable of spilling, open doors, such as the washing machine, drier and oven, which may attract cats by their warmth, open cupboards containing poisons, detergents and cleansers and rubbish bins that may contain small bones that could lodge in a cat's throat. In living areas (2) there are potential dangers from electrical cables that some cats like to chew. Open doors leading to high balconies, objects precariously resting on tables and shelves laden with precious ornaments should definitely be avoided. In general (3) watch out for fires without guards, poisonous houseplants and open drawers in which a cat may be accidentally trapped.

SETTLING IN THE ADULT CAT

The reactions of an older cat to a new environment are similar to those of a kitten. It should be allowed to investigate its new home in peace. If it seems very nervous, it may help to confine it to a single room for the first day or two and allow it to discover the rest of the house in gradual stages as it gains confidence.

Provide a suitable bed, but do not be surprised if the cat prefers to choose its own sleeping place. The adult cat will usually be clean in its habits, but remember that it may not be used to using a litter tray. Make sure that the tray is placed in an accessible position and do not move it from that place.

Under no circumstances should the cat be let out of the house for at least two weeks, unless it is used to walking on a harness. This applies especially to entire (unneutered) animals, which are likely to stray off immediately and not return to their new home. By keeping the cat indoors for a period, you will establish the house as its new territory, associated with food, warmth and comfort. When it is finally allowed to go out, the house will have become the base to which it will naturally return.

If by any chance a cat does not return after being let out, then the first step must be to carry out a thorough search in the immediate vicinity. By following their owners too closely, cats can find themselves locked in outbuildings, garages or sheds, and it is always worth checking such localities. Adult cats are quite hardy creatures, and if they are in good condition, they can survive at least several days without food, although water is a more critical necessity.

Having contacted neighbours, an advertisement in a local shop or newspaper, giving a brief description of the cat and any distinguishing features, may lead to information. Other sources of help to consider are animal welfare groups operating in the area, neighbourhood radio stations, some of which broadcast details of lost and found pets, and possibly the police.

ABOVE LEFT: *The traditional position in front of the fire will attract the cat.*

LEFT: *After a couple of weeks, the cat will feel that your house is the home base to which to return for food, companionship and security, and it can then be allowed to go outdoors without the fear of it straying off again.*

RIGHT: *Cats are comfort-lovers. Although the new home will be strange at first, the cat will soon establish itself.*

RIGHT: *Children and cats need careful adult supervision, but once a cat has established itself in the household, it is surprising what an affinity they can develop with human youngsters. This child is not holding her pet in the correct manner, but it will accept such undignified handling from a child which, from an adult, would meet with much stronger objections. Parents should ensure, however, that children are guided towards treating pets with respect.*

FAR RIGHT: *This kitten has not had any negative experiences with dogs, so it eyes the giant stranger without apparent fear and is prepared to make friends. Introduction of the new kitten to the family dog should be monitored to ensure that the dog does not frighten the newcomer with over-boisterous attentions.*

INTRODUCTION TO THE HOUSEHOLD

If you have other pets already or there are children in the household, a little forethought over the introduction of the new cat or kitten will pay dividends.

In a home where children and other pets are present, it can be useful to construct an enclosed wire pen where the kitten may be safely confined for periods. The cage should be large enough to house the sleeping basket, litter tray and feeding bowls, with enough space for the kitten to move around. Various collapsible models are now on the market, which will store flat when not in use.

A major advantage of such a pen is that it enables the kitten to be fed separately from other cats or dogs. Fights are especially likely to break out over food, and in such instances a small kitten could be easily killed by a dog. In a household where cats are coming in and out, it is also possible to supervise the food intake of the kitten, without fear of the others consuming its meal.

If you have children, they can obtain much pleasure and also practical training in responsibility from having a cat, but you will need to ensure that cat and children do not accidentally harm each other.

Cats and babies generally get on very well together. It is most unlikely that a cat will harm a baby in any way, but to be safe, it does no harm to put a cat net over the crib – cats do love to snuggle up to a warm body if they get a chance. If you already own a cat and are bringing a new baby home, do not ignore the cat or shoo him or her away.

Otherwise, your cat may come to resent the new baby. Make a big fuss of your cat and let him or her become accustomed to the strange 'animal' that has arrived in the house, and all will be well.

A young child will not differentiate between its new pet and its toy animals. Toys can be bashed, kicked around like footballs and squeezed to make them squeak. The child does not yet know that living animals are different and, without meaning any harm, a toddler can terrify, injure or even kill an adored pet. A kitten may be endangered by over-affection, for a young child is quite liable to hug and squeeze it so tightly that bones may be broken or internal organs damaged. A common unintentional injury occurs when a rubber band is wound tightly around the kitten's neck or tail by playful young fingers. The fur conceals the rubber band and, if it is not detected in time it may cut into the flesh, creating a deep wound. A band around the tail may cut off circulation and eventually the tail will drop off.

Just as the child has much to learn, the young kitten probably still has to learn to control the use of its sharp baby teeth and claws. Cats are generally surprisingly patient with children, but if tormented they may lash out.

In order to avoid injury to child or animal, therefore, constant supervision is essential. With a responsible adult keeping watch over their relationship, however, child and animal can develop a friendship from which both will benefit.

You may already have other pets in the household. If you already have a cat, its attitude to the newcomer will depend very much upon its individual temperament.

Cats will either remain wary of each other for a considerable period of time, or settle in quickly together without difficulties. They should not be forced into acquaintance but introduced carefully, preferably after having been fed, with someone present to keep a discreet eye on them. There is much less physical contact between two cats

meeting for the first time than is the case with dogs. Intact toms are an exception and will have to be kept apart in pens at first or serious fighting will be inevitable.

Even if the original cat and the newcomer do not grow to like each other, they will probably learn to live together in relative peace. It is probably best to leave them alone to sort things out between themselves – the presence of the owner often only acts as a source of tension. However, it is wise to keep an eye on them from a distance to ensure that no serious fighting takes place.

If you own a dog, much the same applies, except that a more formal introduction is advisable. In the early days, the two animals will rely on you to mediate between them. The dog's instinct is to investigate and sniff and, if he approves, to bounce around inviting play; you must make sure that he does not frighten the new arrival. The cat will be on the defensive, and you must guard against its sharp claws injuring the dog, especially with regard to the vulnerable eyes.

In normal circumstances, a cat which has never had a bad experience with a dog will be far more likely to welcome, or at least tolerate, a strange canine. One which has been savaged by a dog will always be withdrawn and suspicious. In spite of the popular belief that the cat and dog are natural enemies, togetherness is a perfectly normal way of life for these two species – within limits. The dog is a naturally protective animal and will extend its guard duties in the home to all the inhabitants. The cat, in contrast, is a more solitary creature, but it will accept and, at times, even positively welcome a dog into its home territory.

A final word of warning. The cat will almost always accepts its own family dog, and vice versa, for each is a recognized part of the territory. Because a dog is willing to accept one particular cat, it does not mean that it will welcome others. In fact, it can cheerfully kill a strange cat venturing onto its home area.

RIGHT: *In spite of the popular belief that cat and dog are natural enemies, if they are carefully supervised in the early days these two species will live together amicably.*

CARE OF THE NEW KITTEN

Once your new kitten is safely settled into its new surroundings, your next step is to ensure it gets regular care and attention.

FOOD

Kittens grow very rapidly and therefore require a comparatively large amount of good quality food compared to an adult. A kitten under six months of age will need four or five meals a day, which can be reduced to three by the age of nine months. At first, it is a good idea to allow a kitten to settle into a new home with as few changes as possible, so obtain a diet sheet from the breeder when you collect your kitten and stick to the same diet for the first

few days at least. Once the kitten has settled in, you can gradually change the diet to the type that you prefer – make up your mind how you wish to feed your cat in the long term and get it used to that type of food from an early age. For example, if you expect to feed your kitten on canned food when older, then you should introduce it slowly to one of the brands of complete kitten food available – just as with the adult canned foods, you can be sure that a reputable brand of kitten food will contain all the nutrients your kitten needs. Recommendations as to feeding will be given by the manufacturer on the can. There is no need to feed a vitamin supplement since a complete kitten food will contain them.

By all means feed your kitten on fresh meat or fish if you wish – either regularly, or once or twice a week to add variety to a canned diet. However, it is important that kittens are not fed on fresh meat alone since it is low in calcium and will not provide all the essential nutrients. Be sure that your kitten becomes used to a variety of foods, including a small amount of liver to supply vitamin A, a source of fat such as chopped bacon rind, cooked eggs and cheese. Milk is a useful source of calcium, essential for growing bones, but will cause diarrhoea in some kittens. A balanced vitamin and mineral supplement is a good idea, especially if your kitten does not do well on milk – your veterinarian will be able to advise you on a suitable supplement for your kitten. Do not overdo the vitamin supplements – while it is important that your kitten receives enough of all the essential vitamins and minerals, it is a mistake to suppose that an extra dose of vitamins will be even more beneficial. On the contrary, too much of certain vitamins can be very harmful. In particular, beware of over-dosing your cat with cod liver oil – it contains large amounts of Vitamin A and can cause severe bone deformities.

Obesity is not a common problem in active cats and even less so in kittens that are growing rapidly. Kittens have a relatively small stomach, and it is natural for them to eat little and often – some seem to eat a lot and often! Do not worry if your kitten seems to look decidedly spherical after a large meal, since even a small stomach can be stretched to an alarming size by a kitten with a healthy appetite. You can generally leave it to your kitten to adjust its intake to its own needs – your kitten will probably waste no time in training you to become the perfect cat owner!

LEFT: *A growing kitten needs a comparatively large amount of food containing a wide variety of nutrients. Either a commercially prepared kitten food or freshly prepared ingredients will be suitable, but if you elect to give fresh food make sure it covers all the kitten's nutritional needs.*

VACCINATION AND WORMING

It is important to have your cat vaccinated against infectious diseases. Kittens normally have their first vaccination at about nine weeks of age, followed by another three weeks later. Thereafter, they will require an annual booster. If you have acquired an adult cat, you may receive a vaccination certificate with it; if not, it is safest to assume that it has not been vaccinated and to ask your vet to remedy this.

Vaccines are at present available against feline distemper or infectious enteritis (otherwise known as *panleucopaenia*) and respiratory disease. The latter disease can be caused by several different agents, but the vaccines protect against the two mot important viruses involved. These diseases are discussed in more detail in Chapter 7. If your kitten should catch these viruses, there are no drugs that can be used to kill them. Your veterinarian will only be able to treat the symptoms while your kitten tries to fight them off. Prevention really is better than cure with these diseases, so be sure your kitten is fully protected before allowing him or her outdoors.

If you can be certain that your kitten will never come into contact with other cats then it is most unlikely that it will contract any infectious disease. However, the virus that causes feline distemper is very resistant, and it is theoretically possible that it could be carried into the house indirectly on clothing or shoes. Furthermore, if your kitten grows up in a very sheltered environment and then suddenly comes into contact with disease when older – for example, if it escaped from the house – it would have very little natural resistance to infection. It would probably become very ill indeed – much more so than a cat that was going outdoors all the time and boosting its natural resistance. The kitten would, of course, have to be vaccinated if you wish to board it. Modern vaccinations are very safe, and it is wise to have your kitten protected even if you do not expect to allow it outdoors.

When you visit your veterinary surgeon for the first vaccination, he is likely to recommend worming the kitten at the same time. Kittens may acquire roundworm infection with their mother's milk, although they may show no signs of this at first. Preventative worming will prevent them from developing the debilitating symptoms of a full-scale infestation later on.

LEFT: *Vaccines are usually given by a subcutaneous injection, most commonly under the loose skin of the neck. The procedure is quick and painless, and serious untoward reactions are, fortunately, uncommon.*

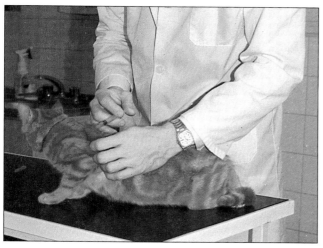

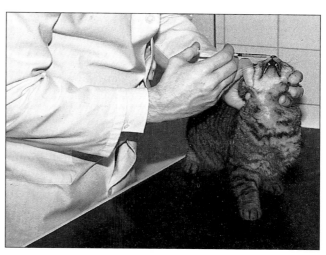

Although subcutaneous injection (**ABOVE LEFT**) *is the commonest means of administering a vaccine, some cat flu vaccines are given as drops directly into the nose.*

(**ABOVE RIGHT**). *Although there may be some side effects, this kind of vaccine provides a very rapid and effective immunity.*

NEUTERING

Neutering is strongly recommended for the pet cat, making life easier for both the animal and its owner. Neutered individuals live longer than their intact counterparts and obesity is not likely to be a significant side-effect of the operation, particularly if the diet is controlled accordingly.

In the case of the male cat, surgery, referred to as castration, can be carried out at virtually any time, although five months is perhaps the best age. At this stage, the blood supply to the testes is relatively small and the risk of post-operative haemorrhage is significantly reduced. Some pedigree breeds, such as the Abyssinian may need to be left intact until they are slightly older. Signs of masculinization of the head will be apparent if the operation is deferred for several months, as some owners prefer but spraying of urine will have already begun.

Castration, even in young cats, necessitates the use of an anaesthetic. This may be given either as an injection or in the form of gas. Recovery from gaseous anaesthetic is invariably quicker than recovery from the intravenous method – as cats can often be conscious again within 10 minutes after gas – but other factors will also influence the veterinarian's decision in this regard. It is preferable to castrate an adult cat outside the breeding season, between September and December. The operation will be less traumatic then, both psychologically and physically, since blood flow to the testes will be reduced at this time. After cas-

tration, sexual drive will be lost but the cat's hunting instinct will not be affected. The risk of abscesses resulting from fights is also significantly reduced. Sexual alopecia, or hair loss, may result from the loss of testosterone from the circulation, but can be corrected by implants if necessary.

Spaying, or ovarohysterectomy, entailing both removal of the ovaries and uterus, is to be recommended for all queens not kept for breeding purposes. While there is a risk of sexual alopecia developing, spaying removes the threat of ovarian cysts and pyometra in later life.

If you do not want your cat to have kittens, she is best spayed before she has her first season, when the womb is small and easy to remove – most veterinarians will carry this out when your kitten is around five months old. It is possible to spay a cat when she is calling, or even when she is pregnant, but the surgical risks involved are greater. If possible, she should be spayed when the womb is dormant. When she is in oestrus, the hormonal changes resulting from oestrus mean that the tissue is receiving a larger blood supply and the uterus itself is more fragile and prone to rupture.

Spaying can be carried out at any age, and it will make no difference whether the queen has already had a litter or not.

The operation can either be carried out through an incision in the flank, or via the mid-line of the abdomen, underneath the body. The area has to be clipped of fur to ensure a sterile environment around the site of the incision, and the fur may grow back paler, particularly in the case of Siamese. For this reason, providing there are no veterinary objections, owners often prefer to have their cat spayed via the mid-line, where the change will be less noticeable.

It is routine for cats to be kept overnight by the veterinarian after surgery. Very few complications result from spaying. Occasionally the cat may take out the sutures (stitches) from its wound and these will need to be replaced. The sutures are always removed about a week after surgery, by which time the site of the incision should be healing well. For the first few days at home the cat should be kept indoors.

Modern anaesthetics and surgical techniques make neutering as safe and trouble-free as any operation can be. However, since it must involve the administration of a general anaesthetic, some risk exists. Complications due to a problem with the anaesthetic, to bleeding directly after surgery, or to secondary infection following recovery from the operation can arise. While anyone putting their pet through any operation should be aware that there are risks, it must be stressed that routine surgery on a healthy young can is very safe and that problems are fortunately very rare indeed. It is probably true to say that the normal risks to the health of a cat simply by going through a pregnancy are greater than the surgical risks of spaying.

NEUTERING

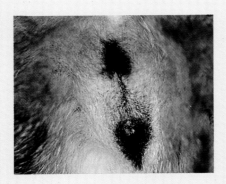

Neutering of a male cat involves the removal of the male sex organs. The reproductive system of the entire male comprises the testes (1) inside the scrotal sac (2), the vasa deferentia, which are the sperm-carrying tubes (3), accessory glands which supply fluid to the ejaculate (4) and the penis (5).

*A castrated male has the testes and part of the vasa deferentia removed. A small cut is made at the base of the scrotum, the vasa deferentia are tied and cut and the testes removed. Stitches are rarely needed and in time the scrotal sacs recede (**ABOVE**), compared with the entire male, (**LEFT**).*

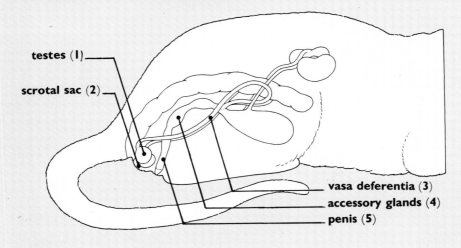

testes (1)

scrotal sac (2)

vasa deferentia (3)
accessory glands (4)
penis (5)

TATTOOING

1

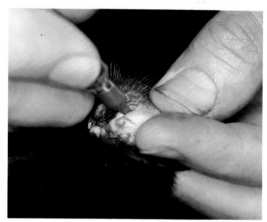

2

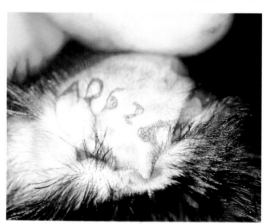

3

Tattooing is a permanet form of identification which can very easily be carried out while your cat is anaesthetized for neutering and may enable a lost cat to be returned to its owner. An identifying number is usually tattooed on the ear. The hair is clipped off the inside of the ear (1). A dye is applied to a special tattooing gun, which actually tattoos the ear (2). The ear is cleaned and the tattoo can be clearly seen (3). This should remain legible for the rest of the cat's life.

SPAYING

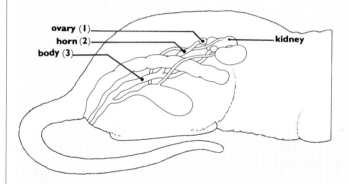

ovary (1)
horn (2)
body (3)
kidney

1 ovary
2 horn of the uterus
3 body of the uterus
4 kidney

ABOVE: *The spaying operation is generally safe and trouble-free, thanks to modern anaesthetics and surgical techniques. Only a small incision is made, either on the flank or midline, and it generally heals rapidly. The stitches are removed after about a week, by which time the fur has already started to regrow.*
The operation is the equivalent of an ovario-hysterectomy in women and involves the removal of the female cat's sex organs – the ovaries (1), horns of the uterus (2) and the body of the uterus (3). This may seem drastic, but it is the responsible way of overcoming the problem of unwanted pregnancies, and a frustrated, confined queen. The queen herself will not suffer by the operation and in fact it is likely to extend her lifespan.

SPAYING

1

Spaying is a comparatively straightforward operation from which cats normally recover quickly.

(1) The veterinarian will administer an anaesthetic, usually intravenously or by gas. The operation site is then shaved of fur and thoroughly cleaned to make a sterile site for the incision.

(2) A small incision is made, either in the flank or along the mid-line of the abdomen, to expose the organs.

(3) The ovaries and uterus are removed.

(4) The small wound is closed with stitches, which will be ready to be removed about a week later.

(5) The cat will remain at the surgery until she returns to consciousness, and will probably be ready to go home the same day. She may be groggy at first, but most cats show little sign of their experience within a couple of days, and once the fur has grown again it will be almost impossible to tell that the operation ever took place.

2

3

4

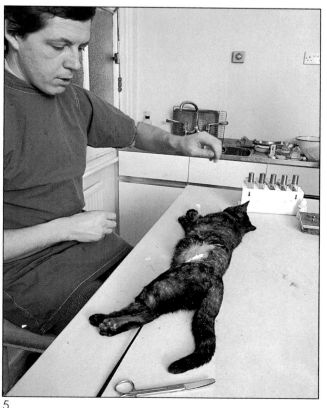

5

It is important to start training your cat as early as possible, for both you and your pets sake. Cats are naturally clean in their personal cleaning and toilet habits, and so training a kitten to use a litter tray, for example, should not be too difficult.

HOUSE TRAINING

Toilet training is one of the first things your cat has to learn. Most kittens will have learnt the rudiments from their mother. While she is nursing them she will keep the nesting box scrupulously clean from faecal contamination, and when they are able to toddle after her towards the litter tray they are likely to follow her example in using it. Orphaned kittens without the example of an adult cat to follow may prove harder to housetrain successfully, but the instinct to cleanliness is still there.

Exactly why cats are conditioned to cover up their waste is a cause for conjecture. It has been suggested that waste is buried to avoid leaving tell-tale signs that might attract larger predators, or that the practice had some evolutionary value in terms of the survival of the species by reducing the chances of reinfestation by the cat's own internal parasites. Whatever the reason, the practice has added greatly to the desirability of cats as pets in man's hygienic world.

Watch your kitten's behaviour, and you will soon learn to recognize the signals that it is about to urinate or defecate. It will start to sniff around for a suitable place, and this is the time to make it clear which place you consider suitable. Pick the kitten up and gently deposit it in the litter tray. It will soon start to scrabble around to dig a suitable hole. The combination of the suitability of the litter for carrying out the digging ritual, and of your praise for its appropriate conduct, will soon encourage the kitten to perform its functions in no other place.

Having adopted its litter tray, the kitten should continue to use it without problems. If an accident does occur elsewhere in the room, there is no point in scolding the animal. It will not understand the reason for such harsh treatment and is likely to respond by losing trust in its owner. It is also likely to repeat this behaviour through sheer lack of self-confidence. The best course of action is to clean the soiled area very thoroughly to remove any smell that might encourage the kitten to use the same spot again, and to persist with patience in encouraging the kitten to use the litter tray.

If the kitten repeatedly fails to use the tray, it is important to discover the reason. It may be because you are not keeping the tray clean enough. Many cats are extremely fastidious and will not use a tray that is already soiled.

Faeces should be scooped out as soon as they are found. If the tray becomes so dirty that you have to do more than just dump out the litter and rinse the tray, then you are probably not cleaning it out frequently enough.

If the box is clean and the kitten still ignores it, it may be the position of the box that is the problem. Try moving it to a more secluded spot, or introducing a second box somewhere else in the room. Of course, if the kitten is suffering from diarrhoea and simply fails to reach the box in time, veterinary treatment will be necessary.

Having spent the early part of your kitten's life encouraging him or her to use a litter box, you may well decide that you would like to dispense with it when your kitten starts going outside. Most cats will prefer to eliminate outdoors once they go out regularly, but you should not be surprised if at first they come running inside to use the box! It is probably best to keep the litter box available for a 'rainy day' when a cat may not want to go outdoors. It might start eliminating around the house if a box is not available.

Some cats may revert to fouling the house when they reach sexual maturity and develop the urge to mark out their territory. The problem is usually cured by neutering.

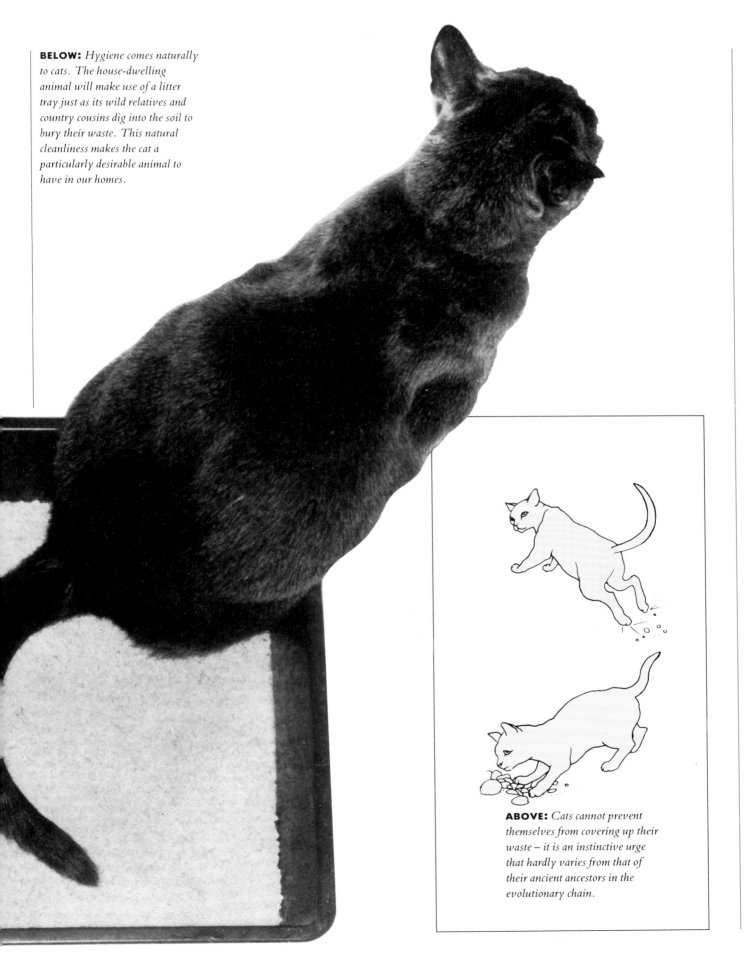

BELOW: *Hygiene comes naturally to cats. The house-dwelling animal will make use of a litter tray just as its wild relatives and country cousins dig into the soil to bury their waste. This natural cleanliness makes the cat a particularly desirable animal to have in our homes.*

ABOVE: *Cats cannot prevent themselves from covering up their waste – it is an instinctive urge that hardly varies from that of their ancient ancestors in the evolutionary chain.*

131

LEASH TRAINING

You may want to teach your cat to accept a collar and lead, so that you can take it with you under circumstances where some restraint is advisable, and this may well prove useful. A cat which is normally kept indoors, as may be necessary in areas with heavy traffic, would benefit from outings on the security of a leash. A naturally extrovert and sociable cat may prefer to visit the veterinarian carried in your arms rather than shut in a box, and here the leash will remove the risk of misadventure. If you wish to take your cat with you on holiday, it will be hazardous to allow it its freedom in a strange place where it might easily be lost, but if it is accustomed to walking on the leash it need not spend all the holiday in confinement.

Although a collar may serve, a harness is preferable for the cat. No cat is ever going to walk smartly to heel like a dog, so it is as well to avoid the risk of uncomfortable pressure around the neck which a collar may cause. In addition, the cat's small head is likely to slip through a collar if it struggles, and a harness which fastens around the body is much safer.

Take an adult cat and put it on a leash, and it will sit and look at your as if you have gone insane! However, if you accustom your kitten to exercising in this manner when it first begins to go outdoors, many will come to accept it as the natural thing to do. It is best to accustom the cat to the harness at home for a few days, introducing the leash only when the harness is fully accepted, and to keep to the home and garden until your pet is quite confident. After this you

LEASH TRAINING

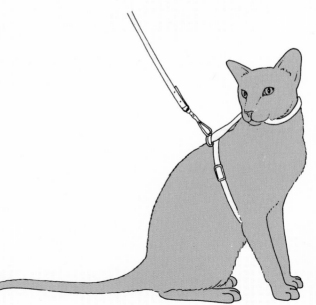

can venture into quiet areas, and introduce the cat to the busy outside world in gradual stages. Some breeds, such as the Siamese, seem to take better to walking on a leash than others: it is not something you can force on your pet if it has rooted objections.

SOCIALIZATION AND HANDLING

Playing with your kitten is a vital part of its socialization. Kittens love attention and a kitten's personality develops more fully if it is handled and played with. However, you should always be gentle when handling a kitten.

Most kittens will rest placidly if they are securely cupped in the palm of a hand and placed over a shoulder. They need to feel secure and not at risk of falling, but at the same time not to feel too restrained.

During play, the kitten is learning important lessons about its relationship with humans. This is the opportunity to teach the youngster gentleness. Whilst playing with its siblings it was able to use its baby teeth and claws because they were protected by fur coats, but the human hand has no such protection and the kitten needs to learn to sheathe its claws and to inhibit its play-bites. It needs to learn that climbing a human like a tree will not be popular. Above all, it is learning to regard humans as friends and playmates, to acknowledge the human hand as a source of pleasurable sensations, and to recognize the different tones of voice that praise it for doing as its owner wishes or reprimand it when necessary.

LEFT: *A litter tray should be available to your kitten at all times and the cat litter should be changed regularly. While a deep litter tray is best for adult cats, the sides of the tray must obviously not be too high to prevent a kitten climbing into it. Fortunately, cats are naturally clean creatures, and toilet training comes naturally to most kittens.*

Cats accustomed to walking on a leash can be taken out and about with the owners regularly, an advantage with a pet kept indoors for its own safety. This also provides a means of exercising the cat in an unfamiliar area without the risk that it will run off and be lost.

HANDLING A KITTEN

Most kittens will rest placidly if they are securely held with the hindquarters supported. Always be gentle when handling a kitten. Most kittens love attention, and the more they are handled and played with, the more their personalities will develop.

133

DISCOURAGING BAD HABITS

Lack of control of claws and teeth need to be tackled early on. The young kitten is accustomed to playing with littermates whose fur protects them from its needle-sharp baby teeth and claws. The thin-skinned human hand is a good deal more vulnerable.

If your kitten has an aggressive personality, it may get rather carried away when you play and start to attack you with teeth and unsheathed claws. Although this may seem cute and harmless in a young kitten, it should be firmly discouraged. Stop playing with the kitten immediately and ignore it. When it has calmed down, start playing with it again very gently, speaking with a soft voice.

The kitten must also learn not to use its claws on your furniture, curtains and carpets. He needs to scratch to keep his claws in good shape, so you should make sure he has access to an approved scratching site of some kind (see page 114).

It is important to get the cat accustomed to using alternative scratching posts when it is a kitten, especially if it is to be an indoor cat. Different cats like to scratch different surfaces, but most will use a fairly large piece of carpeting firmly attached to a piece of wood. Some cats prefer it vertical, others horizontal, but it must be large enough to allow the cat to stretch out when it scratches, and it must be anchored firmly to something so that the cat can pull on it hard without moving it. Scenting the wood by rubbing the crushed leaves of catmint over it is likely to attract the cat's attention. A kitten should be introduced to a scratching site by gently raising its front feet off the ground and positioning them against the wood. It should soon start to scratch here of its own accord. With older cats, any items which have been scratched previously should be removed to divert attention to the new site.

Scold the kitten when you see it using his claws on something forbidden. You can reinforce the scolding with a quick squirt from a water pistol when it is caught in the act. Alternatively, if you can shut the cat out of the room in which it is doing most of its scratching for a while, you may be able to break the cat's habit.

Cats can inflict considerable damage in the garden by scratching the trunks of fruit trees or shrubs. If this occurs, a protective tube of wire mesh should be staked into the ground around the bush by means of canes. Providing the mesh is set several inches away from the bark itself and does not come into contact with it, further scratching at this site will be prevented.

Teaching your kitten claw manners is the only real answer. If you really feel it necessary it is permissible to clip the very end of the claws with nail clippers, but you must be very careful not to cut the quick or splinter the claws, and the effect will not last long. Surgical removal of the claws is possible, and is practised in some countries, but in the United Kingdom most veterinary surgeons would consider this an unacceptable mutilation. Not only is it a fairly painful procedure – akin to having a nail removed for a human – but it undoubtedly handicaps the cat, which depends on its claws for climbing effectively, for catching prey and for defence. A declawed cat is no longer well adapted to roam free out of doors.

The kitten must also learn control of its teeth. Quite apart from unacceptable play-biting, a problem may arise during the teething period, between three and six months, when it may start chewing household objects to ease the discomfort of its gums. It will not discriminate sufficiently

RIGHT: *Stealing food should be discouraged. Never leave food items easily accessible, as the cat is a natural opportunist.*

to avoid gnawing on electrical cables so you should be careful to switch off, and preferably unplug, any electrical appliances within reach.

It is a good idea to provide suitable chewing blocks to discourage damage to household items. The sole of an old shoe is ideal for the purpose, providing there is no risk of pieces being accidentally chewed off and swallowed. Shin bones from cattle are another possible alternative, although these should be checked for any flaking pieces of bone, especially at the ends. The thick chews marketed for dogs also prove acceptable to many kittens. Close supervision or separation will be necessary if there is a dog in the household as well, because jealousies may break out over such items.

Chewing houseplants should be discouraged. This habit is not very good for the plants and sometimes even worse for the cat because common houseplants, such as *philodendron* and *dieffenbachia* are poisonous. A pot of grass or catnip for the cat to chew on may help – this is particularly important if the cat is kept indoors. Smaller plants are probably best put out of a cat's reach. It may be possible to cover larger plants with cellophane until the cat has broken the habit. If you catch your kitten in the act, once again a water-pistol is a useful deterrent.

Some kittens will get into the habit of sucking on material, particularly wool. This should not be encouraged, because the kitten will swallow the fibres which can cause a bowel obstruction. If possible, remove the material that is being sucked. It has been suggested that kittens are more likely to woolsuck when they are hungry, or if they do not have enough fibre in their diet. You could try experimenting with a change of diet to see if that helps – sometimes ad lib feeding with dry cat food seems to stop the problem, but is not advisable as the sole long-term diet. Extra fibre can be given in the form of wheat bran, available from a health food shop, mixed into the meat or canned food.

Stealing is basic to a cat's way of life, and this phenomenon runs right through the feline social scale, from one end to the other. The outcast alley cat has an obvious need to scavenge in such likely places as dustbins, in order to supplement the otherwise meagre diet of anything it can catch. However, this behaviour is mirrored by the fattest domesticated cats. This pampered creature is certainly not above wobbling away from a bowlful of food and a dish of cream – and then stealing the family's dinner while human backs are turned.

Cats will go to considerable trouble to take food, even though it is not needed. Some experts say that it is sheer force of habit. One slightly puritanical theory suggests that some innate part of the cat's make-up dictates that no reward is possible or acceptable without some effort. Quite simply, it is said, the cat cannot really enjoy any meal that it has not begged, stolen or hunted.

Prevention is the only effective cure for this innate behaviour. Train yourself to put food away and to remember that any food left out may be vulnerable. You can make it clear to your cat that if it is seen on surfaces where food is prepared or kept, it will be in disfavour, but the cat is an opportunist who can never be entirely trusted where food is concerned. This also applies to scavenging from dustbins, which need to be securely covered.

You may wish to discourage your pet from hunting wild birds and small rodents. Here again you will be competing against the cat's normal behaviour; even the best fed cat will usually hunt just for the fun of it. A collar and bell may lower the cat's success rate, but most cats can learn to catch wild animals even with a bell on. The best thing you can do is to make sure that you do not assist the cat to catch its prey by siting bird-tables or nest-boxes in vulnerable positions.

The cat can be discouraged from jumping on to tables by a light smack to demonstrate that such areas are not part of its territorial rights. However, cats do not respond to training in the same way as dogs do: the dog is a highly social animal which can feel guilt over wrongdoing, while the cat merely acknowledges your ability to stop it doing what it wants. It is unfair to expect a cat which, in your presence, will not jump on to the table and steal food, to behave in the same way if you go out: it is not in feline nature!

ABOVE: *Chewing houseplants can be a great temptation to cats, but many popular houseplants are poisonous and, in any case, few owners enjoy seeing their plants destroyed, so the cat must be distracted or discouraged.*

Chapter Five

DAILY CARE

Cats are not as adaptable as dogs in terms of the type of food they require, having adapted more absolutely to a strictly carnivorous diet. They need a high level of protein since, unlike many mammals including the dog and man himself, they cannot utilize carbohydrates to make up their energy requirements.

NUTRITIONAL REQUIREMENTS

The protein supplied to cats must also be largely of animal origin, because protein derived from plant sources does not contain the necessary balance of essential amino acids. Proteins are comprised of various amino acids, fused together in chains, and their sequence gives the protein its characteristic nature. Some of these amino acid residues are essential. Because they cannot be manufactured in the body they must be present in the diet if a deficiency is not to occur. Taurine is typical of this group, and is particularly important to cats because it maintains good vision.

Fat metabolism in the cat also differs significantly from that of the dog. As with protein, certain fatty acids are essential. Vegetable fats cannot be converted successfully by cats to meet their essential fatty acid requirement, so fats of animal origin must again be included in their diets. A low-fat diet is easily augmented with such items as raw bacon fat and chop trimings, or even a little margarine. The level of fat will have a direct influence on the palatability of the foodstuff to the cat, and they can consume relatively high levels of fatty foods with no adverse effects.

Fat provides a very concentrated source of energy, liberating twice as many calories as the equivalent amounts of either protein or carbohydrate. In the form of lipids, fats are vital for the correct functioning of cell membranes throughout the body. Fat can also act as an insulator, protecting against heat loss and trauma to vital organs.

Carbohydrates, sometimes referred to as 'starch' (in reality just one form of carbohydrate), are of relatively little significance to the cat as a true carnivore and are not present in significant quantities in their natural prey. Mice, for example, are basically comprised of protein and fat, as well as vitamins and minerals. In mammals, any excess carbohydrate is liable to be converted for storage as fat, rather than to starch, as in the case of plants.

The only form of carbohydrate which cats can digest readily is cooked starch, such as that found in bread or boiled potatoes, but they will rarely accept more than one per cent carbohydrate in their diet, unless it is well disguised by fatty food. Carbohydrate in other forms, such as the disaccharide lactose which is present in milk, may prove indigestible to some cats and could result in diarrhoea.

LEFT: *Cats are highly specialized carnivores whose needs are based on their natural diet of raw flesh.*

VITAMINS

The vitamin requirements of cats are also based upon a meat diet. Vitamins from raw plant sources cannot be utilized by cats. Although only relatively small amounts of vitamins are required, they perform a variety of functions within the body. There are two types of vitamin: fat-soluble, which can be stored in the body; and water-soluble which cannot. Deficiencies, as well as excesses in some circumstances, can have serious consequences.

The cat is known to require at least 13 vitamins, out of which Vitamin A is probably most significant. Cats need relatively high levels of this vitamin, which assists in promoting healthy eyesight and maintaining the integrity of body surfaces against infective agents. Whereas other animals can convert the precursor, carotene, present in plant matter, to Vitamin A, cats must have the actual vitamin present in their food. A deficiency is liable to lead to blindness especially at night, poor skin condition and reproductive failure.

Liver is a particularly rich source of this vitamin, but should not be given more than twice a week, for an excess of Vitamin A causes a condition quite as serious as a deficiency, with damage to the kidneys, fits or paralysis, and abnormal bone development causing lameness.

Vitamin D3 is another significant member of the group of fat-soluble vitamins which are stored in the body, and is found typically in the liver. It is responsible for controlling the levels of calcium and phosphorus, which are especially vital for bone development. A deficiency of Vitamin D3 gives rise to the condition known as rickets, where the limbs appear bowed because the long bones have become distorted during their development. It is most apparent in young animals; in skeletally mature individuals, inadequate Vitamin D3 causes the bones to become fragile and fracture easily. This disease is referred to as osteomalacia.

Cats which have access to direct sunlight manufacture Vitamin D in their skins, which they absorb when grooming themselves, but fish oils are also a valuable direct source of D3. The correct ratio of Vitamin A to Vitamin D3 in a cat's diet should be 10 to one. Because Vitamin D controls calcium storage, an overdose of this vitamin and of calcium means that the cat cannot rid itself of the excess calcium, which will form deposits in the internal organs or blood vessels.

Vitamin E is the other member of the fat-soluble group and, contrary to popular belief, does not appear to improve fertility in the feline. It does however, have an important role in muscle function, and can be inactivated by the presence of fish liver oils.

The water-soluble vitamins include the Vitamin B group, particularly important in metabolic reactions and often acting in association with enzymes. All the B vitamins are found in abundance in the cat's natural diet or raw meat. Thiamin, also known as Vitamin B1, is present in large quantities in yeast, and supplementary tablets can be offered directly to cats, or sprinkled over their food. This is often recommended when feeding fresh items such as raw fish, since a deficiency can easily arise.

LEFT: *Your cat depends on you for regular and nutritionally well-balanced meals.*

TOP RIGHT: *Cats can be very fussy eaters. Conversely, they are not above stealing and scavenging food not intended for them.*

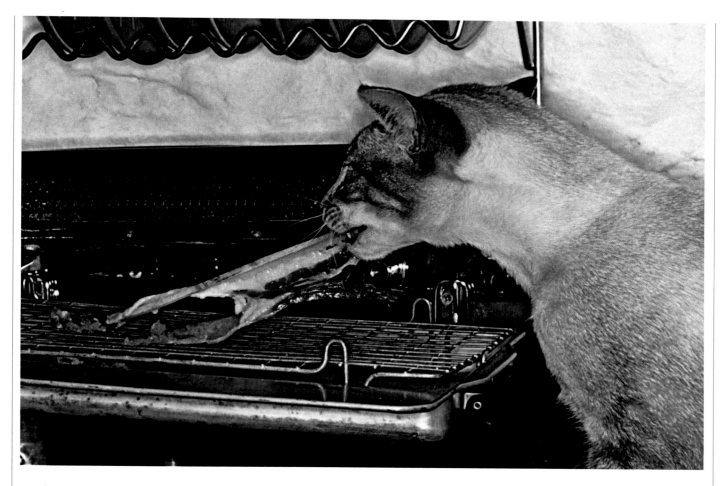

The other vitamin of particular significance is Vitamin K, which is closely involved in the blood-clotting process. Prolonged antibiotic therapy can destroy the bacteria present in the gut which produce this vitamin, predisposing the animal to haemorrhages. Supplementation of Vitamin K, given intravenously at first, will also be necessary in cases of Warfarin poisoning. Cats, unlike humans and guinea pigs, can manufacture their own Vitamin C, and so are not at risk from scurvy.

Because many vitamins are harmful when taken in excess, the responsible owner should aim to meet the cat's vitamin needs through a well-balanced diet rather than relying on supplements, which could lead to overdosing.

MINERALS

The minerals of main importance to the cat are calcium and phosphorus, which shoud be present in a ratio of about one to one: any imbalance is harmful. In some fresh foods, typically offal, this ratio can widen dramatically, to perhaps one to 50 in liver. Pregnant and lactating queens, and kittens, with their developing skeletal structures, are most at risk from a deficiency of calcium. Initial signs may simply be lethargy and mild lameness, which progress to gross bone abnormalities over a relatively short period unless treated. The condition, referred to as osteodystrophia fibrosa, can still occur in kittens given milk, since the relative imbalance of the two minerals may not be corrected. It is most likely to occur in kittens fed on meat alone, but can be simply prevented by adding calcium carbonate to their food, at a level of 8 grains per 3½oz (0.5g per 100g) of meat.

In the natural state, the bones of prey animals provide a good source of both calcium and phosphorus, but domestic cats are rarely fed bones because of the risk of splintering. Milk will provide calcium, if your cat can digest it, and mashed pilchard bones are often acceptable. All prepared foods contain a suitable level of calcium.

Iodine is necessary for breeding queens, and occurs naturally in fish.

Magnesium assumes greater significance for the older cat, especially neutered toms. Prepared foods, fishbones and ox-heart contain high levels of this mineral, which may indirectly predispose the animal to the serious condition of urolithasis, particularly when fluid intake is reduced. Iodine deficiency can occur in cats fed exclusively on meat, while too much manganese can result in a darker fur in the case of partial albinos like Siamese. Such problems, however, are extremely unlikely to arise when the cat is fed a well-balanced diet.

TYPES OF FOOD

Cats may be fed on fresh food, tinned food or dried food. Bearing in mind the cat's specialized dietary needs, any of these will be suitable.

Cats can be faddy feeders, however, and if you feed the same food all the time your pet may decide that it will not consider eating anything else, which can be inconvenient to you and even dangerous to the cat if its particular choice does not meet all its nutritional requirements. It makes sense, therefore, to have some variety in the diet.

FRESH FOODS

If you elect to prepare fresh food for your cat, remember that you must provide a good balance, with the necessary mixture of proteins, minerals, fats and vitamins. Feeding your cat on best fillet steak would be a false kindness, since this lacks fat and certain key minerals and vitamins. Butcher's meat, offal, poultry, rabbit, eggs and fish are all suitable, and may be augmented with suitable household scraps such as the remains of a stew. Alternating between different foods will reduce the risk of providing too much or too little of any vital nutrient; for example, liver is a valuable source of Vitamin A but, fed too often, can give a dangerous overdose of this.

Fish is a useful food but must be carefully filleted to avoid the risk of bones lodging in the cat's throat or lower down the digestive tract. Raw fish is not a recommended food, as it contains an enzyme known as thiaminase, which destroys Vitamin B and can lead to a deficiency, although this enzyme is destroyed by cooking.

Excess fish oils in a cat's diet lead to steatitis, also known as yellow fat disease because of the distinctive colour change in the body's fat deposits. Vitamin E is likely to be deficient in such cases and forms part of the treatment. Affected cats may appear superficially in good condition, but show loss of agility, often preferring to remain in one place, and resent being touched. Their temperature will be elevated, and appetite declines in the latter stages. Young cats are especially susceptible to steatitis, but the disease does not occur when canned complete fish foods are fed, because the Vitamin E level is adjusted accordingly. A similar condition will result from feeding horseflesh on a regular basis.

While it is preferable to cook some fresh foods, overcooking reduces the vitamin value itself. Cats will readily take raw foods such as beef mince, although there is a slight risk of transmitting some diseases, including toxoplasmosis, by this route; poultry, pig-meat and offal should never be offered uncooked for this reason. Eggs, a valuable source of both fat and protein, must also be cooked because biotin, a member of the Vitamin B group, is destroyed in the presence of raw egg white. Once hard-boiled, eggs are quite safe and can be cut up for feeding; eggs can also be scrambled with butter and milk, in the same way as for human consumption. Milk can be given directly, although it should be allowed to warm up for a few minutes if it has been kept refrigerated.

Providing sufficient variety to prevent significant nutritional shortcomings is essential when cats are fed exclusively on fresh food. While the work involved in preparation makes it a tedious task for the average cat-owner on a daily basis, feeding fresh food can prove most economical for those catering for relatively large numbers of cats. As a compromise, it is possible to obtain blocks of fresh food from many larger pet stores. These must be kept refrigerated and, again, do not constitute a balanced diet on their own, but are precooked and can be fed directly. Beef and chicken are marketed in this way.

A reputable vitamin and mineral supplement, or a weekly teaspoonful of cod-liver oil, will help to ensure that the cat's needs are fully met.

ABOVE: *Milk is a useful source of calcium but should be given only in moderation.*

ABOVE: *Your cat's choice of food may not always match its nutritional requirements. To many cats, stolen food is always sweetest, but scavenging should be discouraged.*

PREPARED FOODS

There is nothing wrong with feeding your cat with a balanced diet of freshly prepared foods, but it is not essential. The manufacturers of the reputable brands of commercial cat foods put a lot of work into ensuring that they contain a balance of all the essential nutrients your cat needs. They are convenient in terms both of time and of ensuring that the cat's nutritional needs are met.

It is sensible, however, to vary your cat's diet: if you always feed, for example, one particular brand of canned cat food it is likely that after a while you cat will refuse to touch anything else. Perhaps the best answer is to supplement prepared foods with some fresh food, including suitable household scraps, and to vary the brand you buy.

Prepared foods may be canned, dry or semi-moist. By far the largest proportion of cat food sales in the United Kingdom are of canned foods, with approximately 90 per cent of cat owners feeding it at least once a week. Canned foods comprise a variety of meats, offal, fish or poultry, usually mixed with some carbohydrate. The moisture content is high, comparable to that of fresh foods.

The contents of the cans do vary significantly, however, and some only contain a single ingredient such as sardines. These 'speciality' items do not constitute a balanced diet; if in doubt, the labelling of the can should be checked for the contents. At present the situation in Britain is not as clear-cut as it is in the United States, where descriptions such as 'balanced', 'complete' or 'scientific' on the labels of canned cat food ensure the contents include all the necessary ingredients to keep a cat in good health. Many cans of complete cat food are flavoured, and a 'pilchard variety' should not be confused with a product which clearly states that it is composed entirely of pilchard.

Never be tempted to give your cat canned dog food for a change. Whilst a dog, with its more adaptable digestion, will not come to any harm eating food prepared for cats, dog food is unlikely to contain all the essential nutrients your cat needs. Additionally, some of the dog foods contain preservatives poisonous to cats.

Once a can has been opened, it should be stored between meals in a refrigerator, as must fresh food, and not kept for any longer than 48 hours. It is possible to buy plastic lids to fit the opened cans, to prevent contamination of other foods in the refrigerator.

Canned cat foods are probably the simplest and most satisfactory option for most owners. During recent years, however, the supremacy of the can has been challenged by both semi-moist and dry cat foods. While canned diets are more expensive, they do have the advantage of being generally more palatable, as they are relatively high in both fat and animal protein. It may prove difficult to transfer a cat from canned to dry food, although this depends on the individual concerned. A gradual, rather than sudden change is to be recommended. At least a fortnight should be allowed when introducing dried food so that the cat has a chance to become accustomed to it.

Dry cat foods are convenient and hygienic to fed; they help to exercise the teeth and are ideal to put out if you have to leave the cat alone in the house for a period. They comprise similar ingredients to the canned foods (sometimes with additional carbohydrate), dried in hot air to form small biscuits. The crunchy texture means that they are good for the cat's teeth and gums. The main disadvantage arises from the low moisture content. Fluid, typically water or milk, must be constantly available to cats fed dried diets and the amount consumed should be monitored.

Cats in the wild do not drink large quantities, obtaining most of their fluid intake directly from their prey, and may not readily adapt to drinking the equivalent of a large cupful daily to balance their fluid intake on dry food. If the cat does not drink enough extra water to make up for what it is not getting in the food, this will cause it to produce very concentrated urine. This may lead to urinary problems, especially in neutered male cats.

To encourage cats fed on dry foods to drink adequately, manufacturers include a salt level of three percent in such products, which also increases their palatability. The expanded pellet forms of dry food are most acceptable since they are produced at higher temperatures which gelatinize the starch content, making it more digestible. Fat is then sprayed on directly, increasing the appeal of this type of pellet.

Some cats, especially those already accustomed to canned foods, do not find the dry foods very palatable. However, they are popular with many cats – sometimes too much so. On the whole, most cats are pretty good at regulating their food intake and avoiding middle-age spread. However, a liking for the dry cat foods can easily overcome their natural weight control mechanisms, leading to obesity. On the whole, therefore, dry foods are fine as an occasional treat, but they should be avoided if your cat has had a past history of urinary problems, such as cystitis, or is so enthusiastic that it tends to become 'hooked' on them and refuses to eat other foods.

The semi-moist products are the most recent innovation in the marketing of cat foods and contain significant levels of vegetable protein, augmented with essential nutrients. These brands appear quite succulent and contain about 20 percent water, compared to 75 to 80 percent in the case of canned food. They are treated chemically to maintain their moisture level. Especially for young cats, however, semi-moist food may not be entirely adequate to support their growth and milk must certainly be provided daily as a supplement. The provision of some fresh or canned food on a regular basis will also be beneficial, ensuring that the right level of nutrition is maintained.

LEFT: *Prepared foods are designed to supply the nutritional elements a cat would obtain from eating a natural flesh diet. If your cat eats only dried foods, ensure that it drinks plenty of water as well.*

GREEN FOODS

The cat is a specialized carnivore. Some other carnivores, such as dogs, can manage in the wild on a mixed diet if meat is in short supply, and it is possible to keep a pet dog in good health on a carefully planned vegetarian diet, but cats need meat. They have lost the ability to make certain essential amino acids not found in protein of vegetable origin. A deficiency of the amino acid taurine can cause progressive blindness. Cats also require a much higher fat content in their diet than most other animals and vegetarian diets tend to be low in fat.

It is acceptable to supplement the meat with a small amount of well-cooked and mashed vegetables, or finely grated raw carrot, well mixed in with the meat, if your cat will accept this, but ensure that at least a third of the cat's diet is protein of animal origin.

Most cats, however, will eat grass with enthusiasm. This may be to provide extra roughage, or to induce vomiting to clear the stomach of hairballs or even roundworms. Whatever the reason, cats should always have access to grass. Cats kept permanently indoors and deprived of grass may start eating houseplants, possibly with dire consequences because many can prove poisonous. It is a good idea to offer housebound cats some grass in a pot.

RIGHT: *Chewing grass is a popular pastime with many healthy cats although sometimes it may be a sign of an impending digestive upset. Housebound cats should be offered pots of grass.*

Cats are also enthusiastic about catmint *(Nepeta mussinii)*, also known as catnip, which can be easily grown in a pot or in the garden. It contains a chemical called nepetalactone which seems to have a similar effect to that which a large gin and tonic would have on their owners, releasing their inhibitions and making them more playful than normal. Some toys are also impregnated with this chemical. While the effect seems to be pleasant in most cats, some cats seem to react aggressively, sometimes to the extent of attacking their owners. This reaction is very uncommon, but it would be worth removing anything containing catnip if aggression is a problem.

LIQUID INTAKE

Always be sure that fresh water is available for your cat, but don't be surprised if it chooses to drink elsewhere. Many perfectly normal cats drink very little, getting the fluids they need from their food. The cat's ancestors were desert dwellers and consequently adapted to need less water than many other animals. However, the diet we feed our cats contains less liquid than the natural diet of the wild carnivore, so the cat should be encouraged to drink to avoid damage to its kidneys (see page 220). You may find that, despite the provision of clean water, your cat prefers to drink outdoors, or from less conventional sources such as a running tap, hot bath water, or even from a toilet.

It is essential that cats on a diet of dry foods be encouraged to drink adequately, whether water or milk, to compensate for the reduction of water in their food. The semi-moist foods have a much higher water content than dried foods, but even this may not meet the full requirements of growing youngsters, who must be supplied with milk for additional fluid intake.

Remember that milk is a food rather than a mere source of liquid. Milk is traditionally served to cats: it is certainly not essential to your cat's well-being, but if your cat enjoys it and can digest it (as many adult cats cannot), it is worth supplying, although not in excess, which will encourage obesity. The cream from the top of the bottle is valuable for its high fat content, but homogenized milk is acceptable. Milk can turn sour quickly, so do not leave it out too long.

SUPPLEMENTS

Many vitamins and mineral supplements are available for cats. The simplest rule regarding these is: if in doubt – don't! If a correct diet is provided, the only cats needing any form of supplementation will be those in special circumstances: kittens, pregnant and lactating queens, and cats in poor condition such as rescued strays. Your vet will advise you on the needs of such cases.

ABOVE: *Catnip has an unfailingly ecstatic effect upon cats. Show a cat catnip, and it will show you a change in its behaviour and personality. Even the most reserved animal will purr loudly, growl, roll around and even leap into the air under the influence of this plant. It is not clear why catnip should have this effect, but pet toy manufacturers often utilize it to good effect by filling toys with catnip.*

ABOVE: *Milk and cream are appealing to most cats but some are unable to digest it very well, and may develop diarrhoea if they drink too much.*

RIGHT: *Cats will nibble vegetation in the garden, but care must be taken to ensure that they do not eat any plants which may be poisonous.*

HOW MUCH AND HOW OFTEN?

Cats vary in the amount of food they require, depending upon age, degree of activity and individual metabolism. A kitten will obviously need to eat a good deal frequently, because it is expending much of its energy on growth – four or five meals a day until it reaches six months, and three meals a day thereafter up to nine months, will be needed. A breeding queen will also need additional food, fed more frequently (perhaps four meals a day), since, like a kitten, she cannot consume enough at one time to meet her extra bodily requirements. An older and sedentary cat will require considerably less.

The average adult cat can be fed once or perhaps twice a day, depending upon what best suits your own timetable. A useful guideline is one ounce of food per ounce of body weight while growing, and half that amount for the adult.

In the wild, a cat would not necessarily make a kill every day and would be unlikely to eat regularly. It is useful to establish a regular time for feeding your pet, however. Some owners leave food available throughout the day, so that the cat can return to it at will. While this does not seem to lead to over-eating, it is not advisable. The food may attract flies, particularly in hot weather, and milk rapidly sours if left out; cats will ignore food which is no longer fresh. When food is constantly accessible, this encourages the cat to become fussy, picking at favoured items in small amounts. To ensure that the cat has a regular daily intake, set mealtimes, with the removal of any uneaten food, are preferable.

Since cats are generally good at regulating their own weight, it is usually acceptable to feed a little and often on request. Your cat will quickly have you trained to respond to its demands for food!

With prepared foods, the guidelines set out by the manufacturer on the package should be followed, while with high-protein fresh foods such as mince, a similar allowance in terms of weight to that recommended on cans should prove adequate.

THE FAT CAT

Obesity is not as common in the cat as in the dog, because of the higher intake of protein and fat at the expense of carbohydrate. Fat in particular slows the emptying time of the stomach, acting as a control on appetite stimulus. Neutered cats are more prone to obesity than intact animals because of hormonal changes and a less active lifestyle, but with sensible care, this need not present any problems.

Most cats, therefore, are able to regulate their food intake to maintain normal body weight, but some individuals will over-eat – particularly if they are able to find food elsewhere than at home; it is not uncommon for one cat to be fed by two households.

Because cats are covered with hair, it is sometimes difficult to judge weight; and owners often fail to notice gradual changes. If the adult cat gains only four ounces a year, by the time it reaches an age of 10 or 11 it may be a quarter to a third overweight. You can assess overweight by placing your hands on the sides of the cat and feeling for the ribs; if you cannot feel each rib individually, without exerting

LEFT: *Obesity can kill, and a fat cat is not necessarily a contented one. Although most cats seem to be able to eat just enough food to maintain a normal body weight, weight control in cats can be a problem in those few cats that do not regulate their own intake sensibly, particularly if they are able to find food elsewhere – it is not uncommon for one cat to be fed at two homes. Attempting to fill up the cat's stomach with high-fibre foods may be an answer, but your cat may not agree!*

undue pressure, the cat is probably too fat.

If your cat is overweight, take it to the vet to ensure that there is no underlying physical cause. If the obesity is because of overfeeding, cut the food intake by five to ten percent and keep away from the more fattening items such as dry cat foods and milk. Attempting to fill the cat's stomach with bulky high-fibre foods such as bran may help, but your cat may not agree! Unfortunately, unless your cat is kept permanently indoors, you may have little control over its diet, since it will seek to make up any reduction elsewhere. Exercise will help to increase the speed with which food is burned up, so extra playtime may help.

THE THIN CAT

If, when you feel for the cat's ribs, they feel like pencils, the chances are that it is not being fed enough, or that it is suffering from a condition which needs veterinary treatment. Any sudden weight loss should be taken as a cue to visit the veterinary surgery.

It is common for the elderly cat to lose weight: this may be part of the natural ageing process, or it may be a symptom of some illness requiring veterinary attention.

LOSS OF APPETITE

If your cat is otherwise well, do not worry if it is off its food for a couple of days. Some cats will go without food for a while for no apparent reason. Remember also that your cat may be finding food elsewhere, either by hunting, scavenging, or begging from a friendly neighbour.

A cat may lose its appetite because of dirty bowls or stale food, or during the breeding season if it has not been

THE RIB TEST

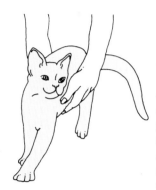

The rib test remains a reasonably effective guide to whether or not a cat's weight is correct. If you cannot feel each rib individually, without exerting undue pressure, then the cat is probably too fat. If the ridges of the cat's ribs feel like pencils, the chances are that it is not being fed enough, or that it is suffering from a condition which needs immediate attention from your vet.

neutered. There are various medical causes for loss of appetite, ranging from a sore mouth to various infections which need veterinary treatment.

A sick cat may need coaxing to eat. Cats can survive for a surprisingly long time without eating, but a prolonged fast is likely to produce nutritional deficiencies which will impede the patient's recovery. With a little ingenuity, you may be able to tempt the cat by offering tit-bits with a strong, inviting smell, such as cheese or pilchards; slightly warming the food may make it more palatable. There are a number of illnesses which cause soreness of the mouth and make the cat, naturally enough, disinclined to eat, in which case soft, sloppy foods should be offered. A very weak cat which lacks the energy to feed itself may be persuaded to lap a little food from your finger, or you can try feeding from a teaspoon. Raise the cat's head slightly with one hand to facilitate swallowing, and slide the spoon into the side of its mouth, giving only a little at a time.

'Fit, not fat' should be the aim. The cat's ribs should be well-covered, not prominent, but not buried under rolls of fat. Most cats will regulate their own diets sensibly, but some individuals seem to lose this ability and may be difficult to keep in healthy condition.

GOOD FOOD GUIDE FOR YOUR CAT

Type of cat	Weight of	Dry food		Semi-moist food		Canned food	
		g/kg of body weight	g/cat	g/kg of body weight	g/cat	g/kg of body weight	g/cat
Kitten							
10 weeks	0.4–1.0	70	28– 70	80	32– 80	200	80–200
20 weeks	1.2–2.0	36	43– 72	42	50– 84	104	125–208
30 weeks	1.5–2.7	28	42– 76	32	48– 86	80	120–216
40 weeks	2.2–3.8	22	48– 84	26	57– 99	64	141–243
Adult							
Active	2.2–4.5	20	44– 90	22	48– 99	56	123–252
Inactive	2.2–4.5	24	53–108	27	59–122	68	150–306
Gestation	2.5–4.0	28	70–112	32	80–128	80	200–320
Lactation	2.5–4.0	70	154–280	80	176–320	200	440–800

*Cats vary in the amount of food they require (**ABOVE**). The chart is based on the findings of the National Research Council and shows amounts of alternative types of food needed by cats at different ages. Dry food contains 90 percent dry matter; semi-moist 70 percent and canned 25 percent. Quantities are given in metric measurements for accuracy.*

BELOW: *It is important to establish a regular eating routine for a cat as early as possible. Cats can be fussy feeders and are easily put off their foods by noise, strong light, other people and even other cats. Since they are clean animals, they are also sensitive to cleanliness; a cat's food bowl should be washed regularly with detergent and then rinsed thoroughly to remove any aftertaste, which may well discourage the cat from eating. As far as actual food is concerned, cats become creatures of habit from early on, so they should be introduced to a selection of foods as quickly as possible and never allowed to become addicted to, say, a single brand of cat meat. Meal times, too, should be fixed.*

ABOVE: *Cats should have fresh water always available and be encouraged to drink. It can be annoying when, with typical feline perversity, they elect to drink from almost any other source than their water bowl, but do not let this stop you from providing the bowl and keeping the water fresh.*

HANDLING YOUR CAT

A cat must be held safely and securely and never hurt during the process. If possible, handle it so that it does not hurt you either, which is sometimes easier said than done.

Young kittens may be held and carried exactly as the mother does it, by the scruff of the neck, for their neck area is strong and their body weight light. As they put on weight, this method will cause pain, and the growing cat will react accordingly.

The adult cat, if placid, can be picked up with one hand supporting the chest and the other under the rump – it can then be cradled in the arms. If the cat is fractious, grasp the scruff firmly in one hand and help support its weight by holding the hind feet with the other hand.

Some cats are almost impossible to handle by the scruff of the neck. The most obvious are full toms in peak physical condition. They have no loose skin to speak of, and their neck and shoulders are muscled like a bull terrier. Few men have enough strength in their fingers to hold an unwilling tom in one hand.

Contrary to popular belief, many of these powerful cats are among the gentlest of creatures, if they are not riled. Try a little soothing conversation with the animal before going any further.

Many elderly cats and some younger ones suffer from arthritis of the spine and neck and simply cannot bear pressure on these joints. The neck area is a typical site of heavy flea-bite infection, or abscesses. One can hardly blame the cat if it responds adversely to squeezing of a painful area. The sensible solution is to look before you reach.

The family pet will often be surprisingly tolerant of children's clumsy handling. Although most children have little knowledge of how to handle a cat, they seem able instantly to communicate their feelings to the animal. Often, even the most disagreeable feline will respond by leaping into the child's arms.

However, in fairness to both cat and child, you should always supervise their interaction. A young child may hug a cat tightly enough to break bones, and of course a hurt or startled cat may lash out with its claws and injure the child.

METHODS OF HANDLING

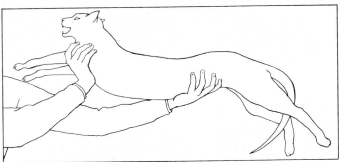

LEFT: *Most cats can be carried like this, with the face and forelegs away from your body so that if they begin to struggle, teeth and claws are not towards you, and the cat can see where it is going.*

ABOVE: *HOLDING FOR EXAMINATION*
This is how a show judge will hold a cat for examination, gripping the forelegs in one hand and the hindquarters in the other.

LEFT: *HOLDING A KITTEN*
A young kitten can safely be held by the scruff of the neck, for its neck is strong and its body weight relatively light. However, it will soon outgrow the stage where this method is comfortable, and will require a hand under the hindquarters to take its weight.

RIGHT: *Playing with your cat will give both of you a great deal of enjoyment. A simple toy like this tennis ball can be batted about for hours.*

*A placid cat can be cradled in the arms, (**TOP**), with the weight supported. A more nervous or aggressive cat (**ABOVE**) should be restrained firmly by its scruff, while still supported below.*

GROOMING

Daily grooming of the fur is essential to the physical and mental well-being of every cat. The majority of cats can manage this themselves without human aid. The short-haired cat can keep its coat in top condition with the specialized grooming instrument that is its tongue. The thick-coated and long-haired types which man has developed through selective breeding do need assistance from their owners, however; most breeders and lovers of these types proudly admit that it requires at least 30 minutes of daily grooming to keep them in prime condition.

Although the short-haired cat does not depend upon its owner for grooming, it makes sense to give it a helping hand once or twice a week, and more often during the moult. Removing loose hair will reduce the risk of fur balls in the cat's stomach, and will enable you to keep a regular check for parasites such as fleas and ticks, and to spot any inconspicuous wounds that might become infected. Grooming should also be a pleasurable activity that reinforces the bond between pet and owner.

The points to remember when grooming are regularity, hygiene and gentleness. Regular grooming is important so that the cat is accustomed to it and will not reject your attentions at times when they are needed, such as during a heavy moult or when a skin ailment or parasite infestation needs attention.

Hygiene is vital to ensure that the brush and comb are not spreading infection. After use, a comb should be thoroughly cleaned and washed. When any cat is thought to be suffering from ringworm, then it must have its own set of grooming equipment, which is not used on the other cats.

Gentleness, it should go without saying, is crucial. You cannot force a cat to submit to grooming: you must persuade it that this is an enjoyable experience. As with children, the introduction must be painless and, if possible, pleasurable. Many a cat which has been gently introduced to combing and brushing will eagerly leap onto the table and purr throughout the proceedings, no matter which part of the body is being combed.

SHORTHAIRS

Grooming a shorthaired cat is a straightforward procedure. You can work with the cat on your lap, or stand it on an even surface with a sheet of paper underneath to help show up any fleas which may jump off and to catch loose debris from the coat. Comb through the fur, starting around the shoulders or at the base of the neck and working backwards towards the tail, making sure to groom the whole body. The legs should be groomed as far as possible in a horizontal manner.

GROOMING A SHORTHAIR

(1) *Stand the cat on a sheet of paper and work carefully through the fur.*
(2) *Work with the fur, not against it. Start at the shoulder and work towards the tail around the body.*
(3) *Rubbing down with a chamois leather pad brings up the coat and is often done before showing.*

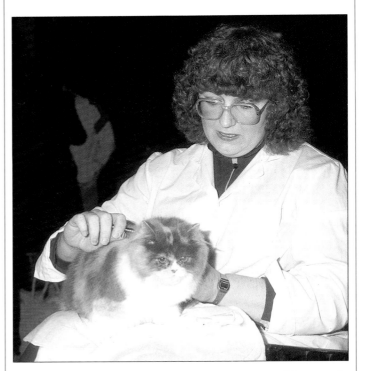

ABOVE: *Grooming should be an enjoyable experience for the cat, an extension of stroking and the direct equivalent of social grooming between two cats of the same group. Be careful as you take the comb through the coat not to tug at any tangles, but tease them out gently, keeping your finger between the skin and the tangle.*

154

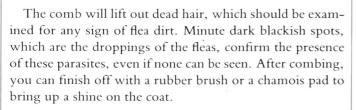

ABOVE LEFT: *The short-coated cat will need only minimal grooming to remove shed hairs and set a gloss on the coat.*

LEFT: *Some breeds fall between the Longhair and Shorthair categories with a medium-length coat but often a bushy tail which will require extra attention.*

ABOVE: *Longhaired cats need more careful grooming than their shorthaired counterparts, since their coats quickly become matted if they do not receive daily attention. There is also the risk that fur balls will form in the stomach as the cat ingests moulted hairs while grooming itself.*

The comb will lift out dead hair, which should be examined for any sign of flea dirt. Minute dark blackish spots, which are the droppings of the fleas, confirm the presence of these parasites, even if none can be seen. After combing, you can finish off with a rubber brush or a chamois pad to bring up a shine on the coat.

LONGHAIRS

Longhaired cats need more grooming, in terms both of time and of care. Every vet, boarding cattery and feline beauty parlour will agree that only a few months of neglect can create such a tangled mess that the only method of restoring order is by cutting or clipping off the whole lot. Nor is that an easy task, for the animal often requires a general anaesthetic.

To prevent that situation arising, grooming should be a regular feature of the cat's daily life, from the time of its arrival in your home.

The young kitten's coat is still quite short and easy to comb through, so by starting when it is young you will accustom both yourself and the kitten to regular grooming in the easiest way. Choose a time when the kitten is relaxed and sleepy, when it will welcome your attentions rather that wishing to bounce off and play, and use your brush and comb to caress the animal.

The adult coat, like long human hair, will be prone to the odd knot and tangle. If you groom every day, you should pick these up before they consolidate into mats and become difficult to deal with. Any knots you find should be tackled before you go on to comb through the rest of the coat. Tease the knot out gently with dampened fingers, taking care not to pull away from the skin, which will hurt the cat and make it extremely uncooperative. More awkward knots can sometimes be eased apart carefully with the end of a tail comb or a knitting needle. If the knot has been missed for a day or so and felted up into a solid mass, you may as a last resort have to cut it out very delicately with a pair of curved scissors. Even with that safeguard, do not snip until your forefinger and thumb are between the blades and the cat. Once you have cut off most of the knot, the rest should be teased apart with ease. If possible, have an assistant to hold and soothe the cat, or you may have to deal with an angry protest, and need first aid.

Having dealt with any knots, comb through the coat in a vertical direction, using short upward strokes, towards the neck. The neck ruff should be brushed up and out to frame the head.

Both long-haired and short-haired cats will need extra attention during the moult, which occurs mainly in the spring, although there may be a secondary moult in late autumn. When moulting, cats will shed many more hairs than usual, which can lead to the formation of fur balls, especially in longhairs. As the cat licks itself, it will ingest large quantities of loose hair, which can accumulate as a mass in the digestive tract causing a blockage. The fur ball

may be vomited successfully, depending on its location, but those which pass lower down the intestines and away from the stomach may cause constipation. A laxative, such as sardines in oil, medicinal or liquid paraffin (which is not the same as combustible paraffin used for heating purposes) given directly on to the food (about a 5ml spoonful twice daily for two days) should ensure any accumulation of fur is passed without difficulty.

During the moult, brush more vigorously to remove as much dead hair as possible. A slightly damp cloth passed over the coat will help to remove loose hairs.

Light-coloured cats will benefit from a little talcum powder or cornflour sprinkled on the coat, rubbed in well and then brushed out.

GROOMING A LONG-HAIRED KITTEN

The long-haired kitten should be accustomed to regular grooming from a very early age, even though its baby coat is not yet as prone to tangles as the adult coat. With a wide-toothed metal comb, start with the legs and then groom the belly, flanks, back, chest, neck and tail, all in an upward direction, fluffing up the hairs. Follow this up by repeating the programme with a brush, and finish off with a polish from a chamois leather.

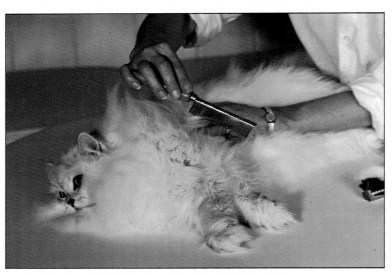

LEFT: *The cat should be thoroughly relaxed and confident as you work through its coat.*

GROOMING A LONG-HAIRED ADULT

By the time the cat is adult it should be familiar with the grooming routine.
(1) The coat is combed first to remove any tangles.
(2) After combing, brush thoroughly in the same manner. Keep an eye out for flea dirt on the brush. You can finish off with a chamois leather if you wish.

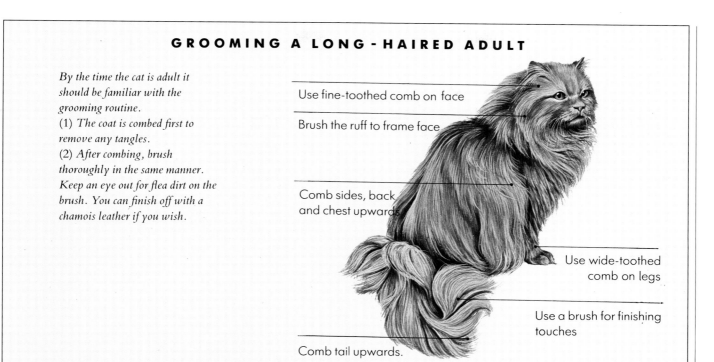

Use fine-toothed comb on face

Brush the ruff to frame face

Comb sides, back and chest upwards

Use wide-toothed comb on legs

Use a brush for finishing touches

Comb tail upwards.

EYES AND EARS

Grooming should include regular inspection of eyes and ears. Any discharge from the corners of the eyes should be gently removed with warm damp cotton wool; of course, if the discharge is persistent, you should seek veterinary advice. Some very short-faced breeds may have blocked tear ducts causing regular watering of the eyes; clean the damp area regularly with cotton wool and warm water, applying a little petroleum jelly to protect the skin if the area round the eyes starts to become sore. Be careful when you inspect the ears not to distress the cat by probing too deeply, but do check for any dirt or waxy discharge, which can be carefully removed with a little warm olive oil on a cotton wool bud. An excess of dark ear wax indicates ear mites, again necessitating a visit to the vet.

If the coat is greasy or dirty, a dry shampoo is useful. An unscented talcum powder, or cornflour, is effective, but a bran bath is as good as any and appears to be enjoyed by the cat. The bran, which is in fact derived from grain husks, can be obtained from many pet stores. Warm it in an oven beforehand and rub it thoroughly into the cat's coat. This will prove a rather messy operation and is best carried out on newspaper outside. Afterwards, groom the coat.

Certain cats produce excessive amounts of grease from sebaceous glands located around the base of the tail, which can give rise to the condition known as stud tail, especially in pedigree toms. The hair in this region becomes matted and unsightly, providing a focus for infections. White cats may develop a yellow stain on the tail. Veterinary treatment may be needed but a regular bran bath helps to remove the secretions before serious problems arise.

DRY SHAMPOO AND BATHS

Bathing is never popular with cats; it removes the natural oils from the coat and carries the real risk of the cat catching a cold unless it is dried very thoroughly, so it should be avoided if possible. However, if your cat manages to become so filthy that normal grooming will not clean it (from rolling in coal-dust for example), or if it has some skin ailment necessitating the use of a medicated shampoo, there may be no alternative.

The task will be easier with two people; the person holding the cat should wear gloves for protection. A large bowl makes the best receptacle, placed on a firm surface. It should be filled with tepid water. Scoop the water over the cat's body, either by hand or using a disposable plastic container such as an old yoghurt carton. Soap the cat with either a shampoo made especially for cats or a mild baby shampoo. Start with the body, working from the neck towards the tail, then wash the underparts and legs, and finish off with the head, being careful not to get soap in the eyes, which will be extremely distressing to the cat and difficult to rinse out. After washing, the bowl should be emptied and refilled with tepid water so that the cat's coat can be thoroughly rinsed. Once this has been completed, the cat should be wrapped in a towel and dried by hand as far as possible. It must be kept warm until its coat is completely dry and then it can be groomed. Rinsing is not always advised if the shampoo is medicated. In such cases, the instructions must be followed implicitly.

If a cat is likely to require regular bathing at any point in its life, it should be given a wash by the age of six months to lessen its subsequent fear of the ordeal.

GENERAL CARE

EARS

Inspect for cleanness. Wipe inside the flap with cotton wool if desired, but never probe. Dark brown wax indicates ear mites.

EYES

Inspect for discharge, cloudiness, discoloration. Third eyelids across eyes indicate illness.

MOUTH

Inspect for sores, bad breath, tartar build-up on teeth. Mouth ulcers may indicate cat flu.

COLLAR AND ADDRESS TAG

Collar must be elasticated or quick-release variety. Check periodically that address tag remains visible.

FUR AND SKIN

Groom regularly – even shorthairs will benefit, particularly during moult. Watch out for parasites, bald patches, wounds. Substances spilled on skin (eg paint) may be toxic and need removing before the cat can ingest them by washing itself.

CLAWS

Provide scratching facilities. Elderly cats may fail to wear their claws down and need (careful) claw-clipping.

STOMACH

Bear in mind the cat's specialized nutritional needs.

FIGURE

Obesity can kill: weight loss may indicate serious illness.

REPRODUCTIVE SYSTEM

Neutering is recommended for all pet cats. Both sexes, if neutered, make equally good pets.

NOSE

Inspect for discharge. Loss of normal colour may indicate anaemia.

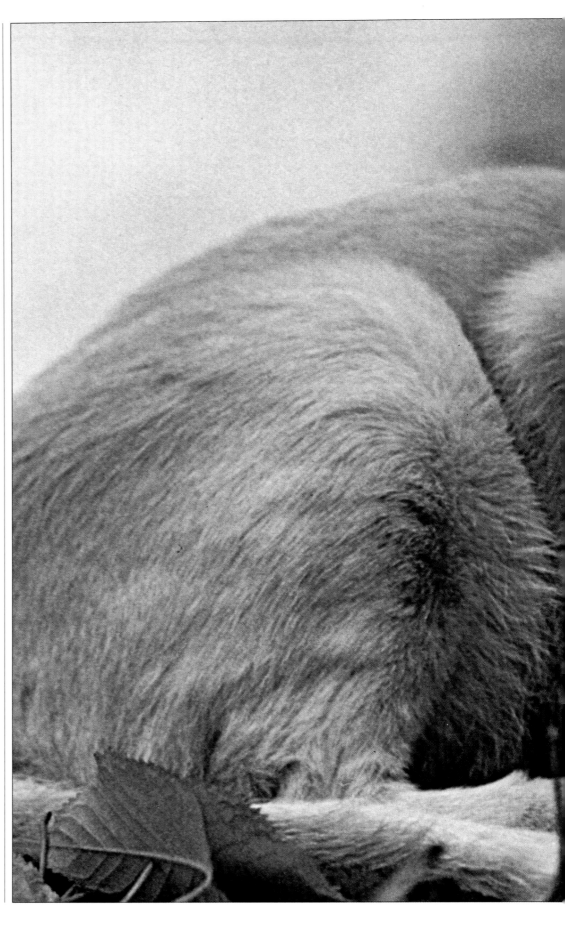

HOLIDAY ARRANGEMENTS

When you go away on holiday, you will need to make arrangements for the care of your cat. Because cats, unlike dogs, generally find security in their attachment to a territory rather than to their owners, it is not usually practicable to take your cat on holiday with you, and of course quarantine regulations preclude this altogether if you are travelling abroad.

Some highly human-oriented individuals, most notably Siamese, do accompany their owners on holiday. Cats are usually good travellers, especially if accustomed to this from an early age. They should never be allowed to wander free while on holiday, but are best kept in a small pen unless someone is present. If by any chance a cat escapes and does not return, as is likely in a strange environment, then the holiday will probably be ruined. Cats travelling in this way should always have an identification tag on them, so that if they do disappear by accident it will be possible for the finder to contact the owner. Cats which will accept a harness and lead can be exercised, preferably in quiet surroundings where there are no dogs in the vicinity. Once a cat has been scared, it will be hazardous to try and pick it up immediately and it should be encouraged to walk back

to safety whenever possible. If you do attempt to pick it up, it will probably scratch or bite.

If you are going away for a short period only, perhaps the best arrangement is to ask someone reliable to care for the cat in its own home. A friend or neighbour may be willing to call in daily to provide food and water. If the cat is accustomed to eating dry food, this is an advantage, as a quantity can be put out and will not deteriorate like fresh or canned food. The cat will have the security of familiar surroundings, and an outdoor cat provided with a cat flap may hardly notice the absence of its family, although it will miss the companionship and may wander further afield as a result.

The obvious drawback of leaving a cat on its own with someone calling in to feed it, is that it may fall ill or be involved in an accident without the owner's knowledge. For this reason, it is safest to keep the cat permanently inside with a litter tray, and ask its temporary mentor to attend to this as well. If the owner supplies canned food, then a suitable can-opener should be left readily available, along with other items such as litter and the feeding bowls. The name, address and telephone number of the veterinarian where the cat is registered should be written on a piece of paper and displayed prominently, in case of emergencies.

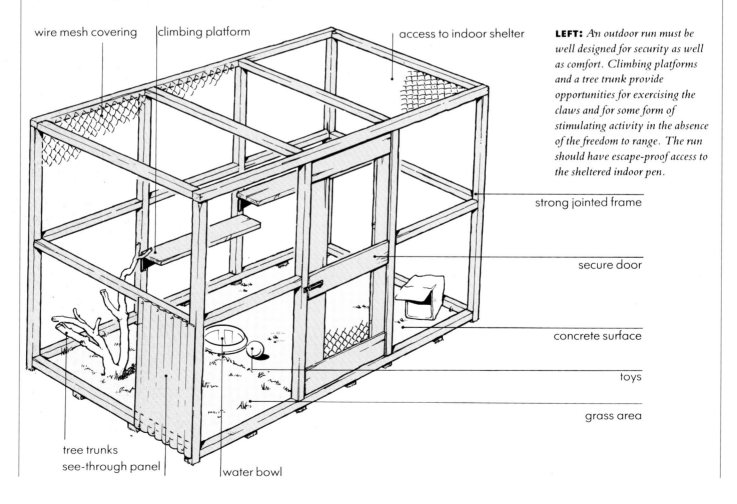

wire mesh covering   climbing platform   access to indoor shelter

LEFT: *An outdoor run must be well designed for security as well as comfort. Climbing platforms and a tree trunk provide opportunities for exercising the claws and for some form of stimulating activity in the absence of the freedom to range. The run should have escape-proof access to the sheltered indoor pen.*

strong jointed frame

secure door

concrete surface

toys

grass area

tree trunks
see-through panel   water bowl

If you cannot make such an arrangement, or if you are going away for a longer period, you will need to book your cat into a boarding home.

In Britain there are licensing requirements for such institutions, but no standardized system of management or fees. It is therefore advisable to seek out a boarding cattery well in advance of the holiday period. As a rule, most satisfied owners return to the same cattery with their pets each year, which may leave few vacancies during peak holiday time, such as Christmas, Easter and during the summer.

Personal recommendation is the best way to find a suitable place. It is sensible to visit the boarding home beforehand and ask to be shown around. Have a good look at the pens; your cat will be spending all its time in one of these, so be sure that they are large enough for the cat to move around comfortably. Ideally they should have access to an outdoor run. Check that the pens are secure, preferably with at least two doors between the cat and the world outside to minimize the risk of escape. Pens should also be well isolated from each other so that boarded cats do not come into contact with each other and risk spreading disease. Hygiene is important: the pens should be designed to be easily cleanable, and it should be obvious that care is taken to keep them clean. Finally, of course, take into account the attitude of the staff. The ideal boarding home owner will take pride in the running of the home and caring for each cat individually. He or she will be eager to discover the likes and dislikes of each boarder and will always be on the look-out for signs of trouble.

The fees vary according to the individual establishment and the services offered. Heating during the winter months and extra services, such as medication, are likely to lead to supplementary charges. It is becoming routine practice for catteries to request payment in advance, because certain owners have used them as a dumping place for unwanted pets, giving false details and then disappearing without trace. Many catteries also have a standard list of conditions for their protection, which the owner accepts and signs accordingly, prior to leaving the cat behind. It is important for both sides to understand their responsibilities.

Some boarding homes prefer owners to supply food, and adjust their fees accordingly. Cats can prove very fussy about eating, particularly when transferred to unfamiliar surroundings. The owner of the cattery should therefore be provided with a diet sheet and, if possible, details where the owners or a friend can be contacted, along with your veterinarian's telephone number. A small proportion of cats do not settle well in a cattery, irrespective of the care lavished upon them, and may appear in relatively poor condition when collected at the end of the holiday. Younger cats usually prove more adaptable, but even they may refuse to eat for the first day or so, due to the disruption in their routine.

Every boarding home should have an arrangement with a local veterinarian for the care of their boarders. You will probably be asked to sign a form to authorize the home to arrange for any essential treatment, although they will probably try to contact you first if possible. It is normal for any such costs to be borne by the owner, but it may be possible to take out insurance while the cat is boarded to cover veterinary fees. If your cat has received treatment recently, be sure the home has the telephone number of your own veterinarian to enable him to find out details of previous treatment given if the need should arise – a letter outlining any treatment given should then be passed on to your veterinarian when the cat is picked up from the home.

Any boarding home worth its salt will insist that all cats are up to date with infectious enteritis and cat 'flu vaccinations – you should be warned of this when you make your reservation. If your cat is going to be almost due for its booster when it goes in, it is wise to have it boosted before it goes, in order to give maximum protection. Be sure your 'Record of Vaccination' has been brought fully up to date by your veterinarian.

You should take the cat to the boarding home in a sturdy carrier (see page 112). Bring any toys that your cat is fond of and its bed, or a familiar blanket, to make the new environment less strange. If it is under any veterinary treatment, be sure to provide information of this and any necessary medications.

ABOVE: *When transporting your cat, a sturdy carrier is essential. Never let the cat, no matter how placid, travel unrestrained in a car, where it could be a dangerous distraction to the driver.*

Chapter Six

UNDERSTANDING YOUR CAT

THE FELINE ETHIC

Because the domestic cat is so familiar to us, it is easy to take its ways for granted. We all know that cats mew for food, enjoy being stroked, bring dead (or even live) mice into the sitting-room and make the nights hideous with caterwauling, but we rarely sit down and think about why they behave like this. Understanding the reasons behind your cat's behaviour can make co-existence easier, for both parties, as well as casting a fresh light on the cat as not merely a household familiar, but an animal every bit as interesting as the exotic beasts we see only on our television screens.

The cat's behaviour, like its physical attributes, has developed from its natural role as a predator, and from the type of predator it is – a solitary hunter rather than a pack animal, a territorial hunter rather than a wanderer, and a dedicated carnivore rather than one with omnivorous tendencies.

SOCIAL BEHAVIOUR

'The cat who walked by himself' is proverbial, and certainly the cat is essentially an animal which hunts alone, the lion being the only member of the family to live and hunt co-operatively in large social groups, but nevertheless cats do have a social pattern which governs their behaviour.

Left to their own devices, domestic cats tend to form small loose-knit groups based on the pattern of one or two queens living under the aegis of one tom, who will not tolerate competition from other adult males. This pattern is much the same as that of the smaller wild cats, where a pair may occupy a territory, with their young. Neither the wild nor the domestic cats hunt co-operatively, and the male does not help to rear the young, although he will tolerate them until the male kittens reach sexual maturity. Within the small family group, however, cats show considerable affection towards each other. It is known that female cats living together will assist each other when kittens are born, acting as midwives, sometimes bringing food to the new mother, and often suckling kittens communally.

In the artificial environments created by man, there are more cats in less space than would ever occur naturally. Feral cats in cities live in quite large colonies for this reason. However large the group, it remains a loose collection of individuals rather than a coherent band with a distinct hierarchy or 'pecking order' such as genuinely gregarious animals develop. Cats have never evolved a complex social ranking system because they are essentially not group animals. There will be some ranking amongst

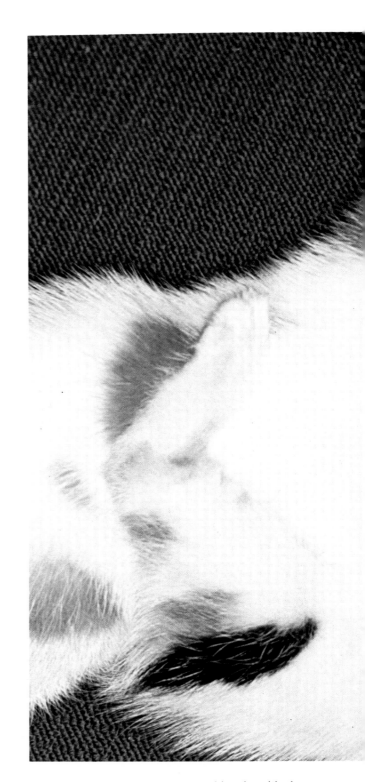

ABOVE: *Although, unlike dogs, cats are essentially not social animals, a family of cats living together will usually demonstrate a close and affectionate relationship.*

toms in practical terms, and in large colonies a dominant matriarch may be identifiable, but dominance in cats depends upon territorial and sexual status rather than individual ranking.

Where cats are concerned, familiarity breeds acceptance. As long as they stay together, cats which have been reared in each other's company will remain on reasonably polite terms. No serious animal behaviourist would ever suggest that cats can recognize their blood relations. This is not to say that such a thing does not ever happen, merely that there is no proof. However, there is evidence that familiarity lessens the normal antagonistic behaviour.

Certainly, cats living communally may not only groom each other, care for each other, and warn of impending danger, but they may even stand together in exceptional circumstances and fight a common foe. This behaviour, which is automatic in dogs, is untypical in cats, for they are not social creatures. Generally, cats may co-operate only when doing so is patterned on normal behaviour. Cats sleep together as adults, just as they did when they were kittens. the act provides natural warmth, comfort, and a high degree of security. The relationship will often go beyond passive acceptance, and two cats kept together may develop a high degree of demonstration, touchingly demonstrated by the distress of one should the other be lost or die.

However, this social bond can be broken down if one cat is absent for several days, to return without the 'home territory' smell it shared with its companion. This process of defamiliarization means that when the former friends are reunited they may meet as strangers, with hostility which will take weeks to break down.

The comparatively unstructured social framework of the cat provides the basis for its non-dependent relationship with man. Domesticated animals react to their human owners much as they would to members of their own species. Dogs naturally live in tightly organized social groups, with a scale of dominance and a clearly acknowledged leader, and consequently it comes naturally to them to accept a human leader. The cat's social structure is quite different. As a solitary hunter with no pack leader, it has no predisposition to cast its human owner in that role.

The cat treats its human family as it would treat other cats in its family group. When you stroke your cat, or when it invites your caresses, this is equivalent to the grooming that takes place between the mother cat and her kittens, and also between group members. The cat rubbing against your legs would rub against other cats in its group in the same way, both as a friendly greeting and also to scent-mark with its head-glands.

The relationship between human and cat partakes more of the mother and kitten bond than the looser bond between two adult cats. The human provides food, security and comfort, with stroking mimicking the caress of the mother cat's tongue. Many cats will respond to this maternal-type provision with a high degree of affection, seeking close contact with their owners and actively seeking attention.

The thoroughly domesticated cat finds much comfort in the company of its family. If that family consists of more than one person, there is almost always a particular individual to whom the cat will devote most attention. This is particularly true of all queens and neutered toms, for in the normal situation, the demands of the reproductive cycle will take up much of the un-neutered animal's interactive capacity.

LEFT: *There is no doubt that these little brothers are on such good terms that even the shattering of peace and quiet will be allowed to pass with nothing more than a pained expression. This may change when they grow up – particularly if they want the same female.*

THE CAT AND ITS HUMAN FAMILY

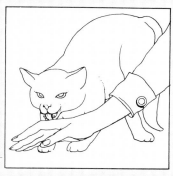

To the cat, its human owner takes the place of feline companionship. (1) Rubbing along the human's legs, the cat offers the same greeting as to a conspecific. The tail is raised in greeting and the action is often accompanied by soft chirruping or purring. As well as expressing friendship, the cat is consolidating 'group scent' between itself and its owner, picking up the human smell on its coat and depositing its own scent from glands on the face.

(2) Face to face contact underlines this message, the cat characteristically sniffing at the human mouth and nose – a contact typically made between friendly cats to mingle their scents. This action harks back to the kitten's earliest social contact with its mother, whose face not only carries the important scent glands but is also associated with the bonding action of grooming as well as presenting the first solid food.

(3) Licking is a social grooming activity which acknowledges a fellow member of the group. Some scientists suggest that the cat also obtains salt by licking the human skin. The rough comb-like texture of the cat's tongue can clearly be felt.

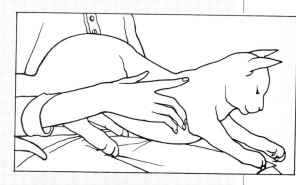

(4) Cats seek the comfort of the human lap, where they feel warm and secure. Part of the attraction may be sitting above ground level, as well as enjoying the warmth of the human body, and there is also the appeal of being well situated to nudge the human hand to continue stroking.

(5) Once comfortably settled, most cats will allow themselves to be cradled in their owner's arms.

(6) The comfortable cat often kneads its owner's lap with its forepaws. This is not always welcomed by owners, especially when the cat's claws are extended. It is an instinctive reaction to a warm, secure position, and harks back to infantile behaviour when the young kitten, while suckling, kneads at its mother's breasts to stimulate the milk flow.

COMMUNICATION

Cats may not be able to talk as we understand it, but they are equipped with a wide range of communication skills, using voice, facial expression and bodily posture.

Cats rely on vocal expression less than dogs, but they possess a distinctive range of vocal sounds which have been classified under three categories. The first group comprises the murmuring sounds, often made with the mouth closed, and reserved for times of intimate contact. They include the little greeting chirrup so endearing to cat-owners, and the soft calls emitted when being stroked. Purring, the sound most closely associated with the domestic cat, comes under this heading. Generally indicating contentment, purring is also heard from injured or even dying cats, perhaps as a way of appealing for comfort.

Biologists have not established quite how the cat makes its purring sound, although it is thought that the additional membranes close to the vocal cords are responsible, and purring results from their vibration. The big cats of the genus *Panthera* cannot purr.

The second set of vocalizations comprises calls which by contrast are more positive and often described as 'vowel sounds'. These are specific calls, made with an open mouth, and with a closing of the mouth appearing to act as punctuation. Such calls are normally used to attract the owner's attention. The cat forms distinct words by closing its mouth to terminate each sound and most cats have a small 'vocabulary' of essential sounds that may mean 'in' or 'out' or 'feed me'. The different way cats pronounce their vowel sounds gives them their individuality and distinctive recognizable voice. Similarly, human voices can be distinguished and differentiated in this way.

The third class of sounds comprises the high-intensity, high-pitched shrieks we call caterwauling. To vocalize these, the cat's mouth is kept open and tensed and changes shape. These shrieks are generally aggressive and reserved for inter-cat communication.

Other feline sounds include the quiet yet distinct clicking sound uttered while hunting, perhaps to indicate to other cats that the individual is in pursuit of prey, and the related curious tooth-rattling stutter of frustration, produced when an inaccessible bird is seen through a window. There is also the 'silent miaow' with which the cat may request food or attention, and which may be interpreted as an expression of submission.

Of these sounds developed for communication within the species, many are easily understood by man to give at least an indication of the cat's mood or needs, and most cat-owners learn to interpret a great deal of their pets' 'talk'. In response, a cat with a close relationship with its human family may become more vocal as it learns to make its needs known.

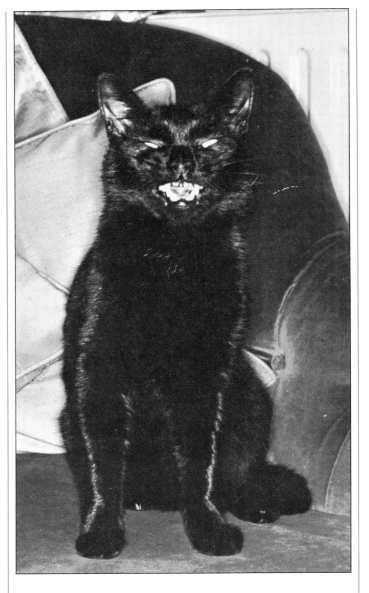

Different breeds of cat vary in the extent to which they are disposed to use their voices. Siamese, which are particularly human-oriented, being both responsive and demanding, are notoriously noisy and are very prompt to raise their raucous voices to inform their owners of their wishes.

Cats also express themselves as it were in mime, using body posture, gesture and facial expression.

Cats are sensual creatures, and their body language is highly developed. Most feline signals have been developed for communication between cats, both within a group, as a means of reinforcing their mutual bond, and between rival

ABOVE: *Although cats rely on vocal expression less than dogs, they have a range of distinctive sounds which owners quickly learn to interpret.*

RIGHT: *The cat will communicate its needs to its owner very distinctly despite the lack of a common language.*

cats, to mark the limitations of their territories, and to attempt to keep intruders at bay.

Feline body language is easily understood by humans. What could be more explicit than the pose of a relaxed cat, portraying contentment with its tranquil posture and calm face, ears and whiskers in their normal alert position, eyes blinking or often closed? Conversely, anger is equally unmistakable, with the whole body tensed and arched, the fur along the spine raised, whiskers bristling, ears flattened and eyes ablaze.

Cats will also use their limbs to communicate. A paw may be extended in friendship, cupboard love, or in a manner indicating danger. Whether in defence or offence, a paw with the claws out is something which must be treated with respect. A gentle pat with a clawless paw is usually a means of letting you know that the cat is ready for a game, or a stroke. Many an owner has been woken up with the gentle, but unnerving, pat on the face.

Tail language also expresses a great deal. The angry cat raises high a tail fluffed out like a bottle-brush. The frightened cat, too, bushes out its tail, but carries it low. In relaxation the tail flows easily and naturally behind the cat, while a feeling of cheerfulness and confidence is demonstrated by a tail carried high and jaunty with the tip gently curled.

During ambush and just before the pounce – whether in play or real hunting – the tail is rigid, with the tip gently gyrating. Some would say that it is like an engine warming up for take-off. The angry cat will also clearly indicate displeasure by swishing its tail from side to side. The abject cat may pull its tail between its legs, rather like a dog.

The way in which a cat walks has a myriad of meanings, most of them quite obvious. For example, the cat which bounds about with all four legs stiffly outstretched, is ready for an energetic game. However, the feline which walks away from a companion, animal or human, in a stiff-legged, deliberately slow fashion, is probably saying, 'You are so far beneath me that you are not worthy of notice at all.'

If this haughty attitude provokes a hostile reaction, the cat will simply become even more infuriating. It will run out of reach and start to groom itself, which clearly says, 'I don't know what the fuss is about. As you can see, I am very busy with my own affairs.'

The face of the cat presents a mirror image of its inner feelings. Eyes, ears and mouth all give clear indication of the animal's attitude to its immediate surroundings, and its companions. When the ears are erect, the cat is expressing annoyance, and the pupils of the eyes are likely to be narrowed to a vertical slit. Flattened ears are suggestive of fear or submission, and are typically evident in the weaker of two cats disputing an area of territory. When actually hunting for prey, the ears are drawn back slightly, contributing to the cat's watchful appearance. A contented cat sits with its eyes semi-closed, while the ears are maintained in an upright position. There are known to be in excess of 20 different muscles controlling ear posture in the cat.

The mouth is also expressive. Cats cannot smile like humans (and some dogs), but the lips express pleasure and distaste. When the animal is pleased, the lips will be relaxed, but when it is suspicious, or disapproving, they may be withdrawn into a thin line. The forehead is also expressive, for it will wrinkle in puzzlement, or if the cat is becoming angry.

Most difficult to interpret are the expressions of the eyes. In the first instance, they are shaped by the objects they are trying to see, and the conditions in which they are viewing. The widely-dilated pupil may be seen as an expression of love, but it is more realistic to assume that the animal is merely gathering all the available images and utilizing all possible illumination.

Anyone who has a cat in the home knows that when the animal is feeling completely secure, it will blink or close its eyes. At such times the cat is saying, 'I trust you, and I don't even have to look at you to know that I am completely safe.' The cat's human companions usually find such displays of affection quite irresistible.

At the other end of the scale, cats will keep their eyes closed when they are involved in fights that they cannot win. This is a protective measure, designed to minimize the damage caused by inevitable defeat.

Finally, mention must be made of the common human phenomenon of jutting out the jaw when being defiant. Cats in aggressive or supposedly superior positions will do exactly the same thing. 'Here I am. What are you going to do about it?' they seem to be saying. Only when the fight begins in earnest will the cat tuck in its chin and go on the attack.

ABOVE: *Tail carriage communicates the cat's mood clearly. A cheerful cat carries its tail straight up in the air with the tip relaxed. The message is one of good humour, and this tail carriage is often employed as part of the friendly greeting.*

FACIAL EXPRESSION

Facial expression shows the cat's mood. From the relaxed face through uncertainty of mood to full-scale warning, the expression is easy to read. The real danger signal is the backwards flattening of the ears, which will only flicker forward when the cat actually springs into attack. However, much of the threat display is bluff, as the cat attempts to frighten off the foe by looking too dangerous to be worth attacking.

BELOW: *Aggression is unmistakable. Ears, eyes, lips and even fur are employed to deliver a clear message that this animal is dangerous.*

TOP: *The curious cat is driven to explore everything in its environment.*

ABOVE: *Anything remotely resembling a hole, such as this laundry basket, must be investigated. Cats will climb into any small dark enclosed space, be it box, bag or even somewhere more dangerous such as under the bonnet of a car.*

CURIOSITY

'Curiosity killed the cat,' we say. Curiosity is certainly one of the cat's outstanding inborn traits, which in its natural state, far from leading it into trouble, is designed to help preserve its life. It is characteristic of hunting animals to take a keen and curious interest in their environment. In the wild, a predator's survival is likely to depend upon investigating anything and everything that takes its attention.

The domestic cat is often quite obsessive about exploring small, dark, enclosed spaces, which seem to hold a limitless fascination for it.

Tubes, tunnels, chimneys, washing machines, fridges, boxes or bags are just irresistible. Some students of animal behaviour make the Freudian suggestion that it is simply a way of returning to the security of the nest. Some say they merely want a quiet place to sleep. A rather far-fetched theory says that contact with the sides of the box or bag gratifies the cat's basically sensual nature.

Bearing in mind the cat's natural role as a hunter, it is logical to associate its passion for anything remotely resembling a tunnel with the fact that, in the wild, tunnels tend to be occupied by small prey animals. An empty carrier bag may not remind us of a mousehole, but it is in fact a hole, and as such stimulates the inbuilt exploratory urge. It is known that many animals respond to what is called a 'supernormal stimulus', that is a stimulus which goes well beyond the normal – for example, the foster-parents of a young cuckoo respond more strongly to the vast gape of the cuckoo nestling than to the smaller and, to them, more 'natural' gape of their own offspring. The cardboard box or open washing machine may carry a similar attraction to the mousehole-oriented cat.

Young cats in particular have a need to investigate and to explore. Strange objects and situations will always be thoroughly examined from a safe distance before closer inspection is felt justified. Final acceptance is a long process. The cat can also quite often be refreshing its own memory, by checking its own domain. If a familiar object has been moved to a new site, it will be subjected to the same detailed scrutiny as a newly-arrived piece.

It has been shown that exploratory behaviour is measurably increased in animals which have constant involvement with humans. Like children in a secure family, they are less afraid to venture into the unknown. Cats from secure homes also tend to live longer than those whose every aware moment is a struggle.

The cat's curiosity extends to almost anything moving, no matter what – a pet goldfish swimming about its bowl, or a picture on the television screen. Its sense of sight is acute, and it is programmed to respond to the small movements which indicate the passage of a prey animal.

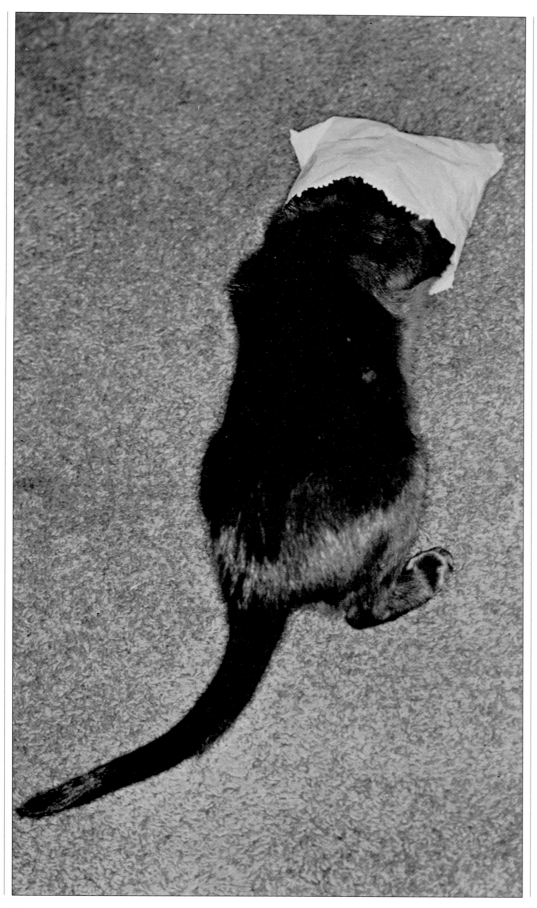

LEFT: *Paper bags are irresistible, even though the cat knows there is nothing inside*

OVERLEAF: *Curiosity may be tempered by caution in the more experienced cat. The mother duck will brook no nonsense from the cat, which recognizes that here discretion is the better part of valour.*

Some of the objects which take the cat's eye may eventually prove unrewarding. Fish swimming about in a tank may be inaccessible, for example. The cat will probably remain fascinated by the movement for some days before it decides that the object is unworthy of further investigation, however, and may return from time to time just in case the movement may really mean something rewarding.

Cats will sit for hours in front of the television set, apparently attracted by the moving images, but how much

LEFT: *Movement never fails to draw the cat's attention. It will be fascinated by the flickering images on the television screen until familiarity leads to the conclusion that there is nothing to be gained from continued watching.*

BELOW: *Of course, sometimes the pursuit of a moving object brings concrete rewards. It is wise to be sure that other smaller pets, such as this goldfish, are well protected from the cat's investigative urges.*

they see, appreciate or enjoy is debatable. The same cat will continue to sit in the same position even when the set is turned off, provided its human family continues sitting in their customary positions.

Cats definitely can see the images on the television, for their eyesight is as good or better than ours. Many learning experiments have shown that they can discriminate between shapes. For example, if they are shown crosses and circles, with one combination representing a reward of food, and another representing shock, they will quickly learn which to choose.

In the same way, cats can discriminate between colours, although not to the same degree as humans. There is no way in which a cat's mind can translate the moving shapes on the screen into any sort of meaningful action.

Probably the cat is initially attracted to the television by its curiosity over the movement on the screen and also the sound. Anything that resembles the sights and sounds of their own lives may evoke a reaction. However, after the initial curiosity has been rewarded by nothing further, most cats nod off in front of the television. Their apparent fondness for it may owe more to the fact that humans usually site the television set in a position where cat finds warmth and comfort.

Other moving creatures, like flies or mice, never lose their fascination for the cat. This is simply because the cat's long hours of watching and waiting are quite likely to be rewarded. Such rewards, no matter how few and far between, are the stimulus for renewed effort. It is not too difficult or unreasonable to draw a parallel with those gamblers who spend hours feeding coins into fruit machines.

HUNTING

Although the pet cat has its food provided by man, its hunting instincts are central to its nature and deep-rooted.

Small rodents, especially mice, and birds, are favoured prey. Kittens are taught to hunt by their mothers; some prove more adept than others in acquiring this skill. Hunting ability appears to be inherited to a certain degree; for controlling a plague of mice, acquire a kitten from a dam who is herself a good hunter. A mother cat will often bring living small prey animals home to her young, even when they have no need for food, apparently in order to teach the kittens how to pounce and kill. When the kittens are more advanced, she will teach them how to stalk their prey.

Cats are extremely patient hunters, and are content to remain motionless for long periods near a mouse hole, waiting for an unsuspecting animal to emerge. Their approach when preying on birds is different; stalking assumes greater importance than waiting. In either case, however, the final pounce must be precisely timed to catch the creature unawares. Whenever possible, the forelegs alone are used to grab the prey, while the hindlimbs remain on the ground for stability. The killing blow is a bite on the back of the neck – the long canines penetrate and cut the spinal cord precisely between two vertebrae. The whiskers have an important sensory function in locating the vulnerable spot; if they are cut or otherwise damaged the cat may have difficulty in killing its prey. Larger prey can present more of a problem and are likely to be pounded first by the feet until the cat achieves its deadly grip on the neck.

Cats are notorious for playing with their prey, especially small mammals like mice. The shocked, disorientated rodent will be released and allowed to run for a short distance before being leapt upon again. It is poked and prodded into further activity, until it either dies of shock or is finally dispatched by its captor. Even then, the cat may continue playing with the corpse, tossing it into the air before actually consuming it. This behaviour probably arises to some extent from the cat's domestic environment, in which the hunting instinct is not fully satisfied by the animal having to provide its own food.

Depending on the animal concerned, the cat will eat part or all of the body. Mice are typically swallowed whole, head first, being chewed in the process. Their fur will not

stick in the throat when ingested in this manner. Feathers, however, are often torn from a bird, which has a thinner skin. Most of the body is consumed, although the legs and skeleton are usually left. Unfortunately, a cat will often return home carrying prey in its mouth for its owner. The cat is identifying with its owner as a member of the colony, who will want to share the kill. The offering should be taken gracefully, and the cat itself rewarded with food.

Preventing cats from hunting is virtually impossible, and their instinct is reinforced by successive captures. There are nevertheless several steps which can be taken to reduce the chances of the cat making a successful kill. If you feed the birds in your garden, you should ensure that the bird table is placed where the cat cannot creep up on it unobserved, and site any nesting boxes well out of the cat's reach.

Some owners attach small bells to their cats' collars, warning birds of their movements. Studies show that the odds favour the prey, however; even experienced cats catch less than 10 per cent of the birds which they actually stalk. Older, or sick individuals are most likely to be taken throughout the years, and in this way, the cat helps to ensure that the overall population remains healthy, and has an adequate supply of food.

THE POUNCE

(1) The cat spies its prey and goes into a crouch, before beginning the slinking run.
(2) Head, body and tail seem to glide along the ground as the cat makes ready for the pounce. Toes dig in, heels rise and the hind legs move back. The tip of the tail twitches with contained energy.
(3) Finally, it pounces, but always keeps at least two feet firmly planted on the ground – just in case it should need a sudden means of retreat. The small drama is complete as it lands upon its prey, seizing it with mouth and forelegs.

LEFT: The cat is an ardent hunter and will spend hours in careful stalking of its prey.

OVERLEAF: Not every attack is successful. This kitten has bitten off more than it can chew in attempting an onslaught on a flock of doves, and every bird has escaped.

PLAY

Play is defined as activity which serves no practical function – mock fighting without real aggression, running and leaping neither to nor from any object but apparently for their own sake, pawing or tossing about an object such as a pebble which is of no value for food, etc. Play occurs in most species of mammal, especially in infancy; playfulness continuing into adult life is perhaps particularly characteristic of predators, and cats are characteristically highly playful creatures.

One function of play is to serve as practice for the serious business of life, keeping muscles and reflexes honed for the vital business of capturing prey. The cat toying with a small object such as a pebble, a straw or a feather goes through the actions it would use functionally when catching small prey. Kittens play-fighting enact in fun the moves they will need to use in serious aggressive encounters as adults. The repetition of actions in play helps to bring them to perfection for the time when they will be needed.

Play also serves a social function. Although cats are not highly social creatures, they will interact with and react to other cats throughout their lives. Immature cats playing together begin to work out a ranking order of social dominance as one kitten's greater boldness or aggressiveness enables it to dominate another shyer or weaker animal. Where cats live in a colony, playing together confirms their social relationship.

Zoologists have always been reluctant to ascribe human-type feelings to animals when seeking to understand their behaviour, and have sought to categorize play as a largely functional activity. However, it would seem to be an over-scrupulous avoidance of anthropomorphism to deny the element in play of sheer fun, the expenditure of surplus energy by an animal which is well-fed, at ease and comfortable in its world.

Kittens start playing with objects and each other from the age of three weeks. At first, they simply jump on their fellows and mother, but gradually they evolve a more sophisticated routine. They start side-stepping and chasing each other more frequently, but do not actually bite at this stage. The mother cat encourages and supervises play amongst her litter. This infantile play is certainly the way that kittens learn actions and reactions they will need in adult life. Watching their mother, they learn to identify her signals and attitudes. The mother appears deliberately to teach her youngsters expressions of threat, and then they try these out on her. Under natural conditions, she will also teach her young to recognize prey, from the age of six weeks onwards. They watch her kills, and she will often bring home live but disabled prey for them to practise on.

It is quite obvious, when a kitten plays with a ping-pong ball, that something important is being learned. The kitten makes a tentative approach and gives the strange object a small pat. The ball moves and in effect is saying to the kitten, 'I am running away and therefore I must be chased.' Usually, within seconds, the kitten learns to dribble the ball.

Similarly, the kitten learns through play what is safe and what is not. It learns to control the use of its teeth and claws as it finds out that its playmates will retaliate if hurt. It learns the limits of its own body by its own efforts. Where is that sound coming from? Is that strange object worthy of note? Can I move fast enough and pounce quick enough to catch and not do myself an injury?

A kitten learns through experience, or trial and error. If

LEFT: *Toys will provide hours of amusement, as the kitten tosses them around, stalks them, chases them, and generally acts out a game of hunting and killing. Even the adult cat will continue to enjoy such play.*

ABOVE AND LEFT: *Any small object will be utilized for play, as the cat manipulates its toy with sensitive paw pads, using all the flexibility of its forelimbs.*

RIGHT: *The human hand becomes a substitute for a feline partner in play. Your hand can be a relatively passive play-object, or can act out the motions of another cat, gently wrestling and, if your playmate does not object, rolling the cat about. If you watch kittens at play, you will see how feline actions can be simulated by your hand. Remember that play needs to be gentle: the roughness of cats' mock fighting is more apparent than real, and if one kitten oversteps the bounds its partner will end the game. Acting out the part of another cat is not only a game, but serves to reinforce the social relationship between you and your pet. It is also a learning exercise for a kitten, as it discovers how to inhibit its play-bites and sheathe its claws in respect for the human's vulnerable skin.*

it accidentally performs an action which proves rewarding it will probably repeat the action in the expectation that the reward will be repeated. If its play leads it into a situation which is painful or otherwise unpleasant, that too is a useful learning experience. A kitten encountering a hedgehog for the first time will probably bounce playfully at it and find out about hedgehogs the hard way; the next time it meets one it will be a great deal more cautious.

Through playful exploration the kitten gradually learns the difference between the many possible expressions of its family of fellow cats, dogs and people. It learns that leaping suddenly on to a dozing human with outstretched claws is not well received and that the dog's tail, although tempting, is safer left alone. After a while, even the most energetic kitten learns that it is best to pause and take stock before rushing in.

Similarly it learns to ignore things which are not dangerous. Falling leaves or shadows may frighten the kitten at first, but it quickly becomes habituated to these and realizes that they can safely be disregarded.

All cats will play long after they have grown out of kittenhood.

The most common forms of play are those which resemble fighting, escaping and hunting, but the distinction between fun and reality is striking.

A simple example occurs when a cat is chased by a dog. If a pack of hounds leaps the fence and heads for the cat to kill, the animal literally has to run for its life and will not stop until it is well and truly out of danger. Even when it has achieved safety, it will remain tense and vibrant for several minutes.

If, instead of the hounds, a friendly neighbourhood dog which the cat knows to be harmless jumps the fence, the chase is more of the nature of a game to both participants. In fact, after a few yards, the cat may turn round and chase the attacker. Throughout the game, claws will remain sheathed and teeth will not be bared.

A further distinction of play is that it will be abandoned if a real problem or need arises. A cat seriously engaged in action takes a great deal of distracting, but play can be set aside without hesitation under another stimulus. The kitten chasing a ball will suddenly forget all about it in order to deal with a flea. A litter of kittens engaged in mock combat will break off in mid-sprawl if they hear the clink of dinner bowls. However, a kitten busy with a serious activity such as eating or stalking prey will be concentrating on what it is doing and will not allow play to intrude.

The inherent playfulness of cats must have been a contributory factor in man's adoption of this species. Hours of entertainment can be had playing with a cat, swinging a toy mouse on a string, rolling a ping-pong ball or allowing the cat to play-fight the human hand.

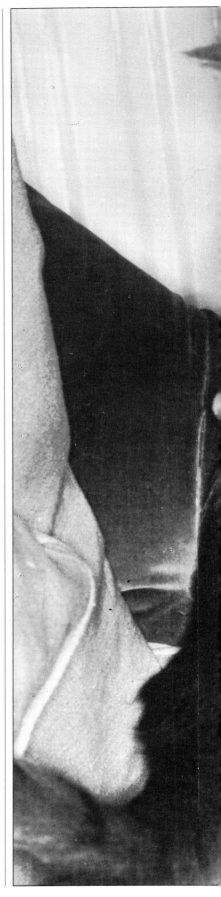

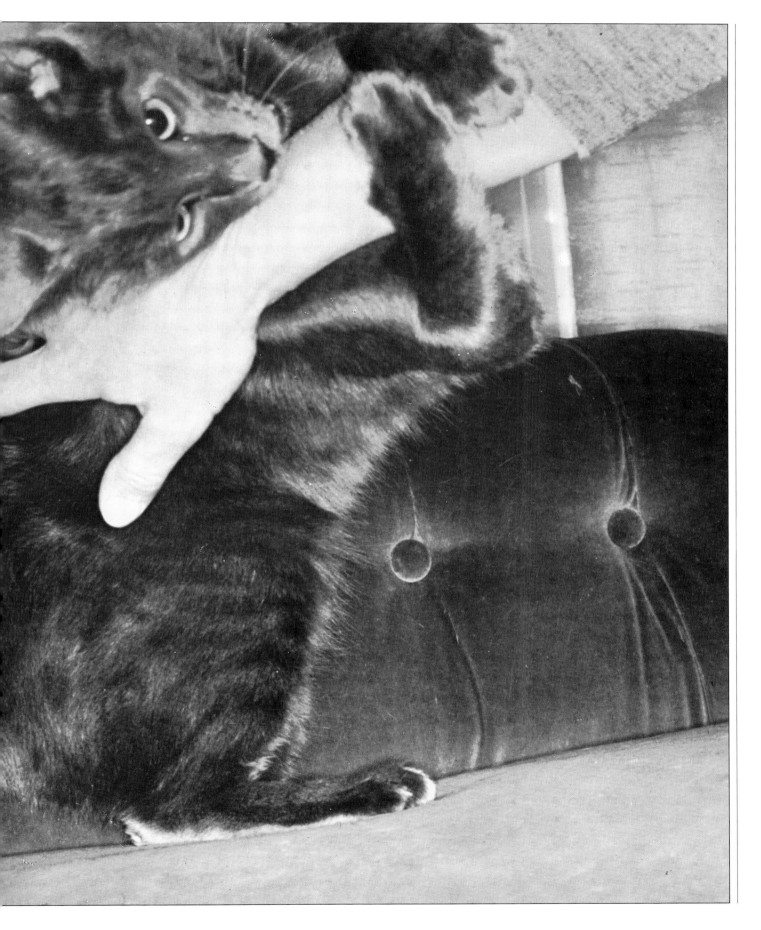

TERRITORY

Cats are intensely territorial creatures, each individual establishing its own territory, centred on the home and extending outwards. In the country, or in the wild, these territories may cover a large area, the rural cat often claiming a spread of about three miles, but in urban areas, where space is more limited and the cat population is high, territories will be smaller. The area around a household where there is no cat will usually be divided among neighbouring cats who will adopt recognized routes to avoid conflict.

Territory size will also depend on gender and also on how shy or bold the individual cat may be. A female neutered before her first season will feel secure only within the confines of her human family, but she may try to establish territorial rights within a short radius of the home. On the other hand, the confident and aggressive tom will have a much broader and more ambitious outlook. In all cases, the boundaries of the territory are firmly fixed. Within them, a stranger runs the risk of attack; on the other side of the invisible lines, it will be left alone.

Any newcomer to the district will have to establish its own territorial rights, probably at the expense of an established claimant. Tomcats are unlikely to object to a new female on their ground, but neuters and queens will often defend their claims vigorously from new arrivals. On the whole, however, serious fighting only occurs in the last resort, as a series of ritualized demonstrations have evolved to resolve many such confrontations without bloodshed.

Domestic cats mark their territory by several means.

Urine provides a pungent scent; toms will spray repeatedly around their territory to establish their boundaries. This habit extends to their indoor territory, which is one reason why owners of tomcats generally prefer to have them neutered. Females and neuters will also spray on occasion, but less frequently and also less pungently.

Other territorial markers include scent, produced by glands on the cat's body. Rubbing the chin or head and tail along fences and railings deposits scent from the glands located in these parts of the body. Scratching posts or tree trunks is another way of visibly marking out a particular area, and also leaves scent behind.

It is often said that the pet cat is more closely attached to its home-as-territory than to its owners. Certainly most cats depend upon their sense of own-territory for a feeling of security, which is why moving house can often be upsetting to them until the new home becomes familiar. This is why, when you go away on holiday, it is often less worrying for the cat to be left in the empty house with a neighbour calling in to feed it than for it to be lodged in a boarding cattery. However, cats do have a greater capacity for affection than they are sometimes credited with, and many individuals show a marked attachment to their owners which outweighs territorial considerations.

LEFT: *Many territorial disputes are settled by a long staring-out contest, from which the weaker cat breaks and flees without any physical confrontation.*

RIGHT: *Scent-marking by spraying urine is a way of staking a claim on an area.*

SUBURBAN TERRITORY

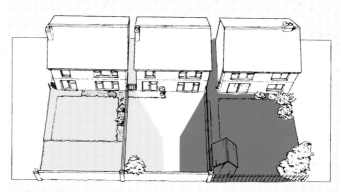

The suburban cat's territory is based around its home. Typically, where space permits, as illustrated here, there will be one small neutral *strip of no-man's-land between territories, but where the cat population is too high to permit this claims will interlock closely.*

SCENT MARKING

Scent glands situated on the face below the ears are rubbed against marking posts at the edge of the territory to deposit the cat's personal signature, and are reinforced by scent glands on the pads of the paws which leave a further message as the cat walks

along. This cat is making a thorough job of scent-marking. First the scent glands of the head are pressed against the railing (1), then the whole body is rubbed along the rail (2), and finally scent is deposited from further glands at the base of the tail (3). The cat's

actions are equivalent to a human setting up printed notices to caution passers-by against trespassing on private property – or simply proclaiming a 'Kilroy was here' type of message!

SEXUAL BEHAVIOUR

The sexual behaviour of the cat is so extrovert, conspicuous and promiscuous that we derive many of our slang expressions connected with sexual activity from this animal. Although the majority of pet cats today are neutered the noisy courtship rituals of the cat are still familiar to most people.

Cats do not mate for life as do some species but are essentially promiscuous. The queen will normally accept a number of mates when she is in season, as the best way to ensure that conception takes place. Such pair-bonding as occurs, as in practice it may do amongst cats living a more or less natural life, is not strong and is based upon territorial interests, the female possessing rights within the male's range.

The domestic cat's breeding cycle is not as rigidly tied to the seasons of the year as is that of most wild animals, but extends over the greater part of the year. Nonetheless, breeding activity tends to die down towards the autumn to prevent young from being born in the inclement winter months, although late litters are not unknown, especially if the weather is mild. Towards the end of winter, perhaps as early as January or as late as April, the cat's hormones respond to increasing daylight and sexual interest flares up again.

When the queen is in oestrus her behaviour often shows marked changes, becoming restless and often abnormally affectionate. The noisy cries of the queen at this time are so characteristic of oestrus that the condition is generally referred to as 'calling'. There can be a great variation between individuals and breeds regarding the amount of fuss she makes at this time – Longhairs are often quite quiet about it, and Siamese notoriously noisy. The queen's calling may come as a shock to the inexperienced owner, who can mistake her howling and rolling around for signs of pain. However, the presence of a queue of tomcats on the doorstep, attracted by her cries and her scent, often gives the game away.

If allowed out, the queen may be gone for some days as

COURTSHIP AND MATING

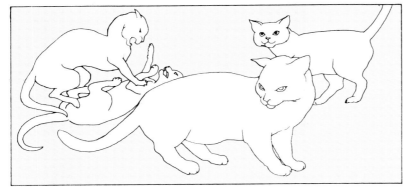

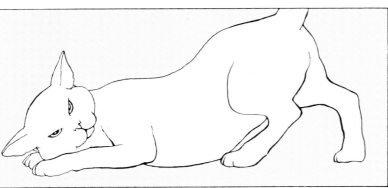

*Competing toms will fight (**TOP LEFT**) for the privilege of being first with the queen on heat. These contests can be protracted, and noisy enough to wake up the neighbours. **LEFT:** the queen rolls around back to give an added come-on to her would-be lovers. The mounted male (**BOTTOM LEFT**) grips the queen's neck with his powerful jaws, to prevent her from escaping.*

she seeks to attract as many toms as possible in the period just before she becomes receptive to mating.

Tomcats will wander far and wide in the quest for queens. The calling queen will attract a following of suitors, rejecting their advances at first while they fight to establish a ranking order, the owner of the territory having a moral edge over his rivals.

When the queen is ready she will choose her mate, often but not inevitably the dominant tom. Copulation is brief and violent, the tom seizing the queen's neck in his jaws. Afterwards she will probably accept each of the other toms in turn – she is capable of conceiving by more than one of these matings, and may even give birth in the same litter to kittens with different fathers. Her receptive period may last for a period of from 12 hours to four days, and this protracted period will maximize the chances of successful fertilization.

When this stage comes to an end, the queen will again reject her suitors and revert to her normal domestic life. The kittens will be her concern alone, perhaps with the help of other females if she lives in a family group, but without any paternal interest on the part of the tom. Where cats live together the tom may allow the kittens to play with him when they are old enough, because even the toughest old tom never fully outgrows the cat's innate playfulness, but at adolescence the youngsters, particularly males, will be pushed into a low ranking position or even expelled from the colony. Individual pet stud cats have been known, exceptionally, to help the mother cat with the kittens, but such devoted fathers are exceptional.

Much of the entire tomcat's behaviour revolves around the need to impregnate as many queens as possible to perpetuate his genes; the entire queen will for much of her lifetime be engaged either with courtship, pregnancy or the rearing of kittens. The common neutering of pet cats not only serves to prevent the birth of unwanted kittens but also diverts the animals' attention from the reproductive drive to more purely social behaviour.

ABOVE: *The queen in season calls out noisily to attract toms, and rolls voluptuously on her back – but she will rebuff suitors until the moment is right.*

LEFT: *The aim and culmination of courtship: a litter of kittens. The queen is generally a devoted mother, and for the first few days will hardly leave them.*

AGGRESSION

The cat-fight is probably urban man's most frequent and vivid reminder of a wilder world than the one he inhabits. In the middle of the city, we notice two cats oblivious of our presence, facing each other down the steely concentration of gunfighters at high noon; in the peace of our own beds we are wakened by unearthly and blood-curdling cries shattering our sleep.

Cats fight over territory and over potential mates. Although these confrontations sound murderous, many go no further than vocal threats. There is considerable ritual inolved in most animal aggression. It would not be in the interests of the survival of the species if creatures equipped to kill made a habit of using their equipment on their own kind, and so most predators have evolved a high degree of ritualization in their conspecific aggression.

The aggressor cat makes itself look and sound as intimidating as possible. With arched back, fluffed-out fur and tail, lips retracted to display the fangs, eyes narrowed with contracted pupils, and ears flattened parallel to the head, it hisses, snarls and lets out the drawn-out howls we call caterwauling. The weaker cat takes up a defensive crouched posture. The two cats may hold their positions for a long time, with direct eye contact. Often the confrontation ends with the weaker cat dropping its gaze and turning to flee. The 'fight' is typically a duel of glares only, without physical contact.

Only if neither cat is prepared to back down, or if the flight path of the weaker is barred, are they likely actually to come to fighting. The threatened cat will then adjust its stance to show resistance, curling its tail and taking up a more aggressive posture, although its pupils may remain dilated and its ears down.

The aggressor may then choose to advance on its rival, who rolls over to meet the challenge with the claws of all four feet tensed and its sharp teeth ready. The first cat lunges with open jaws, usually aiming for the neck, and the two cats engage, gripping and slashing with their paws. The actual engagement is of short duration, with the loser breaking away, usually pursued by the victor for a short distance.

In urban areas man has created an artificially high population density of cats, and consequently confrontations are more frequent and often more deadly than in the natural state. Under these artificial circumstances fights may occasionally even be pursued to the death.

Fighting is more of a problem with entire tom cats than other cats because these toms will try to defend a very large territory. But it can occur with neutered cats as well, particularly when a new cat moves into the area. This is normal feline behaviour and cannot be stopped, but the cats will usually settle down once they have decided on the territorial boundaries. Of course, if your cat is a tom, you should have it neutered. You may have a problem with a neighbour who refuses to neuter his own cat.

When ritual gives way to action, the fighting cat is equipped to do considerable damage. In normal circumstances the weaker cat will normally break away and flee before serious injury is incurred. In areas with an unnaturally high cat population, however, confrontations will be more frequent and often more violent.

Never attempt to separate fighting cats with your bare hands, as the aroused cat is an undiscriminating and deadly fighting machine, and cat scratches and bites are always potentially dangerous because of bacteria carried in the cat's mouth and on its claws. The traditional bucket of water is as good a way of breaking up a fight as any, but often the human presence alone will suffice to separate the combatants.

ABOVE: *The angry or frightened cat erects the hair along the spine and tail and arches its back, making itself appear larger and more threatening. All the factors that go to display aggression are designed to deter the would-be attacker.*

RIGHT: *The aggressive cat seeks, if possible, a higher position than its opponent's from which to appear dominant.*

EXPRESSION AND GESTURE

*The full lexicon of facial and body language is used to express mood.
(1) The relaxed cat displays tranquillity in its whole pose.
(2) With the appearance of something alarming, fear is demonstrated by muted gestures of hostility, the head lowered and ears and whiskers flattening.
(3) This may be followed by flight, or may develop into the full aggressive display with arched back, bristling fur, whiskers standing out, ears back and teeth bared.*

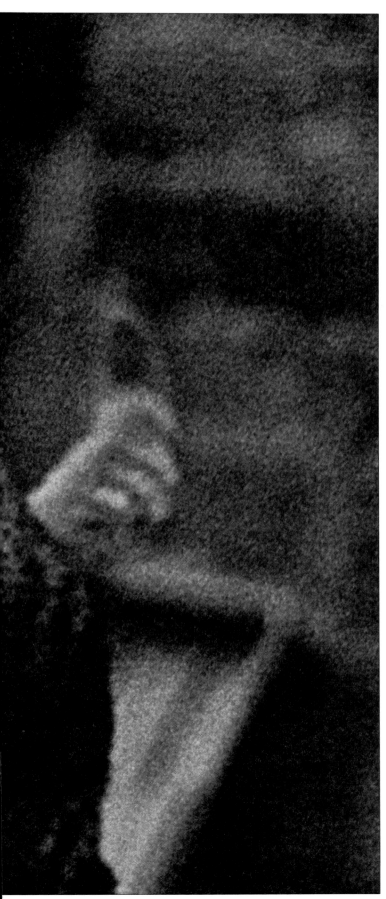

There are four common reasons why cat fights cat – the introduction of a stranger into the home territory; competition for a queen in season; protection of the young; the release of pent-up energy. Obviously, a new cat in the home, or in the house next door, is a threat to established felines, and they will fight for superiority – unless the newcomer is a kitten.

GROOMING

Throughout the animal kingdom, the process of grooming occupies only slightly less time than sleeping. Furred animals have little option in the matter, for they must constantly strive to keep their covering in the very best of condition. This is partly a matter of comfort, but its more important function is to maintain their coat's unique qualities of insulation and waterproofing.

Grooming is an instinctive activity for cats and kittens, and provides the first active relationship between the mother cat and newborn kitten. Within seconds of birth, the mother is using her tongue and teeth to loosen the kitten from its enveloping membrane, stimulate breathing and dry its soaked body. She will groom her youngsters almost constantly in the early days, to keep them clean, healthy and comforted. It is vital for the kittens' development that she remove any parasites such as fleas, which congregate around the mouth and eyes of the helpless infants and, without her help, would sap the kittens' strength. Her grooming also serves to stimulate evacuation in the kittens, and to consolidate the maternal bond as she sets her own body scent upon them.

Grooming is one of the first activities that the kitten is capable of performing on its own. In one study of 40 kittens under laboratory conditions, the eyes opened at 12 days, walking began at 22 days and grooming a day later.

Kittens reared without their mothers, in separate incubators, began grooming at 15 days, two days before they began walking. It was difficult to evaluate, for the kittens tended to perform sucking movements on their own bodies soon after birth.

Throughout its life, the cat will spend a great deal of time in grooming its fur. The flexibility of its spine enables it to twist itself around into astonishing yoga-like contortions so as to reach almost every part of its body with its rough tongue, which acts like a comb working through the fur. Very little of the cat's coat is inaccessible to the tongue. However, to groom the face and head it uses its forearm, cleaning the limb itself afterwards with its tongue. Many other species of animal use the palms of the forepaw to wash their faces, but the cat's paws, with their close-set pads and long claws, are ill-designed for this method.

Grooming performs several important functions in the cat. The most obvious of these is coat maintenance: the tongue with is little backward-pointing projections combs out shed hairs, scrubs off dirt, teases out mats, helps to control the numbers of skin parasites such as fleas, and aligns the individual hairs correctly with each other to maximize the insulating action of the fur. Grooming also stimulates the skin glands to produce their natural oily secretion and spreads this over the coat to waterproof it.

In hot weather, cats groom themselves to keep cool. Saliva licked on to the fur fulfils the same function as sweat helping to control body temperature by its evaporation. Sweat glands of the type widely distributed in humans are confined exclusively to the feet in cats, and are thus of little significance when it comes to losing excessive heat from

LEFT: *Cats groom every part of their bodies thoroughly, and spend a good part of the day doing so. The rough surface of the tongue combs through the fur and realigns every hair so that the coat offers maximum insulation and waterproofing.*

RIGHT: *Social grooming is an important element in communication between cats, starting out as the necessay care a queen gives to her kittens, but continuing in adult life as a confirmation of group membership.*

GROOMING

The cat's physical flexibility enables it to reach most parts of its body with its tongue. The few remaining areas are groomed using the forearms.

ABOVE: *The cat's supple spine enables it to twist around to reach every part of its body with ease.*

BELOW: *The forearms are carefully cleaned after being used to groom the face and head.*

the body. The cat has to rely on grooming and panting to cool itself.

Yet another benefit of grooming is that the cat's tongue passing over its fur takes in Vitamin D manufactured naturally by the skin in the presence of direct sunlight.

A cat will often wash itself when it is irritated or frustrated. At such times grooming may consist of short, sharp strokes of the tongue delivered in a recognizably edgy manner rather than the normal long, caressing strokes, or it may consist of a mere stilted licking around the lips. This has nothing to do with functional grooming but is termed a 'displacement activity'. The cat cannot find a satisfyingly appropriate response to the situation, but finds relief in ritualized grooming actions as an alternative. A cat which has skidded on a wet floor or miscalculated a leap will nearly always sit down and wash: in this case the response to the irritant stimulus is also a means of comforting itself.

Self-grooming, termed *autogrooming*, is a matter of bodily maintenance and comfort. In common with many other species of animals, cats will also solicit grooming by others, or *allogrooming*. This has a practical value in that another cat can wash those areas out of reach to their owner, licking the face and ears. The grooming animal will also pay special attention to any inaccessible wounds, which will benefit from the disinfectant properties of its saliva. The most important benefit of allogrooming, however, is the social aspect of this activity.

Grooming is first experienced by a cat as a helpless infant when its mother repeatedly washes it. The pleasurable sensation is associated with comfort and security. In adult life, cats living together will regularly groom each other, establishing and reaffirming a 'family' bond.

Cats which live as a group will, in addition to their individual scents, acquire a group smell which identifies members of the colony to each other in much the same way as a football team is identified by its colours. The cat washing its companion picks up the smell by licking and 'reads' the confirmation of group membership. When it licks its own coat the message is repeated as it identifies its companion's smell on its own fur. Mutual grooming is therefore a vital social activity, enabling the group to function as a whole.

This social and pleasurable aspect of grooming spills over into the cat's relationship with man. The stroking action of a human hand is the direct equivalent of the action of another cat's tongue. It is obviously a source of great enjoyment to the cat, and you are likely to see the animal actively setting its scent upon its owner by rubbing its head-glands against hands or clothing, and also 'reading' the human scent on its coat by subsequent washing.

BELOW: *Grooming by the owner not only serves to keep the coat in good condition but should be a pleasurable experience which reaffirms the social bond between cat and human in the same way as mutual grooming between two cats confirms their friendly relationship.*

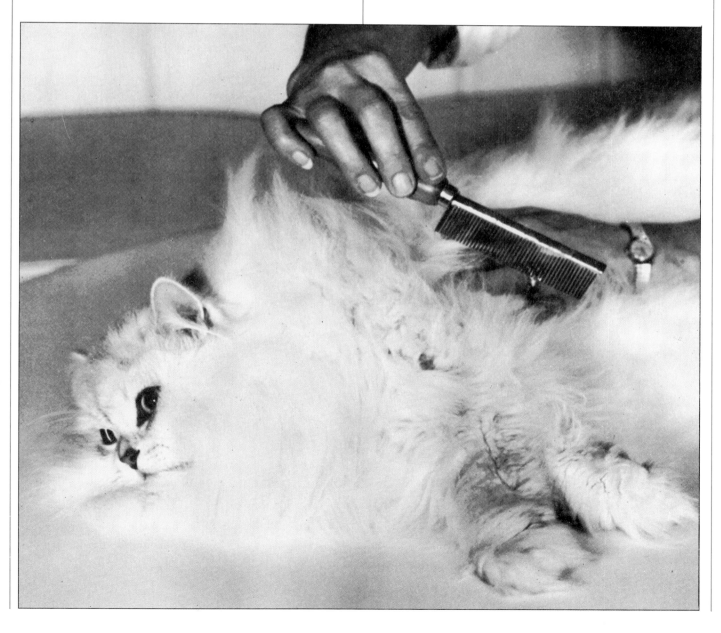

SLEEPING

Whereas human beings spend about a third of their lives asleep, the cat averages more than sixty per cent. Scientists do not know the causes or the functions of sleep but they do know that prolonged interruptions of the cycle of rest periods can produce illness.

Sleep may be light, fairly light or deep. The lightest level is that shallow, easily-disturbed dozing state that is so characteristic of the cat that we call it cat-napping. The cat seems able to drop into a cat-nap anywhere and at any time, and is as easily awakened.

During light sleep the cat moves its limbs frequently. In deep sleep it will move very little, except for the eye muscles and the ends of the limbs, but the electroencephalogram will look very similar to that of the cat when it is awake. This form is known as *paradoxical sleep*, and this is when dreaming occurs. The adult cat spends about 15 percent of its life in paradoxical sleep. Kittens, immediately after birth, spend over 90 percent of their sleeping time in this state, but by the time they are four weeks of age they are down to the adult level. Very old cats, like kittens, revert to sleeping for a greater part of the day.

The pattern of sleep is nevertheless variable, being influenced by external factors such as the companionship available. A cat left on its own tends to sleep more, making use of unstimulating periods to log up more rest, unlike the dog which, left alone, displays loneliness and boredom by crying or destroying the furniture.

The cat's sleep pattern, like so much of its behaviour, derives from its natural lifestyle as a hunter. A predator can obtain its food and fill its belly comparatively quickly and has no need to continue the search for food until its meal has been digested, unlike, for example, the large herbivores, which need to spend much of their time eating to obtain the large quantities of vegetation needed to supply their wants. More highly socially organized animals than the cat also need a certain amount of waking time to devote to social interaction. The cat's needs are comparatively small. As a predator itself it has no cause to avoid excessive sleep periods as a time of vulnerability, so what better way to fill up the surplus hours than the comfortable doze?

THE STRETCH

Most humans make do with one all-embracing stretch. Cats usually embark on a whole series of movements, designed to loosen almost every area in the most pleasant and satisfying manner. This process is presented as a public performance, unlike so many feline activities, and it will usually commence with a joint and muscle-loosening extension of the front legs. No respecters of such trifles as your upholstery, cats will dig their claws in to give themselves an effective anchorage. This is followed by the arching of the back, in which the animal squeezes itself into an amazing and concertina-like posture, before completing the acrobatic and, at times, almost balletic spectacle. The finale is usually reserved for the rear legs, which are each stretched out in turn. The whole show can be accompanied by a further selection of face-twisting yawns.

A cat-nap can be taken anywhere; for deeper sleep the cat is usually particularly attracted by a soft, warm location such as a bed. Many cats choose odd nooks and crannies such as cupboards or half-open drawers to sleep in, along with the traditional spot on the family armchair. This is because, unlike dogs which flop down anywhere, cats need security before sleeping.

The cat will soon learn to fit its routine of sleeping and waking around the pattern of its human household. Regardless of the seasons and the weather, alarm clocks ring and activities begin at the same hour each day. The cat soon learns that all this jangling activity is the prelude to its breakfast. That is, for five days of the week. But there may be two days of the week that this frantic bustle does not happen. No matter how hungry, or how piteously it miaows for its breakfast, the whole ritual is postponed for no clearly decipherable reason. The mature cat knows that it might just as well roll over and go back to sleep, saving its energy for a more worthwhile time.

The temperature of the body drops slightly in warm-blooded animals. Bats become almost cold-blooded during sleep. When they wake they must stretch and exercise to raise their temperature to a normal level. Similarly, the waking cat (if it has not been startled) will go through a leisurely ritual of yawning and stretching. These yoga-like exercises are performed with a thoroughness that relatively stiff-muscled humans envy and try to emulate. Every single joint from the top of the head to the tip of the tail appears to be moved. This has the function of restoring full circulation and instant readiness for action to every part of the body. It may also be one of the ways in which an apparently sedentary creature keeps itself superbly fit.

TOP: *The cat seeks out cosy, secluded places for deep sleep. Cupboards or drawers left open are favourite sites.*

ABOVE: *Young kittens spend nearly all their time in deep sleep, reserving their energy for warmth conservation and growth.*

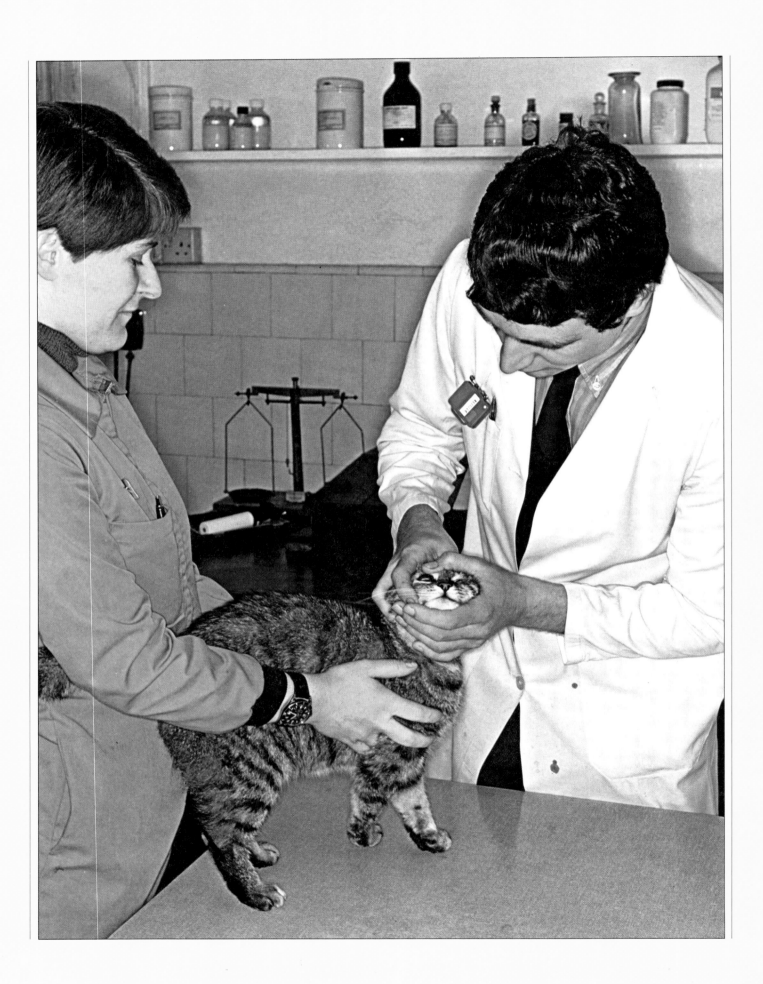

Chapter Seven

HEALTH CARE

YOU AND YOUR VET

After acquiring a new kitten or cat, it is sensible to make an appointment with a veterinarian as soon as possible. The choice of veterinarian will be influenced by various factors, such as personal recommendations and proximity to the surgery, but all veterinarians have undergone a rigorous and extensive training, and this decision will not be critical to the cat's subsequent welfare.

A large multi-vet practice may be able to offer more elaborate facilities than a single-handed practice, but you may find a larger practice more impersonal. If you do decide to attend a multi-vet practice, find out whether you can arrange to see the same veterinarian each time for routine problems. Do not be afraid to ask about the facilities that are available at the office, whether the practice is prepared to make house calls if necessary, and about emergency services – every practice should offer a 24 hour service to its clients for urgent cases. The fees charged may well relate to the standard of facilities offered – every veterinarian has to charge a consultation fee for his time, not only to cover his own income, but to pay for the ancillary staff, the capital invested in buildings and equipment, and the day to day overhead expenses such as heating, electricity, taxes, vehicle expenses and disposable items used. While the fee for a five or ten minute consultation with the veterinarian may seem high, only a small proportion of that amount actually goes to pay the salary of the veterinarian himself. While it should therefore be obvious that it is unwise to select a veterinarian on the basis of the fees charged alone, it does not necessarily follow that the most expensive practice in your area will be the best equipped – you must make a judgement as to which practice appears to offer the best service for the level of fees charged.

Initially, you will want to visit your vet to arrange for the vaccination, worming and probably neutering of your new pet (see Chapter 4). Thereafter, you can expect to make at least an annual visit for vaccination boosters, when your vet will probably also carry out a check-up on the cat's overall health.

If the cat at any time shows any distressing or unusual symptoms, you should arrange an appointment with the vet at once – early treatment of any illness will increase the chances of a full recovery, reducing the period of discomfort to the cat and the size of the vet's bill for you.

It is possible to take out insurance against veterinary fees, and most veterinary surgeons can provide information on this.

This protection can be particularly valuable for those with show cats or people with large numbers of cats in their care. Insurance will not, however, cover 'routine' costs such as vaccinations.

It is wise to look at the cover provided by several companies – the price and the degree of protection offered may differ between policies, and some companies may offer insurance cover for cats at a lower premium than that for dogs. Of course, the insurance companies can only make a living if the value of overall claims is less than the total premiums paid, but on an individual basis, pet insurance does offer cat owners the assurance that they are not going to have to pay a large bill unexpectedly and that any necessary treatment can be carried out regardless of the costs involved.

If you should find yourself facing the prospect of a veterinary bill which you cannot afford to meet, the most important advice is to discuss the problem with your veterinarian at the outset – he may be able to arrange for you to stagger your payments over a period of time or to take your cat to one of the animal charities' clinics that exist to help owners genuinely unable to afford veterinary fees. While most of these clinics used to be poorly equipped and poorly staffed, and some still are, many of them are able to deal with even the most complicated of cases. Please remember that these facilities are provided entirely by voluntary donations – do not use them unless you are genuinely unable to pay for private veterinary fees because you may well deprive another pet owner who really does need help. If you are unable to manage, simply make a donation.

SIGNS OF ILL HEALTH

The best health care is preventative. As well as regular visits to the veterinarian for vaccinations and check-ups, prevention includes providing a clean environment and a good diet, combined with a degree of vigilance.

Cats are creatures of habit, and you will soon become familiar with the normal behaviour pattern of your own cat. Any sudden change may be an early indication that trouble is brewing. For example, while most owners are not aware of how much water their cat drinks they will often notice if the cat starts to drink more than normal, or if a cat that has not drunk much at all suddenly starts drinking from the tap or the garden pond.

Other indications of health problems that might attract your attention include persistent vomiting, diarrhoea or constipation, or repeated bouts of coughing or sneezing. Any of these symptoms is the cue for an appointment with the vet.

Regular grooming sessions, as well as helping to maintain the cat's coat in top condition (see pages 154–157), provide an opportunity to carry out an overall health check.

Starting at the head, the eyes should be clear and bright:

dull sunken eyes indicate illness. Some cats have a little 'sleep' in the corners of the eyes occasionally, and some, particularly light-coloured longhairs, may show tear-stains on the fur below the eyes, which should be gently bathed with cottonwool soaked in warm water. Any soreness of the eyes or heavy discharge should receive veterinary attention.

If your cat is feeling 'low', its eyes may shield them-selves with an extra eyelid. This may look alarming, but it is a useful warning sign, and will disappear as soon as the cat's ailment has been identified and successfully treated. If the eye is simply watering, or has a discharge, bathe it with dilute salt water, then take the cat to the vet.

The ears of a healthy cat should not need cleaning, although it will do no harm to wipe inside the ear flap with cotton wool buds, never probing deeper into the ear than you can see. Any discharge, irritation or unpleasant odour will indicate a problem calling for veterinary aid, as will unusually frequent scratching or twitching of the ears.

Check that the nose is clean. A discharge from one or both nostrils should not be ignored, particularly if it is thick and yellow. If the skin on the tip of the nose loses its normal pink colour, the cat may be anaemic or in shock.

Inspect the mouth for sore and inflamed gums, ulcers inside the cheeks or on the lips, dribbling or bad breath. Sore gums indicate a heavy build-up of tartar on the teeth. This will need to be cleaned off by a veterinarian, who will be able to check whether the underlying tooth has decayed as well. Tartar is a possible cause of bad breath, although another more serious reason may be kidney failure, especially in an older cat. Both are likely to lead to a loss of appetite. Ulcers within the mouth are a common symptom of cat flu (see page 214). Any swelling on the lips them selves, particularly in white cats of any breed, must be viewed with concern. Rodent ulcers, possible caused by an infection or tumours, may be the underlying cause. Per-sistent salivation may indicate a dental problem, or even poisoning or cat flu, again calling for veterinary inter-vention.

The condition of the cat's coat is a good indicator of its health. A healthy cat has a glossy coat: poor health is reflected in a 'staring' coat which has lost its shine and lies in an open, spiky fashion. Watch out for parasites – fleas leave characteristic little dark gritty particles in the coat. An irritation of the skin could indicate mites or an allergic reaction to fleas. Balding patches might indicate ringworm. The skin should be elastic and loose over the body – if the cat is dehydrated, the skin will lose its elasticity and stay in a 'tent' when lifted from the body. Any abnormal swellings on any part of the body may be abscesses from a fight with another cat and need not necessarily be tumours.

The claws should also be checked by gently holding the pad and pressing the retracted claws out. Cats normally keep their claws in good shape, but if they seem long, it is advisable to have them clipped by a veterinarian. The claws receive a blood supply; if too much dead nail is removed, they will bleed quite profusely. It is important to use an adequate tool for cutting purposes and not just scissors, since these may actually cause the nail to split, rather than cutting it cleanly.

All these points take a good deal longer to describe than to actually check out during the course of grooming. If you train yourself to make an automatic check of these simple health pointers whenever you handle your cat, many a potential health problem can be tackled before it becomes serious.

PARASITES

Parasites, whether external such as fleas or internal such as roundworms, are an unfortunate fact of life that an out-door cat is likely to come into contact with from time to time. Although some may have a very minor effect upon the cat – wild animals are generally riddled with parasites of one kind or another, and carry on their lives nonetheless – the problem should never be ignored. Some parasites are intrinsically dangerous to the cat's health; others, less immediately damaging in themselves, can build up their numbers into a severe infestation; and quite a few carry a degree of risk or unpleasantness to the cat's human owners.

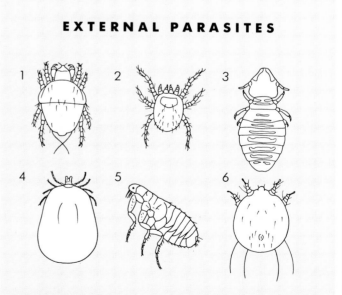

EXTERNAL PARASITES

Some common external cat parasites are illustrated above:
1. Cheyletiella, *fur mite*
2. Trombicula, *harvest mite*
3. Felicola, *cat louse*
4. Ixodes, *sheep tick*
5. Ctenocephalides felis, *cat flea*
6. Fly maggots, *which may infest open wounds ('fly strike')*

FLEAS

Fleas are the commonest external parasites found on cats, and most cats which are allowed outdoors will manage to pick up fleas at some stage.

Scratching is one indication of the presence of fleas. Individual cats vary in their sensitivity to flea bites, some being relatively untroubled and others suffering acute discomfort, but repeated scratching should always be investigated. When you groom your cat, always inspect the combings for flea dirt – tiny blackish-red droppings. You may actually see the fleas jumping out of the cat's fur. Fleas have a particular predilection for the area just in front of the cat's tail, and this region should always be combed carefully.

Fleas are an apparently minor nuisance that must be dealt with promptly to prevent worse problems arising. Although the actual flea-bites are slight – a flea consumes only a tiny amount of blood, less than a drop, once or twice a day – some cats will develop a sensitivity to them. Some individuals may simply show signs of heavy moulting and a dry, scurfy coat, whereas allergic cats may develop *miliary dermatitis*, which takes the form of small scabs, usually along the back. Continual licking by the cat will often wear away the hair and cause patches of baldness, which may become infected with bacteria, causing severe weeping.

Fleas can also infect the cat with tapeworm, which uses the flea as an intermediary host for its larvae. The larvae are swallowed with the carrier fleas when the cat grooms itself. And, of course, the flea is no respecter of persons and is likely to move on to the human members of the family. Although the cat flea cannot complete its life cycle in humans, it will be quite happy to vary its diet.

Individual fleas that you catch will prove extremely difficult to kill; the only sure method is to squeeze them hard with a finger nail to block their respiratory pores, which causes them to explode with a slight popping sound. When combing your cat for fleas, have a disused margarine tub or similar container half-filled with water on hand to immerse loose fleas in, until they can be flushed down a toilet.

Control of fleas necessitates both treatment of the cat and also of its bedding. Any dogs sharing the same household must be dealt with simultaneously, because fleas can be transmitted from one creature to another. Powders provide the most direct means of reducing the flea population present on the cat. Care must be taken to ensure that the preparation chosen is safe for cats and, if necessary, can also be used on kittens. Cats are especially susceptible to the toxic effects of such insecticides because of their licking and grooming habits. Aerosol sprays are also available, but often prove considerably more expensive than powder; apart from the unpleasantness of using them, aerosols are

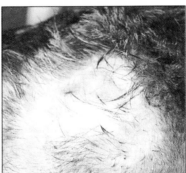

*The first indication of a flea infestation is commonly repeated scratching (**TOP**), and excessive licking and biting of the irritated area can lead to a localized skin ailment (**ABOVE**). This may then become infected with bacteria, causing severe weeping of the skin. Regular flea treatment with an appropriate powder or spray is advisable for all cats, on the basis that prevention is better than cure. If a cat has a flea infestation, its environment will also require treatment.*

liable to scare the cat more than applying powder.

It is vital to treat the cat's surroundings as well as the animal itself, because fleas typically lay their eggs away from their host, although *Ctenocephalides felis* is an exception: its eggs rub off the body very easily and are often transferred to the cat's bedding. It is quite possible for a single female flea to lay up to 800 eggs in its lifetime, although 500 is an average figure, with the complete life cycle taking four to five weeks. In order to break the cycle, the cat's blanket should be either discarded or thoroughly washed and treated as necessary. While sprays may be easier than powder to use around the home, care should be taken if there are other creatures such as fish in the same room. Fish may be inadvertently poisoned unless their tank is adequately covered before and after treatment, until the particles have settled out from the air. Vacuuming will not remove all flea eggs from a carpet and eggs may occur in large numbers right up to the walls.

Your vet will be able to provide a spray designed for use on carpets and furniture. Faced with a heavy domestic infestation of fleas, it is sensible to call in pest control agents to treat the home. Some local government authorities run a service of this nature and the treatment should keep the home free of fleas for some months.

Flea collars impregnated with toxic compounds are available for cats but are not recommended as they are not completely reliable and can cause an allergic reaction.

TICKS

Ticks are blood-sucking, wingless insects that are occasionally picked up by cats in long grass. On farmland they usually come from sheep or cattle, but animals such as hedgehogs may carry them into domestic gardens, Ticks bury their heads into the cat's skin and, since they are fixed and do not move, can easily be mistaken for small cysts, although on close examination the legs can be seen close to the skin.

The cat's head and neck are the most common sites of attachment. Under normal circumstances, only one or two ticks will be encountered, but for one cat to have as many as 100 is not unknown. In such large numbers, these parasites are likely to cause anaemia.

Great care should be taken when removing ticks, as it is easy to pull off the body and leave the head embedded in the skin, where a sore is likely to develop. You can loosen their grip by dabbing them with alcohol, or with grease such as petroleum jelly or butter, and after a few moments remove them with tweezers. However, it is probably safer to kill them first by spraying them directly with a veterinary flea spray – they will then shrivel up and drop off within 24 hours or they can then be pulled from the skin easily, complete with the head. These animal ticks do not usually affect humans.

TICKS

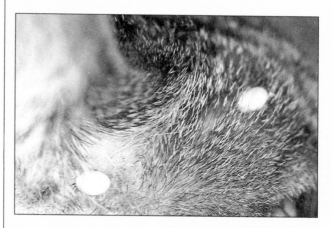

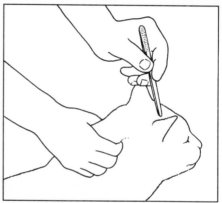

Ticks bury their mouthparts in the cat's skin to attach themselves firmly while sucking blood **(TOP)**. *Attempts to pull them off will generally leave the mouthparts still attached, causing a sore to develop. Their grip should therefore be loosened by an application of grease, which prevents them from breathing through the body's pores, before they are removed, carefully, with tweezers* **(ABOVE)**.

MITES

Various mites can affect cats, with skin mites giving rise to the condition commonly referred to as mange. These microscopic creatures cause local irritation, leading to excessive washing or scratching of the affected area. Baldness and spots are also associated with cases of mange. *Notoedres* mites occur especially on the sides of the face in the region between the eyes and ears, but can spread up to the neck and down the back if left untreated.

A mite which causes no noticeable symptoms in cats and yet can give rise to an unpleasant dermatitis in humans is *Cheyletiella parasitivorax*. Cheyletiella mites are sometimes called 'walking dandruff mites' because they are small and white and just about visible to the naked eye: it looks as though the cat has dandruff moving on its back. These can be picked up from other affected cats, dogs or rabbits. They live on the surface of the skin, sometimes digging shallow tunnels into it, and attach their eggs to the hairs.

As with other mite infections, the parasite responsible can be detected by means of a skin scraping carried out by a veterinarian. This involves scraping the surface of a suspected area of skin with a sharp blade and examing the sample under a microscope. Obtaining a scraping is not a painful procedure and no sedation is normally necessary. Shampoo preparations must be used regularly to clear the problem.

EAR MITES

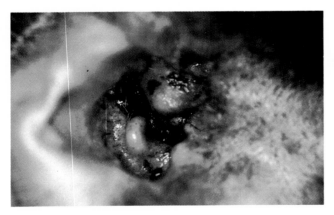

*Frequent scratching of the ears (**LEFT**) often indicates ear mites. Inspection is likely to reveal an accumulation of dark brown wax (**ABOVE**), often accompanied by an acrid smell. Veterinary treatment at an early stage will prevent further infection or damage to the ear itself.*

Harvest mites are small orange or red mites that are just visible to the naked eye and sometimes cause irritation of the head, ears or legs, particularly in the autumn. A flea spray will normally clear them.

Mites remain in close proximity to their hosts throughout their life cycles, but *Trombicula autumnalis*, commonly known as 'chiggers', is an exception. The adult form of the mite is free-living, and resembles a minute red spider, but the larval form is parasitic and will attach to the cat, often between the toes, causing a great deal of irritation. The larvae appear as minute orangish-red spots and may be seen elsewhere on the body where the skin is both relatively thin and hairless. Infection with these larvae only occurs during the summer months and is localized to particular regions where the adult mites naturally occur.

Veterinary advice should be sought without delay in cases of suspected mite infections. Treatment consists of the application of a suitable preparation to kill the mites and soothe the affected skin, so the cat will not mutilate itself by continually scratching at the site of irritation.

Mite infections of the ear are also extremely common; if a cat rubs its ears repeatedly, they should be examined carefully with a torch. Grass seeds may occasionally become lodged in the ear canal, then the mite known as *Otodectes* is likely to be responsible. An unpleasant smell is usually associated with such infections.

Ear mites are transmitted from cat to cat by close contact and cannot affect humans, although they can affect dogs, in which case they often cause even more irritation than with cats. Your veterinarian will be able to diagnose the problem by the nature of the wax and by looking in the ear with an auriscope to see the mites. He or she will prescribe ear drops to kill off the mites. It is important that all in-contact dogs and cats are treated at the same time, and that treatment is continued for three to four weeks to kill off the eggs of the mites as they hatch out.

Ear mites should be taken seriously. Although some cats do not seem very troubled by mites, others find them very irritating, and their persistent scratching can cause a lot of inflammation and secondary infection. the cat's scratching and head-shaking in response to the irritation can rupture blood vessels in the ear, causing a painful blood-filled swelling called a haematoma which will probably need surgical treatment. Another danger from ear mites is that infection may enter the middle ear. This can cause loss of balance and a tendency to move in circles, and the chances of a successful recovery are not always good.

LICE

Lice are occasionally seen, mainly in kittens. The adult louse, another wingless insect, lays its eggs and attaches them to the hairs – the small white eggs are often visible and are called nits. The whole of the life cycle is therefore spent on the host, so that regular treatment of the cat itself should clear the problem. Infection can occur from cat to cat only by contact, although lice can be transmitted on shared grooming implements. They are very fussy about the species of host they choose and cannot affect human hair.

ROUNDWORMS

Roundworms are very common in cats, especially kittens. they may be vomited or passed in the stool, and look like lengths of white thread. The eggs are shed in the stool, but they are so small that they are not visible to the naked eye; your kitten may well have roundworms without your knowing.

Roundworms can be passed on directly without the need for an intermediate host. The immature worms, called larvae, lie dormant in the tissues of the pregnant queen and infect kittens by passing through the breast tissue into the milk, ensuring that a large proportion of kittens become infected before they are weaned. Since roundworms can cause such problems as potbelly, tummy upsets, or even intestinal obstruction, it is wise to treat all kittens regularly against roundworms. Your veterinarian will be able to supply you with a suitable drug.

The larvae develop into worms in the bowel, and the worms shed eggs into the stool. These eggs are very small and invisible to the naked eye – so that a cat may have worms without the owner being aware of them. The eggs lie on the ground and develop into larvae, which are then either eaten by another cat, or eaten by a wild animal such as a mouse, which is in turn eaten by a cat – and so life goes on!

Adult cats are less likely to come to harm through harbouring roundworms, but an annual worming will do the cat no harm and prevent the build-up of serious infestation.

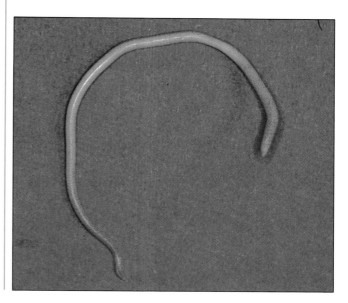

LIFE CYCLE OF THE ROUNDWORM

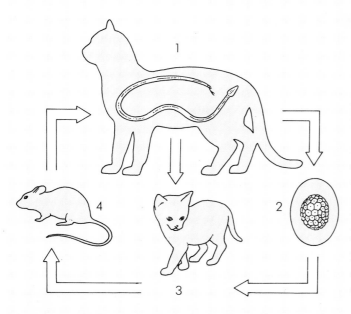

Ascarid roundworms grow in the intestines of a cat (1) and feed on the digested food there. Their eggs (2) are passed on via faeces, which may be swallowed by another cat, and if this happens, the larvae hatch in its intestines. The danger to a newborn kitten is that the larval stage of the Toxocara cati *species migrate to the mother's milk at the onset of lactation and infect the kitten (3).*
Alternatively, the eggs of either of the known species of roundworm, Toxocara cati *or* Toxocascaris leonina, *in the faeces may be eaten by another animal – such as a beetle, bird, rat or mouse (4) –*

that a cat may prey upon and so in turn infect the cat.

ABOVE: *Roundworm are white, long and round, growing to a length of up to 4 ins (10 cms). Common symptoms in a kitten are weakness, a dull, dry coat, a pot belly and sickness and diarrhoea which may contain visible worms – a help in diagnosis. Kittens infected at birth can be treated when they are two or three weeks old.*

TAPEWORMS

Tapeworms are also very common in the cat. The adult worm looks long and flat, like a piece of tape, although on close examination it can be seen that it is divided into segments. The adult tapeworm has hooks and suckers on its head to attach it to the wall of the bowel where it feeds on the food that the cat is so obligingly digesting on its behalf. Mature segments break off from the end of the adult worm and are shed in the stool. They resemble grains of rice and can sometimes be seen to move. These segments burst, releasing tapeworm eggs which cannot be taken in directly by another cat, but have to pass through an intermediate host first. The hosts are usually fleas but can also be lice or wild rodents.

Tapeworms do not usually produce serious disease, but can lead to a noticeable loss of condition and may cause stomach pain, mild diarrhoea and possible irritation around the anus. Owners are more often aware that their cat has tapeworm, because the segments may be seen in the stools or around the cat's bottom. Tapeworm can be more resistant to treatment than roundworm, and it is best to obtain a suitable treatment from your veterinarian, together with an insecticidal spray to clear any fleas or lice if appropriate.

TAPEWORMS

LEFT: *Tapeworms spend their larval stages in other animals which must be eaten by the cat before it can be infected. The most common species are* Dipylidium caninum *and* Taenia taeniaformis.

LEFT: *The most significant sign of a heavy infestation of tapeworm in a cat is the appearance of whitish tapeworm segments in the faeces and in the area around the anus. When dry, these resemble grains of rice.*

LIFE CYCLE OF THE TAPEWORM

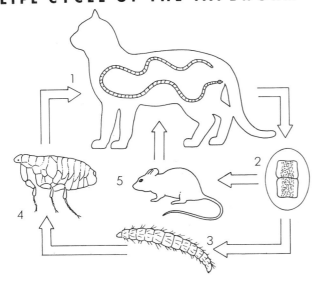

Inside a cat, tapeworms can grow up to 3½ ft (100 cm) long (1) and consist of egg-filled segments that are passed in faeces (2). Dipylidium caninum eggs are eaten by lice or flea larvae (3)

and infect the cat via the adult flea parasite (4). Eggs of Taenia taeniaeformis *may be eaten by a rodent (5) and infect a cat that preys on the rodent, for example a rat.*

OTHER WORMS

Lungworms have become more widely recognized in cats during recent years. One survey found a level of infection of 9.6 percent, based on a sample study of 125 cats. A mild case of lungworm may produce few apparent symptoms, but coughing and signs of respiratory difficulty, such as laboured breathing, could be indicative of this parasite. The disease has been seen in both domestic and wild cats and can be treated, although the drugs used are rather toxic. Examination of the faeces for the lungworm eggs, together with perhaps a blood test, should serve to confirm a diagnosis before treatment. As with many other parasitic infections, the eosinophils, which form part of the white cell group, are raised in number in such cases. Various other lungworms may occasionally be seen in cats in other areas of the world.

Heartworms occasionally occur in cats, although more commonly found in dogs. They are transmitted by insect hosts such as mosquitoes, and infest the pulmonary artery as well as the right ventricle of the heart. They may actually block off the circulation, leading to sudden death, or cause circulatory disorders such as fluid collecting in the tissues, a condition which is technically referred to as oedema. Treatment of heartworms is extremely hazardous, because destroying the adult worms *in situ* can itself cause an obstruction. Regular preventive dosing of both dogs and cats is therefore carried out in areas where the infection is present, typically Australia, the Mediterranean region and the warmer parts of North America.

Other worms occur in the warmer parts of North America and Australia. Both threadworms (*Strongyloides* species) and whipworms (*Trichuris* species) are in this category, but respond well to treatment. Diagnosis of such infections is based on examining the faeces of a cat for eggs. Tablets are the normal method of dosing at present, although injections may be developed in the near future, a treatment becoming more routine for controlling such parasites in farm livestock.

Flukes, which are classified as trematodes, do not usually affect cats, although they can be a problem in certain areas of North America. The intermediate infective hosts are usually fish and, where flukes are endemic in the local fish population, such food must be cooked before offering to cats. Flukes develop in the bile ducts of the liver and can cause jaundice, as well as affecting the pancreas.

Treatment of any worm infestation, along with regular preventive worming, is best undertaken with veterinary guidance, although preparations can be purchased in pet stores. It is important to select the correct medication for the particular parasite concerned, and if any course of treatment is purchased from a pet store, it is important to follow the instructions on the packaging.

PROTOZOAL INFECTIONS

Protozoa are microscopic organisms, some of which are parasitic upon the cat, causing various diseases.

Isospora catis gives rise to the disease known as coccidosis. When present in large numbers it causes diarrhoea which may be tinged with blood, and also fever and general depression. Coccidosis occurs most commonly in cats living together in cramped, dirty conditions, since it is spread by faecal contact. Treatment of coccidosis can be carried out quite successfully with sulphonamide drugs, although the dehydration resulting from the diarrhoea can prove fatal, especially in kittens, unless it is corrected early.

The protozoan *Toxoplasma gonadii* is particularly significant because it can be transmitted to humans with pregnant women especially at risk. Symptoms of infection in the cat are rather vague and may resemble those of panleucopaenia or bronchopneumonia, even if they become apparent. Clinical tests will be necessary to confirm this illness. After becoming infected, either by consuming contaminated raw meats or rodents, the cat then excretes the oocyst or dormant stage in its faeces four or five days later, and may continued to do so for up to three weeks. The oocysts themselves, once outside the body, take between two and four days to become infective. They may then survive in the environment for months, although they can be destroyed by boiling water and certain chemicals. The risk to humans comes when these oocysts are accidentally ingested, once they have had an opportunity to become infective.

In order to prevent this hazard, contact with cat faeces

LIFE CYCLE OF THE LUNGWORM

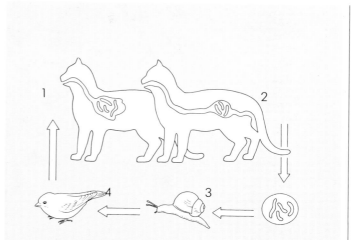

The adult lungworm lives in the lungs of cats (1). It lays eggs in the air passages, which are then coughed up and develop into larvae which are passed out in the motions (2). The eggs lie on the ground, until they are ingested by a molluscan intermediate host such as a snail (3). It is thought that these infected molluscs are then eaten by birds (4), which are then in turn eaten by cats (5).

should be kept to an absolute minimum. Gloves should always be worn when emptying a dirt tray, the contents of which should be disposed of before sporulation can occur. Infection may also occur in sand pits or gardens where cats are known to have defecated. It is particularly sensible for pregnant women to wear gloves when working in such areas because of the possibility of the protozoan crossing the placental barrier in the body, to affect the unborn child in the uterus, perhaps even causing a miscarriage. If possible, cats should be prevented from gaining access to sources of *Toxoplasma*, but in practice this is often not feasible if they are allowed outside at all.

An insect-borne protozoal infection, with a worldwide distribution, seen in cats is feline infectious anaemia. The organism itself, known as *Haemobartonella felis* or *Eperythrozoon felis*, is transmitted by biting insects such as mosquitoes. Male cats for some reason appear more at risk than females, especially those between four and six years of age. The parasites destroy the red blood cells, giving rise to the anaemia and causing debility and fever in the process.

The organism can usually be seen if the blood of an infected cat is examined under the microscope, but not always because sometimes the organisms can be found only intermittently in the blood of infected cats. The disease tends to be of a recurrent nature, with bouts of infection following periods of stress, and it is frequently associated with concurrent feline leukaemia virus infection. It will usually respond well to treatment, although a long course of drugs may have to be given, sometimes in combination with a blood transfusion.

SKIN DISORDERS

Most of cats' skin disorders are caused by parasites and, apart from ringworm, other skin disorders such as balding and stud tail are non-contagious and easily cleared.

RINGWORM

Ringworm, despite its name, is not caused by a worm but by a fungus that grows on the skin and hairs. Characteristically, it causes white, scaly, bald patches, especially around the head region, but some cats carrying the fungus show only mild symptoms such as a somewhat scurfy coat, and indeed some individuals can carry ringworm without actually having the infection themselves.

It is important to identify and treat cases of ringworm, as the condition is easily transmitted to humans either by handling an infected cat or from its environment.

There are three recognized type of ringworm which may affect cats, the most common being *Microsporum canis*. Distinction between these forms is of more than academic interest. In cattle, ringworm infection produces typically distinct whitish circular patches on the coat, whereas the only trace of infection in cats may be a few broken hairs, barely noticeable without a very close inspection.

*Signs of ringworm on a cat are usually subtle and may only be visible as a small patch of broken hairs (**ABOVE**). Certain cats may even be carriers of ringworm without having the infection themselves.*

Cat ringworm can usually be identified by your vet without having to take skin scrapings or cultures, by means of a special ultraviolet light known as a Wood's Lamp. It may also be visible on the hairs under a microscope. The most accurate form of diagnosis is to take a hair sample and try to grow the fungus in the laboratory, but this can take up to three weeks to produce a result.

Treatment of ringworm is also long and laborious. Certain medical preparations can be used for localized problems, but affected cats usually have to be treated with tablets of an antifungal drug called griseofulvin. This drug protects the cat by being incorporated into new hairs as they grow, so initial clipping of the hair followed up by three months of treatment may be necessary. Griseofulvin cannot be used with safety in pregnant cats, since it may well cause malformations in the developing kittens. A fungicidal shampoo for the coat itself may also be recommended because, while griseofulvin works up to the skin surface, it will not act against fungal spores actually present on the hairs. Even when a case appears to have resolved successfully, tests are advisable to ensure that no trace of the fungus remains.

The disease is not uncommon and since the spores of the fungus are resistant to disinfectants and can stay in the environment remaining infectious for a long time, ridding the household of the fungus can be difficult. The cat's bedding must be destroyed and its surroundings treated as recommended by your vet. The cat itself should be handled with rubber gloves to minimize the risk of its transmitting the infection to its owners, and care should also be taken when handling its feeding bowl and litter tray.

Ringworm infections in humans do not always prove severely irritating, but are nevertheless unpleasant. If an infected cat has been handled accidentally without gloves, washing with soap using cold water is recommended. This is thought to lessen the risk of the disease developing, since the skin pores will not open so readily when cold water is applied to them, and the fungus will not gain easy access to the skin itself. If circular red patches do appear, particularly on the hands or arms, medical advice must be sought. Human treatment is also likely to involve a prolonged course of griseofulvin.

ULCERS

Unpleasant thickened and ulcerated skin lesions termed eosinophilic granulomas are not uncomon in cats and are often called rodent ulcers. They occur most often on the upper lip. The condition is not malignant like the rodent ulcer encountered in humans, although cancerous growths actually within cats' mouths are not uncommon. The cause of these ulcers is obscure, although they may be caused by excessive grooming by the cat, and therefore fleas could be a contributory factor.

Veterinary treatment is necessary to prevent the condition from becoming severe. Most cases respond well to medical treatment, but surgery is sometimes necessary. Cryo-surgery may be recommended, which entails freezing the affected area using a liquid nitrogen probe, to kill the diseased tissue, hopefully ensuring subsequent healthy resolution. Healing in all cases is likely to take several weeks, and recurrences are not unknown.

ALLERGIES

Some skin problems may be caused by an allergy, but it is not always easy to discover the predisposing factor. A process of elimination is often necessary, taking away one item, such as milk from the diet, and then noting any improvement. Confirmation can be achieved by reintroducing a small amount of the substance held responsible, and seeing if the condition then reappears.

Sunburn can also cause skin irritation. This is most common in white cats, with the ears often becoming inflamed following prolonged exposure to the sun's rays.

OTHER SKIN DISORDERS

Neurodermatitis, which again may resemble military dermatitis, is due to excessive licking and grooming of the coat by nervous cats. Affected cats may respond to tranquillizers or to attempts to make their surroundings less stressful. This condition is most common in Siamese, Burmese and Abyssinian breeds of cat.

Feline acne is a thickening of the skin due to infection of the lower lip. It is probably caused by an overproduction of natural oils of the skin glands in that region. It may be possible to clear the problem with topical treatment applied to the skin, or antibiotics may be prescribed.

Stud tail is a baldness and thickening of the skin on the tail near its base. It is usually seen only in entire tom cats, and is due to large numbers of special skin glands that develop in that area. In some cases, the area may become infected and sore and should be cleaned regularly with a surgical scrub.

ENDOCRINE ALOPECIA

This is a localized loss of hair caused by a hormonal imbalance, and occurring predominantly in neutered cats. Bald patches of skin appear, usually on the stomach and flanks. This can look like miliary dermatitis (see page 204), but tends to be more symmetrically placed and the skin is not itchy or sore. The bald areas appear because the hair fails to grow properly, not because the cat is continually licking and pulling it out. This can be a seasonal problem, and if it is severe, the cat may need hormone treatment to control it. This problem should not be confused with a thinning of the hair in front of the base of the ears, which is usually completely normal.

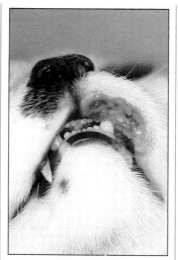

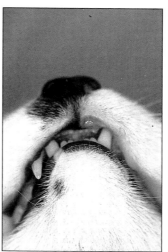

*Rodent ulcers are deep skin sores on the upper lip (**LEFT**). Their cause is not known, although they may be aggravated by continual licking of an initial skin irritation. Most cases respond quite rapidly to anti-inflammatory treatment. (**BELOW LEFT**). However, if your cat does not respond rapidly to treatment, it may be necessary to take a small biopsy specimen from the lesion so that it can be examined under the microscope to rule out any other possible causes, such as skin cancer.*

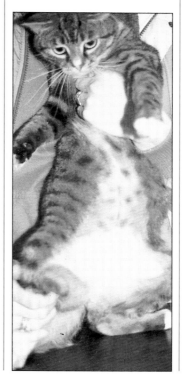

LEFT: *Localized baldness, especially on the lower abdomen and flanks, is caused by hormonal alopecia. The skin is not itchy or sore, and the baldness is caused by a failure of new hair to grow after moulting. The problem may be seasonal.*

*A protrusion of the third eyelid (**LEFT**) is a sign of a general illness rather than a disease in itself. The eyelid normally sits tucked away in the inner corner of the eye and can be drawn quickly across the eye to protect it.*

ABOVE: *Conjunctivitis is an inflammation of the membranes surrounding the eyes, caused by infection or irritation or sometimes associated with a generalized disease such as cat flu.*

EYE DISORDERS

Apart from *conjunctivitis*, the inflammation of the membranes around the eye, diseases of the eye itself are relatively uncommon in the cat. Protrusion of the third eyelid across the eye is not usually a sign of eye disease itself, but signifies that the cat is generally unwell in some way (see page 202). Sometimes it does occur on its own without any other signs of illness, and is probably due to a virus affecting the nerves that control the third eyelid. Some cats bred with a short nose, such as Persians, may have an obstruction to the flow of tears down over the face. In some cases it may be possible to clear the tear duct surgically, but it is usually sufficient to clean around the eyes regularly with cotton wool and warm water. If the area starts to become sore due to the tears, a little petroleum jelly will help to protect the skin.

Any sign of discharge from the eyes may indicate a viral infection and requires veterinary attention.

Conjunctivitis, an inflammation of the membranes surrounding the eyes resulting in soreness and discharge, is not uncommon in cats. It may be caused by a localized infection that affects only the eyes, or by some irritating agent such as excessive dust, or pollen in allergic individuals, or it may be a symptom of a more generalized disease, particularly cat flu (see page 204).

Most cases of conjunctivitis respond well to treatment with an antibiotic ointment, sometimes combined with a drug to reduce the soreness. However, a few cases prove to be very resistant to treatment and may require long-term therapy.

The surface of the eye, the cornea, is vulnerable to infection and to injury. Any damage to the cornea will cause soreness, often cloudiness of the clear cornea, and usually cause the cat to hold its eye shut or partially shut. Any damage to the surface of the eye is potentially serious, since there is a risk that if the damage is deep it may perforate the cornea, which would probably then result in permanent blindness in that eye. The veterinarian will often put a special green dye called fluoroscein into the eye to highlight any corneal ulceration. The cornea can usually repair itself rapidly if the cause of the damage is removed and antibiotic ointment applied to control disease.

Any noticeable change in the colour of one or both eyes will also require immediate veterinary attention, as it may indicate a serious viral infection. Enlarged pupils which do not appear to widen and narrow in response to changing

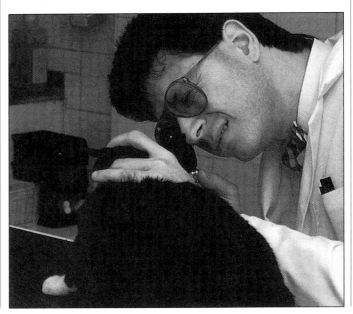

levels of light may also indicate a condition requiring veterinary treatment.

Occasionally serious damage to an eye may mean that it has to be surgically removed. Such cases tend to be more traumatic for the owner than for the cat itself. The fur quickly grows over the eye socket, so that its appearance is not unsightly, and cats adapt perfectly well to the loss of an eye, although obviously it becomes important to take extra care to ensure that the other eye does not develop problems.

Blindness in both eyes will naturally pose more of a problem. If it has developed slowly, cats can learn to function in familiar surroundings quite happily. But, if it has happened suddenly, as in a road accident, it is likely to cause the cat much distress. The cat is probably best put to sleep if there does not appear to be any chance of its sight returning.

EAR DISORDERS

The ear consists of the ear flap, or *pinna*, the outer ear canal which leads down to the ear drum, the middle ear behind the ear drum which contains the three bones that transfer sound vibrations, and the inner ear, deep within the skull, which contains the organs responsible for hearing and balance.

The external ear flap is easily injured, perhaps in a fight or perhaps through the cat scratching an irritation too fiercely. This may sometimes lead to bleeding within the ear flap itself, causing the ear flap to swell up and form an *aural haematoma*. If this occurs, the cat will require an operation to drain out the blood. If left untreated, the ear will become misshapen – a 'cauliflower ear' and this in turn may lead to obstruction of the ear canal and consequent irritation.

White-haired cats are prone to sunburn on the ear flaps in warmer months of the year – this may progress to a skin cancer in that area if left untreated. Frequent applications of a barrier suntan cream and keeping the cat indoors when the sun is bright will help to prevent the problem. In severe cases it may be necessary to remove the tips of the ear flaps surgically.

Infection of the outer ear canal is not uncommon, and is indicated by irritation, inflammation, discharge and, frequently a distinctive acrid smell. It is often caused by ear mites (see page 206) but may become further infected. Treatment will usually entail ear drops.

LEFT: *The veterinarian examines the eye with an ophthalmascope, which shines a bright light into the eye to give a magnified image of its structure. It may be necessary to administer eye drops first to dilate the pupil.*

*An auriscopic examination, using an illuminated magnifier (**RIGHT**) to see inside the lower part of the cat's ear, enables the veterinarian to identify the basic cause of an ear problem.*

It is very important to follow the directions given by the veterinarian carefully and take the cat back for re-examination if requested. It is very tempting to stop treatment as soon as the symptoms disappear, but if the infection has not fully cleared it will soon be back with a vengeance.

Because the balance organ is situated in the inner ear, any infection here will affect not only the cat's hearing but its sense of balance. This is most commonly manifested by a head tilt to one side, often causing the cat to walk around in circles. Such deep ear infections are distressing for the cat and the owner and require long and extensive treatment if a return to normality is to be hoped for.

*Persistent scratching around the ear can lead to self-injury and the formation of a skin haematoma (**ABOVE**) or blood blister, which will need veterinary treatment.*

VIRAL DISEASES

The cat is unusual in that a large proportion of its disease problems are caused by viruses. Viruses are exceedingly small organisms that cannot reproduce themselves, but invade the cells of the victim and cause the cells to manufacture more virus particles on their behalf.

They are transmitted from cat to cat not only by direct contact but by insect bites, human hands, shared food and litter trays and even borne on the wind, and can remain dangerous for up to a year after being shed by an infected cat.

If your cat shows the general symptoms of ill health – lack of energy, loss of appetite, a dull 'staring' coat and dull eyes – a viral infection may be suspected. Sometimes, however, a cat may harbour a virus without displaying symptoms, and successfully develop antibodies against it. Unfortunately a cat which has fought off a viral infection, with or without overt symptoms, and built up antibodies may still carry the virus and be infective to other cats.

Vaccinations have been developed for several of the most serious viral diseases – feline infectious enteritis (otherwise known as feline distemper or *panleucopaenia*) and the two most important forms of cat flu – but not as yet for others such as feline leukaemia. It is vital to give your cat as much protection as possible by maintaining annual vaccination boosters and by a high level of hygiene in the home. Viruses shed by infected cats can be destroyed by disinfectant, so litter trays and food bowls should be regularly and scrupulously disinfected. Any cat suspected of incubating an infection should be isolated to protect other cats.

Viruses can be passed on by a queen to her kittens before birth via the placenta and after birth via her milk, so particular care should be taken of breeding queens. Kittens are especially vulnerable to infection, particularly during the period after maternal antibodies received from the mother's milk have begun to wane, at around 6 weeks, and before they are old enough for vaccination at 10/12 weeks. They should therefore be kept isolated from other cats until they are protected by vaccination.

FELINE INFECTIOUS ENTERITIS

Feline infectious enteritis (FIE) affects the cat's digestive tract and is often fatal to unvaccinated animals. The main symptoms are weakness, severe vomiting, loss of appetite and, at a later stage, diarrhoea, and more than half the cats that pick up the virus will probably die from it despite treatment.

The incubation period is between four and 10 days; the cat will lose its appetite as its temperature rises and may start vomiting. After this stage, severe diarrhoea occurs resulting in serious dehydration, despite the cat's attempts to drink to compensate for the loss of fluid. The term

TRANSMISSION OF A VIRUS

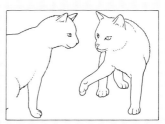

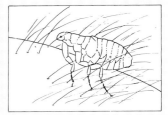
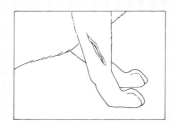
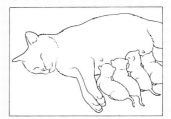

There are several ways that a virus may spread from cat to cat. It may be airborne (1), in droplets that are coughed or sneezed, as in the transmission of cat flu. Some of the more resistant viruses such as feline panleucoplaenia may simply be transmitted on contact (2) or indirectly on contaminated items such as feeding bowls. Feline panleucopaenia is also transmitted *by being ingested in food and swallowed (3). Other kinds of diseases are spread by bites from insects or other animals (4), or by open cuts and wounds (5). A particular danger to developing kittens is that some viruses pass across the placenta, or contaminate the mother's milk and infect newborn kittens (6).*

'panleucopaenia' refers to the characteristic alterations in the numbers of white blood cells (leucocytes) present in the circulation during the disease. The leucocyte count falls sharply and very few cells of the lymphoid group remain in severe cases. All rapidly dividing cells in the body are attacked by the virus; the resulting damage to the intestinal cells can be so severe that absorption of nutrients is permanently impaired. The cat may suffer intermittent bouts of diarrhoea for the rest of its life, if it manages to survive at all.

A pregnant female can infect her kittens while they are still in the womb, killing them or causing *cerebellar hypo-*

FELINE IMMUNOLOGY

When viruses enter the body, they stimulate the host to produce antibodies that attach to the organisms and neutralize them(1).

These antibodies are produced both at the site of entry – the nose or intestines – and in the bloodstream by white blood cells, the

lymphocytes (2). Once neutralized, the organisms can be engulfed by other white cells in the blood, the macrophages, and

broken down (3). A vaccine stimulates the body to produce antibodies so it can respond more quickly to future infection (4).

plasia, which affects the brain and makes the kittens unco-ordinated and wobbly from the time of birth.

Newly born kittens can also be infected. To ensure a good level of immunity is present in the dam's colostrum or first milk, she should have been vaccinated with a killed preparation, preferably just prior to mating.

Because FIE is caused by a virus, it will not respond to antibiotics, although these will help to prevent secondary bacterial infection. Antibiotic treatment is of particular value since the cat's own defence system cannot function effectively with low levels of leucocytes. Fluid and electrolyte replacement to offset the effects of the diarrhoea, given as a drip and coupled with a blood transfusion, generally offers the best hope of recovery.

The virus can remain infective for up to a year once shed from the cat's body, and it is not easy to rid a house of the virus once it has been contaminated – a 1 in 32 solution of bleach, together with some dish-washing liquid is effective in killing the virus, but is not very pleasant for use in the household. If you should be unfortunate enought to have had a cat die from the disease, you should disinfect the house and wait at least six months before introducing a successor, who should have been vaccinated before arrival: it will not be safe to introduce an unprotected cat or kitten for at least a year. Fortunately the vaccine is very effective.

CAT FLU

Cat flu is a disease that can be caused by several different agents, but about 80 percent of cases are caused by one of the two feline respiratory viruses – *feline herpesvirus* (FHV) and *feline calcivirus* (FCV). Cats cannot catch influenza or cold viruses from humans. These two types of virus are much less resistant than the feline panleucopaenia virus,

and, while they can be spread indirectly, they are usually spread by direct cat-to-cat contact or by aerosol inhalation due to sneezing. Contaminated food bowls or litter trays, or cat bites, are further sources of infection.

Typical symptoms include runny eyes, a runny nose, sneezing, a sore mouth, and a loss of appetite, but the nature and severity of symptoms will depend upon the nature of the virus and the condition of the cat: a healthy, well-fed and unstressed animal will be less severely affected than one which is neglected and/or stressed.

FHV is the most severe form and may be fatal, due to associated dehydration or a secondary pneumonia. Young cats are particularly susceptible and can show signs of infection for up to six weeks in bad cases, coupled with severe weight loss. In pregnant queens, abortion may well result from infection. FCV is not quite so severe, but typically causes painful ulcers to develop on the tongue, nose and mouth.

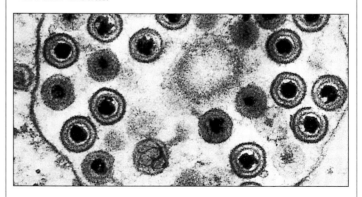

ABOVE: *Feline* Herpesvirus *is one of the viruses causing cat flu. This electron micrograph shows its structural characteristics.*

There is no real treatment for cat flu. Affected cats should be kept in a warm room and encouraged to rest, and recovery will depend upon antibiotics to prevent secondary infection, multivitamins to try to improve the cat's resistance, and careful nursing to keep the cat's strength up while it is trying to fight off the virus. Both viruses may linger in the nerve cells for many years, multiplying and causing bouts of illness when the cat is stressed and its defences are lowered. The damage caused by the viruses may also leave the cat with a long-term conjunctivitis or runny nose (known descriptively as 'chronic snuffles').

The virus itself can be destroyed by most common disinfectants or even by sunlight, but in multi-cat households it may be virtually impossible to identify and eliminate the cats that are carrying the viruses.

Cats should be vaccinated against FHV and FCV. Any place where large numbers of cats are brought together such as shows and catteries carries an increased risk of infection and animals exposed to this sort of hazardous environment are in particular need of protection. Unfortunately, very occasionally the vaccine may prove unreliable. Whilst ensuring that your cat has the best protection available by keeping up its vaccinations, do not ignore flu symptoms on the assumption that immunity is absolute.

FELINE LEUKAEMIA VIRUS

Feline leukaemia virus (FeLV) is very common in cat populations and is probably the most common cause of death in adult cats, aside perhaps from the automobile. The virus cannot live for very long outside the body of its host, and transmission from cat to cat is by close contact, with the virus shed in the saliva in fairly large amounts. Spread is therefore most noticeable in areas where cats are kept together in a confined environment. It is also possible for queens to infect their unborn kittens.

After exposure to the virus, 60 to 70 percent of cats will recover without problems, either because they are naturally resistant or because they develop effective antibodies. The remainder of infected cats are unable to overcome the virus and these are likely to succumb to its effects, especially leukaemia and lymphosarcomatosis. Resistance to other infections will also be lowered. The incubation period before the onset of symptoms may be as long as several years. The tumours associated with the disease most commonly affect the intestine and kidneys in the abdomen, while the thymus gland in the neck is a common site in younger cats. The symptoms vary according to the organs affected: in the case of the thymus, the cat may have difficulty in swallowing and breathing.

Lymph nodes are often enlarged in this condition and this will help a veterinarian to diagnose the disease. A blood test is useful for diagnosis. The disease can then be confirmed by removing a small section from a lymph node for

ABOVE: *Cat flu virus typically causes runny eyes, a runny nose, sneezing, a sore mouth and a loss of appetite. It can be fatal, especially to young or weak cats. Most cases can be prevented by regular vaccination, however,*

study under a microscope.

FeLV is often suspected as an underlying cause of many non-specific illnesses and of infertility, and veterinarians will often carry out a blood test for the virus if they suspect FeLV could be playing a part in the problem. It is also common practice nowadays to give regular blood tests to cats that live in large groups, where the disease is most common. The owner of a pedigreed cat will often be asked to have his or her cat's blood tested before a visit to the stud tom. The stud tom should also have been regularly tested, since mating is an ideal opportunity for the virus to spread, and there is very little that can be done to treat FeLV infection once it has become established.

Some cats that show a positive result on the blood test are fighting off the virus and may not become carriers – cats that are positive on one test should be isolated and re-tested after 12 weeks. The second test may prove negative, indicating that the cat has overcome the infection and is now immune. A second positive test shows that the cat is still infective and is also likely to succumb to the disease.

There is no cure for FeLV, and it is better to have a cat suffering from this illness put to sleep rather than to permit it to infect others. A vaccine against FeLV is available in the United States, but it is expensive and thought to protect fully only about 80 percent of the cats to whom it is given. It is hoped that cheaper and even more effective vaccines against FeLV will soon become available worldwide.

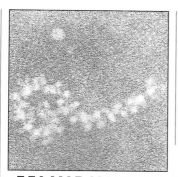

LEFT: *Feline infectious peritonitis has been known in the cat world for many years, but the virus responsible for this serious illness was only identified in 1966. It is known as* Coronavirus, *and is shown here, within a body cell, magnified 712,000 times by an electron microscope.*

FELINE INFECTIOUS PERITONITIS

Feline infectious peritonitis (FIP) is another serious viral disease for which there is no vaccine and no hope of recovery once symptoms are apparent. It affects the peritoneum, the lining of the abdominal cavity and its contents.

The disease often starts with non-specific symptoms, such as a lack of appetite and a high temperature, but the cat then goes on to develop an accumulation of fluid in the abdomen and sometimes on the chest. The abdomen becomes swollen, and breathing may become laboured. The nervous system can also be involved, leading to a loss of balance and convulsions; there may also be impairment of vision.

Examination of the fluid is often enough to confirm the diagnosis and, although a blood test is available, the results may be difficult to interpret. Some cats develop a different form of the disease (without the production of fluid) and have a wide range of symptoms due to the virus affecting the kidneys, liver, eyes, or nervous system. Diagnosis of these cases may be difficult. Once the disease is confirmed, it will only be a matter of weeks before death occurs; it may well be kinder in the latter stages to have the cat painlessly put to sleep by the veterinarian.

RABIES

Rabies is one of the most feared of all diseases. The rabies virus can affect all warm-blooded species, including man. Although most people think the main risk to humans comes from the dog, in areas where rabies is established in the wildlife population, a large percentage of human contacts with the disease come via the domestic cat. Infection usually occurs from a bite wound, with the virus initially multiplying in the wound and then travelling up a nerve to the brain. Although most animals develop symptoms about three weeks later, the incubation period may last for several months.

Rabies is an insidious disease; in many parts of the world, such as North America where infection is endemic in the wildlife, cats can be routinely vaccinated against the disease. Britain is currently free of rabies and has very strict controls on the import of cats and other mammals to maintain this status. Vaccination here is not normally permitted unless the cat concerned is being sent abroad to an area where rabies occurs, and must be authorized by the Ministry of Agriculture, Fisheries and Food.

Any animal suspected of being infected should not be handled if at all possible. Veterinary advice must be sought immediately. When approaching such an animal, protective clothing, including gloves, will be necessary. If there is any likelihood of human infection, the wound should be washed out at once, preferably with ethanol, or else water, followed by an application of tincture of iodine solution. A doctor must, of course, be contacted at once.

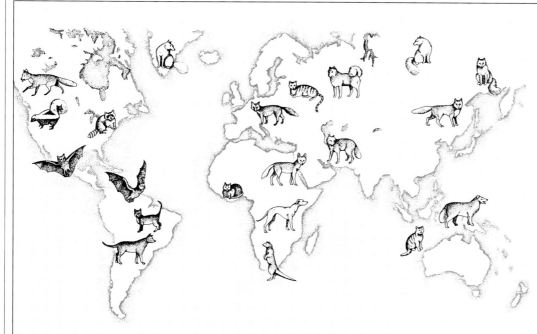

ANIMAL VECTORS OF RABIES

The distribution of rabies is worldwide and in places where the disease occurs regularly there is usually a 'reservoir' of the infection in wild animals – foxes in Western Europe, skunks and racoons in the United States, mongooses in South Africa, India and the Caribbean and vampire bats in Central and South America. Australia, the United Kingdom, Antarctica and Hawaii are the few rabies-free places in the world – thanks to their isolation by water and extremely strict import controls.

DIGESTIVE DISORDERS

Digestive problems may be caused by the cat's diet, but are often a sign of something wrong in the cat's system.

DIARRHOEA AND CONSTIPATION

Diarrhoea is a symptom associated with a variety of diseases rather than a condition itself.

It may simply be a reaction to something the cat has eaten. Most cats will develop diarrhoea if they eat too much of certain foods such as raw liver which have a laxative effect. However, other cats will develop diarrhoea if they eat even small amounts of food to which they are sensitive. Some individuals cannot digest some or even all brands of tinned cat foods, and others respond badly to milk. The immediate treatment is to withdraw food for twenty-four hours. If you can identify the offending food, remove it from the cat's diet.

Intestinal worms (see page 202) can sometimes cause diarrhoea, but this is usually only a problem with kittens.

Diarrhoea may also be caused by an infection, when it tends to come on suddenly, may affect other cats in the same group, and often causes the cat to run a temperature and appear unwell.

The treatment of any case of diarrhoea is likely to involve, initially, the removal of any milk or milk products from the diet, and a bland diet of something such as freshly cooked chicken, or white fish fed in small amounts but often. This regime can be tried before veterinary advice is sought in mild cases if the cat is otherwise bright and eating well, but assistance should be sought if the problem persists after 48 hours, both to establish the cause of the problem and to prevent dehydration, which can be particularly debilitating in kittens.

Constipation is rarer in cats and can usually be dealt with by giving a mild laxative, such as one recommended for fur balls. It can be aggravated if the cat swallows a lot of hair, so keep an eye on the coat for signs of any problem that might be causing excessive moulting, particularly fleas, and help the cat out with regular grooming. Constipation is commonest in elderly cats, which may develop a 'lazy bowel'.

Do not confuse straining due to constipation with straining due to urinary obstruction – the latter is a serious problem and requires immediate veterinary attention (see page 219).

VOMITING

Vomiting can be a natural function in cats to rid themselves of unwanted substances. Fur balls, or the feathers or bones of prey, may be vomited up quite naturally; some cats seem to be intolerant of certain foods and will vomit if fed them and sometimes a cat will eat its food too fast and then vomit it up to eat it again more slowly. Again, vomiting (often with diarrhoea) may occur as a natural function if the cat has eaten poison or some unwholesome food. Suppression of these symptoms at an early stage may mean that more of the harmful substance is absorbed into the body.

Prolonged or severe vomiting, however, is an indication that something is seriously wrong and may pose a major threat to the life of the cat. Veterinary treatment is called

THE DIGESTIVE SYSTEM

The digestive system in a cat is similar to ours. Food is taken in at the mouth (1), and after very little chewing is passed down the oesophagus (2), to the stomach (3), where it is mixed with acid and digestive enzymes. It passes on down the small intestine (4), where digestive juices from the liver (5) and pancreas (6) work, together with intestinal enzymes, to break down and absorb the food. Water is then re-absorbed from the large intestine (7), and the faeces are excreted.

2 oesophagus
3 stomach
6 pancreas
5 liver
7 large intestine
1 mouth
4 small intestine

for, both to establish the cause and to prevent dehydration.

If food is regurgitated rather than vomited, this is likely to indicate a disorder of the oesophagus, the tube that carries food from the mouth, through the chest and down to the stomach. Regurgitation can be distinguished from true vomiting as it is less violent, with less heaving and contraction of the abdominal muscles. It usually takes place soon after eating, and the food brought up is undigested, often in a 'sausage-shaped' mass.

Persistent regurgitation of food can be caused by a dilation of the oesophagus, by something sharp that the cat has eaten getting stuck on the way down, by a constriction of the tube itself that may either have been present at birth or developed later on, or by an inflammation of the oeseophagus following an infection or the ingestion of hot or caustic substances. As with so many disorders, the first step should always be to try to determine the cause of the problem so that it can then be resolved.

GASTRITIS AND ENTERITIS

An inflammation of the stomach is called *gastritis*, and may often be part of a generalized inflammation of the alimentary tract, *gastro-enteritis*. Enteritis primarily causes diarrhoea, possibly with blood in it. The cat may also have abdominal pain, strain to pass stools, and lose weight. It can either refuse food because it feels unwell, or eat more than normal to try to compensate for the food that is not being digested properly.

URINARY DISORDERS

The urinary tract begins at the two kidneys, where urine is produced. It then passes down small tubes called the ureters to the bladder where it is stored until it is passed out via a single tube called the urethra. Disorders of the urinary tract are quite common in cats.

The cat's urinary system is designed for maximum fluid conservation, so the urine is naturally highly concentrated. This means that any factor which increases the already high concentration – overlong retention of urine by a lazy cat, or simply a low fluid intake – can easily lead to problems. Cats should therefore be encouraged to go out frequently and to drink as much as possible.

It is important to recognize when your cat is having problems urinating, as urgent attention may be essential. The cat is likely to spend time attempting to urinate without success, often crouching rather than taking up the normal squatting position – the symptoms may easily be mistaken for constipation.

THE URINARY SYSTEM

The urinary system in cats, in both sexes, consists of the paired kidneys (1), ureters (2), bladder (3) and urethra (4), which opens at the tip of the penis in the male, whereas in the female (**ABOVE**) it opens at the vulva (5).

CYSTITIS

Cystitis, an inflammation of the bladder, is not uncommon in cats. It may be brought on by cold, wet weather, but the most common cause of cystitis and blockage of the urethra is the *feline urolithiasis syndrome*, or FUS. The disease is due to the accumulation of a fine 'sandy' material in the bladder and urethra which irritates the lining of the bladder to cause cystitis. In male cats it will often cause an obstruction to the flow of urine down the urethra – the urethra of the female is much wider and therefore less prone to blockage. The precise cause of FUS is not clear, but it is known to occur most commonly in obese and inactive males fed a high proportion of dry foods.

Cystitis can be recognized by the fact that the cat strains frequently to pass small drops of urine, and they appear blood-stained. Very often the urinating habits of the cat will suddenly change; normally clean cats will urinate on the rug. If the cat has a urethral obstruction, it will strain repeatedly to pass urine, but none will be passed. It is important to recognize this, and not to confuse it with constipation as a urethral obstruction is an emergency and must receive immediate veterinary attention. Severe illness from the build up of toxic waste in the body and dehydration will be noticeable within 24 hours of the problem developing.

The veterinarian may have to give the cat an anaesthetic, in order to insert a draining tube, or catheter, up through the urethra into the bladder, cautiously breaking down the obstruction in the process. Pressure on the bladder itself has to be exerted extremely carefully because of the risk of rupturing it. In severe cases where catheterization is not possible, the bladder may have to be emptied directly.

Intravenous correction of the dehydration which accompanies the obstruction is likely to be necessary; subsequently, the cat should be encouraged to drink as much as possible to dilute the urine and reduce the irritation to the bladder wall. Salt can be sprinkled on food but it may promote diarrhoea in some cats. Gravy is another possible alternative; it is also sensible to change the diet to canned and fresh food, both of which have a relatively high water content. A veterinarian may also recommend a urinary acidifier such as ammonium chloride, although this unpalatable to many cats. By increasing the acidity of the urine, these chemicals will make the compounds responsible for the blockage more soluble and less likely to crystallize out in the urethra.

In the case of a very severe or recurrent condition, your vet may advise an operation called a *perineal urethrostomy* which converts the narrow urethra of the male cat into a wide tube, resembling the female urethra so that it is less likely to become blocked with small stones.

KIDNEY DISEASE

Kidney disease is commonest in elderly cats in the form of chronic interstitial nephritis (see page 236). Younger cats occasionally suffer from similar forms of this complaint, with similar symptoms, to be treated with a low protein diet.

There is, however, a type of kidney disease known as *glomerulonephritis* which produces the *nephrotic syndrome*. The main symptom is the appearance of fluid under the skin of the legs and the lower part of the body and it is sometimes referred to as 'dropsy'. It is important to differentiate this from the usual type of kidney failure because the symptoms are caused by an excessive loss of protein from the blood through 'leaky' kidneys, and a high protein diet must be fed – exactly the opposite of the low protein diet that should be given in the case of chronic interstitial nephritis.

CIRCULATORY DISORDERS

Although heart disease is relatively rare in cats, there are a number of diseases of the blood. Any disorder of the circulatory system is potentially serious, and many blood diseases need samples to be taken by a veterinarian for efficient diagnosis and treatment.

HEART DISEASE

Heart disease is fortunately not very common in cats. They are spared from coronary thrombosis, which so often causes heart attacks in humans, and do not suffer from heart valve disease, a very common problem in older dogs. Heart diseases may be congenital or acquired.

Certain congenital defects, such as hole-in-the-heart, are occasionally encountered in kittens, but are fortunately very rare – about 1 in 1000 kittens – and when they do occur may be mild and not cause any symptoms or illness. However, they may cause kittens to fail to thrive as they grow and if severe, usually necessitate the kitten being put to sleep.

Valvular problems occasionally occur, often as a result of bacterial infections, but do not produce severe symptoms, which is fortunate since treatment is not easy. Digitalis, which is commonly used for other species, produces toxic effects, including vomiting, at very low dosage levels in cats.

Elderly cats are sometimes affected by a degeneration of the heart muscle, leading to thrombosis.

ANAEMIA

Anaemia is a reduction in the number of red blood cells circulating in the blood. It is not a disease itself but a sign of illness that can have many possible causes. The red blood cells are responsible for transporting oxygen in the blood; affected cats will tend to be breathless and lethargic. Since haemoglobin, the pigment in the red blood cells, gives the blood its red colour, anaemia will tend to make the cat 'pale' – this is best seen by examining the membranes that line the eyes and mouth, the tongue, and the tip of the nose if it is not too heavily pigmented.

If the cause of the anaemia is not obvious from an examination of the patient, the veterinarian may have to carry out a blood test, or even a test of a sample of bone marrow, to diagnose the cause correctly and undertake treatment.

Anaemia may be caused quite simply by a loss of blood, either externally due to injury or blood-sucking skin parasites, or internally due to internal injuries, tumours, or disorders of the normal clotting mechanisms of the blood. Some rat poisons may cause the latter. In these cases a blood test will usually demonstrate that the cat is frantically trying to make new blood cells to compensate.

A common type of anaemia, which unfortunately does not respond well to treatment, is caused by a failure of the bone marrow to manufacture red blood cells. The most likely causes of this are kidney failure, particularly in the older cat (see page 236) and feline leukaemia virus (see page 216).

Anaemia can also be caused by an infestation of the protozoan parasite *Haemobartonella felis* (see page 209), which can be treated with antibiotics.

*Anaemia can be caused by one of many different diseases. It is often necessary for the veterinarian to take a blood test (**LEFT**) to examine the blood to determine the cause of the problem. The blood is usually taken from the vein that runs along the front of the forearm, a procedure that generally causes very little pain or distress.*

RESPIRATORY DISORDERS

Diseases of the respiratory system – nose, throat and lungs – may evince themselves in apparently minor systems such as a runny nose, coughing or wheezing, or laboured breathing, but should always be taken seriously. They can be divided into upper respiratory disease, affecting mainly the nose and upper air passages, and lower respiratory disease, affecting the lungs.

UPPER RESPIRATORY DISEASE

The most serious of upper respiratory diseases is cat flu (see page 215), requiring veterinary treatment and careful nursing.

Any inflammation of the nasal passages that has become well established over a period of time is termed *chronic rhinitis*. It may be caused by a foreign body, such as a grass seed, lodged in the nose, by a fungal infection or by a growth in the nose, all of which will respond to early treatment, or it may follow secondary bacterial infection after a bout of cat flu.

Diagnosis of the cause of 'chronic sniffles' may involve the use of X-rays, blood tests, and a culture in the laboratory of the bacteria present in the discharge. Treatment will involve trying to clear the cause of the problem, together with drugs to help alleviate the symptoms. Unfortunately, once the lining of the nasal passages have been severely damaged, a complete cure is often impossible, and the cat and its owner have to learn to live with the problem.

Cats can also suffer from bouts of *pharyngitis*, sore throats, causing discomfort when swallowing, and *laryngitis*, which may cause the cat to lose its voice, a source of great worry to some owners, and of great joy to others! Both conditions usually respond well to antibiotic treatment.

LOWER RESPIRATORY DISEASE

A cough is relatively uncommon in cats, and disease of the lower respiratory tract usually manifests itself in the form of *dyspnoea*, or laboured breathing. This may be accompanied by other symptoms such as the cat feeling unwell and being reluctant to eat or to exercise.

When cats do cough, it is usually due to disease of the trachea (windpipe) or the bronchii – the larger airways into the lungs.

Bronchial asthma, an allergic chest problem, can cause cats to cough, but the cause may also be an infection. Chronic coughing, rather like chronic rhinitis, can often be a difficult problem to cure completely, and treatment often has to be continued on a permanent basis to control the problem.

Lungworms (see page 209) may also cause a cough and are quite common in young cats, but only rarely do they cause serious disease. Diagnosis of lungworm infection relies upon examination of the cat's stool under the microscope to identify the larvae of the worm, and specific drugs effective against lungworm must be used for its treatment.

Dyspnoea is generally a symptom of a fairly serious lung disease, especially since breathing in cats usually does not become laboured until the underlying disease is well advanced. There are several possible causes, and the first step is usually to take an X-ray to establish whether there is fluid on the chest or whether any other possible cause of the breathing problem such as a growth is visible. If fluid is present, the veterinarian will probably wish to drain off a sample for analysis. Causes of an accumulation of fluid on the chest include a chest infection, feline infectious peritonitis (see page 217), a tumour within the chest, or heart disease (see page 220). If the cat has been involved in an accident, the veterinarian will check for damage to the diaphragm, the muscular sheet that divides the chest from the abdomen (see page 227). Some of the causes of laboured breathing such as most growths within the chest and feline infectious peritonitis are incurable, and any of the other causes are likely to require intensive treatment.

DISORDERS OF THE NERVOUS SYSTEM

There is a wide range of congenital diseases of the nervous system that may affect kittens, such as *hydrocephalus*, a build-up of fluid around the brain, and *congenital vestibular disease*. The latter affects the balance of kittens and is thought to be hereditary in certain breeds of cat, including Siamese, Burmese, Birmans and British Creams. There is often very little that can be done to treat such cases, but kittens that are only mildly affected may improve with time.

FITS

Fits occasionally occur and are very alarming for the spectator. The cat may jerk and cry out, lose coordination or even become temporarily paralyzed; it may vomit or involuntarily void its bladder or bowels. It will not be in control of its actions and may well bite if handled.

If your cat has a fit do not touch it but leave it alone in a darkened room and contact your veterinarian.

A cat may have a fit once in its lifetime and the cause may never be established. However, the commonest causes include poisoning, brain tumours and infections that affect the brain, all of which can prove fatal, so do not delay in obtaining veterinary assistance.

Poisoning (see pages 230–231) by drugs such as metaldehyde, commonly used as a slug pellet, can sometimes be tackled, when the cat has recovered from its convulsions, by inducing vomiting as a first aid measure. If the fit is caused by a brain tumour, this is often a result of lymphosarcoma due to feline leukaemia virus (see page 216) and the prognosis is not good. Infections that include the brain include a form of feline infectious peritonitis (see page 217), also a fatal illness.

Fits may also be caused by injury – either directly following a knock on the head or as a delayed response days or weeks later – or by epilepsy, fortunately rare in cats. Some other diseases which could be responsible include some forms of liver disease and terminal cases of kidney failure (see page 236).

If the underlying cause of the fits can be identified and treated, it may be possible to cure them. More often than not, however, it is necessary to resort to control with drug rather than cure. It should be remembered that a fit is usually more distressing for the onlookers than for the person or animal having it. It is best to leave an animal having a fit in a quiet and dark place until it subsides and then seek veterinary advice. If a fit has lasted for more than ten minutes and shows no sign of subsiding, however, immediate veterinary attention should be sought. If a cat is having only infrequent fits, your veterinarian may decide against keeping the cat on permanent medication, but if fits are frequent and severe, long-term therapy may be essential. If a cat is receiving long-term medication for fits, it is important that treatment be given regularly and that it does not stop suddenly, otherwise very serious fits could follow.

STROKES

Strokes in cats are not usually thought to be due to blood clots in the brain as in humans, but they may nevertheless appear very similar. Depending on the part of the brain affected, they may produce severe uncoordination, apparent blindness, or continual circling and problems with balance. These cases do not usually respond to any treatment that is given, but, as with human stroke victims, the function of damaged areas of the brain can slowly be taken over by other undamaged parts. Problems with balance may also be caused by inner ear disease, when infection has spread either from an external ear infection or a throat infection into the organs of balance in the inner ear deep within the skull. Inner ear disease will often respond to drug treatment, although surgery to drain the deeper parts of the ear canal can be necessary in some cases.

ABOVE: *Key-Gaskell syndrome causes a paralysis of the central nervous system. This cat shows the distinctive dilated pupils, unresponsive to light, typical of many cases.*

KEY-GASKELL SYNDROME

Key-Gaskell Syndrome, or *feline dysautonomia,* is a disease affecting the cat's nervous system which was first identified in the early 1980s and has become quite widespread. The cause of the disease is completely unknown, but it leads to a failure of the autonomic nervous system, the part of the nervous system that unconsciously controls body function such as tear and saliva production, bowel movements and urination.

All cats seem to be susceptible, although a higher incidence of disease has been noted in young shorthairs. The illness can strike kittens as young as 10 weeks old and there is no difference between the sexes in susceptibility. The disease may not be infectious, since often only one cat in a multi-cat household will develop symptoms and those living permanently indoors on their own can also be affected.

Symptoms include vomiting and loss of appetite, dry eyes and nose and noticeably dilated pupils. The third eyelid often protrudes across the eye. Diarrhoea may also be apparent; in the more protracted cases, constipation is likely to be noted, and in severe cases the cat may be unable to urinate normally. Symptoms may at first resemble an upper respiratory tract infection, with sneezing being evident. Weakness of the hindlimbs or more generalized loss of mobility is also observed in many cases.

Many cases show only some of these symptoms, and it is often necessary for the veterinary surgeon to establish his diagnosis by taking X-rays of the oesophagus, the tube that carries food to the stomach, which is almost always enlarged in cases of this disease. Sometimes more than one case occurs in the same household, but very often it does not, so it is not yet known whether the condition is infectious.

Since the actual cause of the Key-Gaskell Syndrome has not been discovered yet, treatment is restricted to alleviating such symptoms as constipation, loss of appetite and insufficient secretion of tears and saliva. With time, up to a third of cases may recover to lead a fairly normal life, but any damage done to the nervous system is irreparable and some signs, such as dilation of the pupils, may never disappear.

The disease is most distressing for owners, since a lot of nursing care and patience is necessary if the cat is to have any hope of recovery, and even then a fair proportion of cats will continue to waste away until they die or are put to sleep. The only encouraging aspect of this depressing disease is that the recovery rate does seem to be improving, partly perhaps because of a better understanding of how best to treat these cases, and possibly also because the disease itself is becoming milder.

Research into the Key-Gaskell Syndrome is continuing. The possible role of fleas and their control has been a focus of attention, with one suggestion being that the disease may be linked as a sequel to treatment, but this has not yet been confirmed and the most recent work tends to dismiss this theory. When a case is diagnosed, it is probably sensible to keep the cat isolated and disinfect its environment thoroughly, in case the illness could infect others.

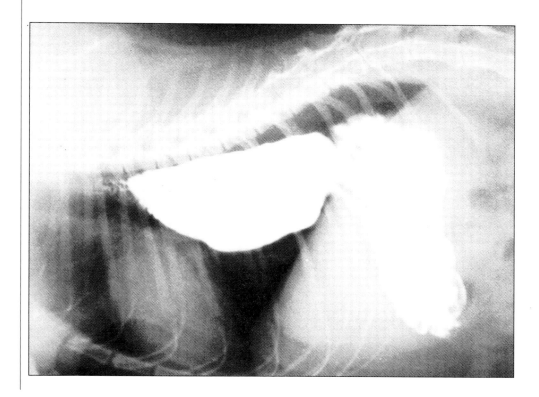

LEFT: *Some sufferers from Key-Gaskell syndrome show none of the typical symptoms, and the disease can only be identified by the dilation of the oesophagus, or gullet, found in all cases. The cat is given a barium swallow and a radiograph is taken immediately afterwards.*

LIVER DISORDERS

Liver problems are not very common in cats, and when they do occur, the diagnosis and treatment may be somewhat complex.

Cat owners should, however, be able to recognize jaundice, a yellow pigmentation of the skin, because it may be a vital clue that all is not well and that veterinary assistance should be sought. Rather like anaemia (see page 220), jaundice is not a disease in itself, but a symptom of disease which can have one of several causes. it is due to excessive levels of pigment produced from the breakdown of red blood cells, which are normally processed by the liver and then excreted into the stools, giving them their characteristic dark brown colour.

Jaundice can therefore be due to an excessive breakdown of red blood cells as might occur in feline infectious anaemia (see page 214), or to a failure in the processing system of the liver itself, or to a blockage of the normal route of excretion of the bile from the liver into the intestines. Yellow discoloration is often best noticed in the whites of the eyes, although it may also be visible inside the mouth, and in advanced cases, on the hairless areas of skin, such as on the underside of the abdomen.

This jaundice will normally only occur if a fairly serious disease is present, and the cat should always be taken to your veterinarian for further examination to determine whether it has contracted a serious ailment such as hepatitis or pancreatitis.

REPRODUCTIVE DISORDERS

Tomcats allowed to roam free will often disappear for long periods in quest of females, and suffer particularly during the latter part of the breeding season, often reappearing in very poor condition during August. This condition is largely due to lack of interest in food while they are impelled by the reproductive urge. They have usually lost considerable weight and their relatively large kidneys may be evident as swellings in the abdominal region, either side of the vertebral column. They should, however, respond well to good feeding, and soon put on weight again.

The queen is more prone to problems directly linked with her reproductive system. If she has not been spayed but is not permitted to breed, she may suffer *endometritis* in her middle years. This is an inflammation of the lining of the uterus, which is often linked with a vaginal discharge. If the uterus becomes full of pus, the condition is referred to as *pyometra*. This is most commonly seen in older cats, 14 or 15 years old, which are not actually breeding yet still cycling regularly.

Pyometra is a serious condition which requires urgent surgical treatment. Symptoms include a pronounced enlargement of the abdomen, lack of energy and increased thirst. In the 'open' form there will be a noticeable vaginal discharge but in some cases the cervix remains closed, preventing the escape of matter. The only treatment for pyometra is a rapid ovarohysterectomy (spaying), and providing this is carried out without delay, the chances of recovery are likely to be good.

Pregnancy failure in cats may be due to endometritis, or it may arise from feline leukaemia virus infection, both of which can cause the death of foetuses. This may be apparent to the owner when spontaneous abortion is seen to occur, or the dead foetuses may be resorbed back into the body. Repeated small litters may also indicate a similar problem. A blood test should be taken to rule out FeLV infection as a cause of infertility or low fertility; in the case of endometritis this may respond to antibiotic treatment. It is also wise to allow the queen to call without being mated for two or three cycles before attempting to breed her again. While nutritional problems and hormonal imbalances may frequently get the blame for such cases of infertility, neither seems to be a common cause.

Cats are exceptionally healthy creatures, and very few queens miscarry or abort a pregnancy unless they are carrying an infection. A serious fall, an attack of flu or enteritis could cause this, however. If the miscarriage occurs in the early stages of pregnancy, the cat may show little sign of discomfort. As with humans, a miscarriage in the later stages is a more serious matter and will certainly require a visit to your veterinarian.

Sometimes an unmated cat, or one which has mated successfully but lost her kittens at a very early stage, may undergo a false pregnancy. Such a queen will show all the symptoms of a true pregnancy, with abdominal enlargement, the appearance of milk, the maternal behaviour such as making a nest and cuddling up to objects as if they were kittens. She may also become morose, neurotic and aggressive and refuse her food. The only difference between this condition and a true pregnancy is that there will be no kittens. Most cases of false pregnancy will sort themselves out if left alone. If it seems to be making the queen uncomfortable, or if she is producing a lot of milk, it may be necessary for the veterinarian to provide hormone treatment.

RIGHT: *Surgical operations can be carried out at most practices when necessary. The operating theatre is usually highly up to date, and many a cat's life has been saved by modern surgery and nursing techniques.*

FAR RIGHT: *The modern veterinary practice is equipped with facilities comparable to those in human hospitals, enabling sophisticated treatment of animal disorders.*

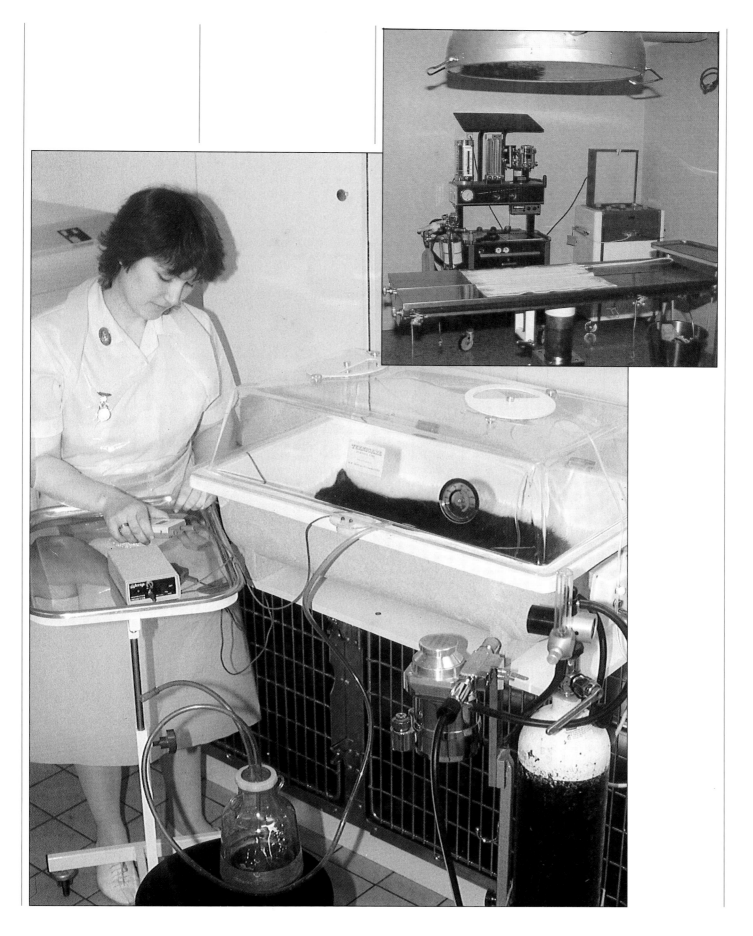

ACCIDENTS AND INJURIES

Cats are as prone to accidental injury as any other creature, and their independent lifestyle exposes them to such hazards as traffic. If your cat is injured, you can do a great deal to help it before the vet arrives, and some basic knowledge of first aid may mean the difference between life and death to your pet.

ROAD ACCIDENTS

Road accidents are sadly not uncommon, especially in urban areas. Even minor accidents should be taken seriously, as internal injuries may not be immediately apparent, and even if the cat is only slightly injured the accompanying shock may be fatal.

The instinct of an injured cat is to run away and hide, so it is important to act quickly to catch it. Pain and fright may make any animal dangerous, so handle a hurt cat with caution, grasping the scruff of the neck with one hand and supporting the hindquarters with the other. If the cat is struggling wildly, cover it with a towel or blanket and place the whole bundle in a strong box or cat carrier. Extreme care is vital, not only to protect yourself from the cat but to avoid further damage to the animal.

Try to control any severe bleeding with a pressure bandage placed on the wound. It is important to keep the cat warm until veterinary assistance is available, to minimize the effects of shock, which can be fatal in itself. Wrap the animal loosely in a blanket; if you have some of the plastic bubble type of wrapping material to hand, this makes an ideal insulating wrap.

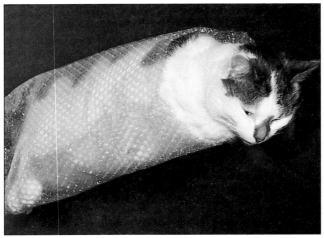

ABOVE: *An injured cat should be kept warm to reduce the risk of severe shock symptoms. It can be loosely wrapped in a blanket, or, as shown, in 'plastic bubble' wrapping material, which has excellent insulating qualities.*

If the cat is unconscious, ideally it should not be moved, but in practice you will probably have to get it out of the way of other vehicles on the road. Move it with great care to avoid exacerbating its injuries. A blanket makes an ideal stretcher: slide one hand under the chest and one under the rump and ease the cat on to the blanket without twisting the body. Make sure that the airway is not blocked, clearing any vomit or blood from the mouth and pulling the tongue well forward. Do not allow the cat's front end to hang down, as a relatively common injury is a ruptured diaphragm, through which the intestines could slip from the abdomen into the chest cavity.

It can be difficult to distinguish between unconsciousness and death. If the cat has been killed outright, breathing will have ceased, the heartbeat will have stopped, the pupils of the eyes will be widely dilated and fixed and the cat will not blink if the surface of the eye is lightly touched. You may be able to feel a heartbeat by placing the hand on the cat's chest in the region that lies below the elbow when it is drawn back over the chest, or to see the movement of

MOVING AN INJURED CAT

Always approach an injured cat from behind so that it does not claw you. To alleviate the possibility of putting unnecessary pressure on any internal injuries, use both hands outspread, gently coax them under the cat's rump and chest to distribute its weight, and, avoiding any twisting or bending of the cat's body, lay the cat down onto a towel or blanket (1).

Alternatively, if the cat is restless, gently pick it up by the scruff of the neck, and supporting the rump, place it into a cardboard box or suitable carrier (2). If the cat struggles violently it is a good idea to wrap it up in a towel (3), prior to placing it in the cat carrier.

body hairs, if the heart is still beating. However, if the heartbeat is very weak, it is difficult for an inexperienced person to detect it. If you are in any doubt, it is always best to have the cat examined by a veterinarian to confirm death.

Road accidents often cause injury to the rear of the cat, commonly resulting in either a fractured pelvis or femur (thigh bone). Advances in veterinary orthopaedic surgery mean that today much can be done to repair injuries that would once have been considered beyond repair. Fractured limbs can be splinted externally, but often require internal fixation, for example by the insertion of a metal pin down the cavity inside the bone to support it while it knits. Once the vet has set the break, such fractures normally heal well, but careful observation is needed in the early days to make sure that there are no associated internal injuries.

One relatively common internal injury caused by road accidents is a ruptured diaphragm. The diaphragm separates the chest from the abdomen, and if this is torn the cat will have difficulty in breathing, and the internal organs may slip into the chest. The tear can be repaired by surgery, although the anaesthetic risk is quite serious.

Another common road accident injury is a ruptured bladder, allowing urine to escape into the abdomen. If this is left untreated, the poisons from the urine will be absorbed into the cat's system and make it ill. It is important, therefore to be sure that any cat which has been involved in a road accident is urinating normally afterwards. If there is a likelihood that the bladder has been damaged, your vet will need to take X-rays and possibly blood tests to establish whether surgery is needed.

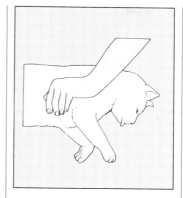

FINDING THE HEARTBEAT
The heartbeat can be felt by holding the lower chest just behind the shoulders between the fingers and thumb of one hand, or you may be able to see the hairs moving in this area as the heart actually beats. It can be very difficult for an inexperienced person to detect if the animal is shocked and the heartbeat weak.

BANDAGING
Wrap the wound with surgical gauze, cover this with cotton wool and then bandage tightly.

STOPPING BLEEDING
Pressure on the site of an open wound will often serve to stem the blood loss.

FALLS

Although the flexible skeleton and agility of the cat enable it to fall from considerable heights without injury, accidents to happen. Cats living in high-rise apartments are obviously at risk from falls. Kittens in particular are liable to overbalance from a windowsill, or miscalculate a leap up on to a high surface, If a cat suffers a fall, even if it seems undamaged a veterinary check-up may be a wise precaution. If it is knocked unconscious, cannot walk normally, or is bleeding heavily, particularly from the mouth or anus or in the urine, immediate veterinary attention is needed.

Falls may cause muscle strains and sprained ligaments. In such cases the cat will be reluctant to move, may hold itself tensely in a hunched posture, and show lameness. The condition will usually right itself with rest, but if it persists your vet will be able to give antiinflammatory treatment.

If a cat falls from a great height, it often makes a 'five point landing' on all four feet and its chin. This may result in a fracture of the hard palate in the roof of the mouth, or of the jaw bone, which will need to be surgically repaired.

WOUNDS

Wounds are common, and all but minor scratches (which the cat will treat itself with its naturally anti-septic tongue) are best checked by a veterinarian. If they are gaping open and exposing tissues underneath, of if they are bleeding heavily, immediate attention is called for. Bleeding can be staunched by pressure on the wound, using a pad of gauze or similar material; a temporary bandage can be used to hold the pressure pad in place while awaiting veterinary aid. In severe cases, it may help to apply a tourniquet above the wound.

Fight wounds are rarely emergencies unless they penetrate a vital organ, but it is wise to have any deep bite treated with antibiotics to prevent infection developing, as bites inflicted by other cats introduce bacteria from the assailant's mouth. In summer in particular it is important to ensure that wounds are kept clean and dry to prevent attracting flies, which will lay their eggs on the broken skin, leading to 'fly strike' (maggot infestation). Dusting with an antiseptic powder combined with an insecticide, which your vet can supply, will prevent this problem.

Because bites are often puncture wounds, with little

bleeding, they may be inconspicuous at first and may not be spotted until an abscess has developed. This should be treated by your vet, who will open and drain the abscess and prescribe antibiotics. If the abscess bursts before the cat can be taken to the vet, wipe away the discharged matter with cottonwool soaked in warm water and bathe the wound in a solution of one teaspoon of salt to a pint of warm water to encourage draining, or wash it out with a solution of hydrogen peroxide. The cat should then be treated by the vet to prevent a further abscess forming.

Gunshot wounds occasionally occur, especially from airguns and .22s in the hands of irresponsible youths. The pellet may make only a small and harmless-looking skin wound, but it may then cause serious infection or damage to internal organs.

ABSCESSES
These should be bathed two or three times a day with a wad of cotton soaked in a solution of a teaspoonful of table salt to a pint of water. The solution should be used as warm as the cat will comfortably tolerate, and the wound should be gently squeezed to drain out any pus.

ABOVE: *An infected fight wound is probably one of the most common veterinary problems of all, in cats. Although they are not often dire emergencies, it is probably wise to have all deep bites treated with antibiotics to prevent sepsis developing.*

DROWNING

Drowning is not very common. Cats are able to swim, although most will avoid doing so, but occasionally a cat may be trapped in water and drown. If a cat is rescued from the water and shows no signs of life, resuscitation can be attempted while veterinary attention is being sought. Hold the animal by its hindlegs, head downwards, and swing it gently back and forth to drain water from the lungs. The mouth must be kept open, and the tongue should be pulled forward to ensure that it is not blocking the airway.

If the cat does not begin to breathe, lay it on its side and press the chest, behind the elbow, rapidly several times, then pause to check whether the cat has begun breathing again. Repeat the process twice a second until the heartbeat can be felt. It is worth continuing for two or three minutes if no response is evident, although, as time elapses, the chances of success will almost certainly be reduced.

Alternatively, mouth-to-mouth resuscitation may be attempted. Pull the cat's tongue out to clear the airway, cup both hands around the open jaws and breathe into them.

BURNS AND SCALDS

Cats are especially at risk in a kitchen, where they may jump onto hot surfaces – especially ceramic cooking surfaces – or be splashed with hot liquids or cooking oils. They may also manage to singe themselves by lying too close to a fire. It is essential to cool down the skin as quickly as possible by immediately running cold water over the affected area or applying a pad soaked in cold water to it, to decrease the inflammation. Anything other than the most minor of burns will require veterinary attention.

Occasionally a cat may be burnt by caustic chemicals. Treat as for burns, additionally washing the coat to remove the chemical.

Cats, and especially kittens, may receive burns from chewing an electrical wire. You can reduce the risk of this by keeping electrical appliances unplugged. If it does happen do not touch the cat until the current is turned off, or you could electrocute yourself. Sometimes the electric shock may kill the animal outright, but usually it causes severe burns to the mouth and veterinary attention should be sought without delay.

SWALLOWING FOREIGN BODIES

Kittens in particular may swallow dangerous objects such as a needle and thread. These may lodge in the throat, causing gagging and choking. Open the cat's mouth and investigate: the offending object may be accessible for removal, but in many cases it is best to seek veterinary assistance as it is easy 'accidentally' to push the object further down the airway or to cause bruising and tearing to

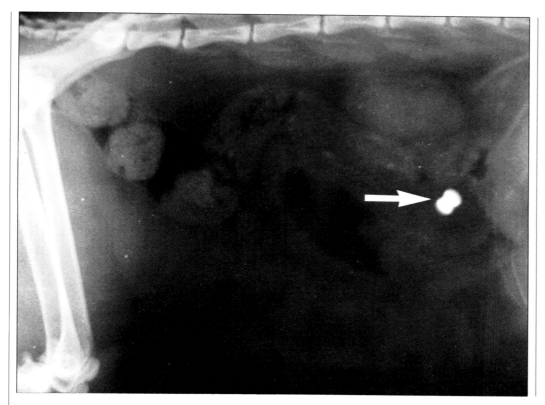

the delicate tissues, quite apart from the risk that the cat may well be uncooperative and even bite. Fortunately, while the cat may be very distressed, it is unlikely to suffocate before veterinary treatment can be obtained.

If a foreign body is actually swallowed, especially in the case of sharp objects such as pins or bones, there is a danger that they may lodge in the digestive tract and perforate the gut. In such cases the veterinarian will be able to locate the offending object by X-ray and may need to operate to remove it.

SNAKE BITES

Britain has only one venomous snake, the adder, but in countries such as the United States or Australia snake bites are a more common hazard. Snake bites should be treated by applying a tourniquet, if possible, to prevent the poison from entering the general circulation, and placing an ice-pack over the swollen area, before seeking veterinary aid.

INSECT BITES

Insect bites are common, especially in the summer, usually occurring on the face or feet and resulting in pain and swelling. Bee stings should be bathed in a solution of bicarbonate of soda and the sting removed if found; wasp stings should be bathed in vinegar. Most stings are not serious and the cat will recover naturally, but if the sting is in the mouth, breathing may be impaired and you may need to seek veterinary aid. Some cats may show an allergic reaction with alarming swelling, and here again veterinary attention will be required.

DROWNING

If the cat shows no signs of life when it has been pulled out of the water, resuscitation can be attempted while veterinary assistance is awaited. Hold the cat upside down by its hindlegs and swing it gently to and fro to drain the lungs of water. If the cat is still not breathing, lay it on its side and press the chest rapidly several times. Keep doing this, pausing at intervals to check the heartbeat.

TRAPPED CATS

Contrary to popular belief, cats rarely find themselves trapped in trees or similar locations. An apparently trapped cat is usually capable of descending on its own, but may be reluctant to do so for some time if it is frightened. If it is still up its tree after 24 hours it may require help. You may be able to rescue it yourself with a ladder, taking care to position the ladder securely and to wear gloves to protect your hands if the cat does not welcome your assistance; however, rather than take unnecessary risks, it may be advisable to call your local fire station for help.

Occasionally a cat may become trapped in a drainage duct or ventilation shaft. Rescue in such cases may be difficult because the cat is likely to panic and struggle violently when handled, and it may be necessary for a veterinarian to administer a sedative injection before the cat can be freed.

The instinct to investigate enclosed spaces can lead to cats being accidentally shut in sheds, garages or empty houses. A cat trapped like this may survive for up to six weeks without food or water, but when rescued is likely to be in very poor condition. Its stomach will be unable to cope with an immediate return to normal eating and drinking habits, so give frequent small amounts of water and of bland, well-moistened food. Veterinary advice may be needed. If the cat is unconscious when rescued, it should be rushed to the vet, who may be able to save it by intravenous drip feeding.

HEAT STROKE

Heat stroke is rare in cats, which can adapt to high temperatures better than dogs, but a cat left in an enclosed space such as a car parked in direct sunlight may suffer from this. Symptoms are panting, vomiting and signs of shock. The cat should be cooled down quickly with tepid water and immediate veterinary assistance sought.

POISONING

Cats are susceptible to a wide variety of poisons, including many found in the home. Veterinary advice should be sought immediately if you believe your cat has eaten a poisonous substance, or even if it has picked up a harmful substance on its coat or paws, since it is likely to ingest this when grooming. The treatment will depend upon the nature of the poison, so it is important to find out as much about it as you can.

Probably the commonest cause of poisoning is careless use of rodenticides, which cats may swallow directly or ingest by eating poisoned rodents, and also of certain insecticides.

Many rodent poisons, such as Warfarin, are anti-coagulents which interfere with blood clotting, causing internal bleeding. Side effects include anaemia and lameness. Repeated small doses are more dangerous than a

ABOVE: *Many wood preservatives are dangerous to cats. If fences or sheds are being treated, seek a preservative that is known to be safe or shut your cat indoors for a few days.*

single large quantity. The presence of this type of poison can be detected from a urine sample, and the effect can be counteracted with Vitamin K injections if the condition is identified in time.

Alphachloralose, commonly used as a mouse bait, may also be ingested by cats. It can cause either over-excitement or drowsiness and kills mice by lowering the body temperature to a fatal level. An essential part of the treatment, therefore, is to keep the cat warm while it is recovering.

Fortunately, the use of highly toxic poisons for killing rodents, such as strychnine, thallium and fluoracetate, is strictly controlled in the United Kingdom. Many drugs that are used are now colour-coded with dyes to aid in their identification, so inform your veterinarian of any unusual colour seen in a cat's vomit.

Slug bait pellets are sometimes eaten by cats, although some modern brands contain substances to repel pet animals. They usually contain metaldehyde, which causes weakness and lack of co-ordination, muscle twitching and excessive salivation, and may lead to collapse and unconsciousness. This poison also affects the circulatory system and may cause death through respiratory failure.

Many insecticides contain organo-phosphorus compounds, with controlled amounts being present in flea collars. These cause muscular tremors and excessive salivation, as well as vomiting and diarrhoea. Recovery is possible with veterinary treatment.

Not all cases of poisoning can be successfully treated, as some compounds have no reliable antidote. These include paraquat, the rat bait ANTU (Alpha napthyl-thiourea) and zinc phosphide.

Some weed-killers are harmful to cats, especially sodium chlorate, which causes diarrhoea, abdominal pain, blood in the urine and sometimes even death.

Insecticides used to control parasites on cats should be applied with care. Always read the instructions thoroughly before using an insecticide, and do not apply more than one drug at a time - a particularly common error if you forget that the cat is wearing a flea collar. Ensure that you keep dosages correct and do not use drugs specifically approved for cats. Remember that the cat will lick its coat: if you are directed to brush, for example, flea powder, out of the coat, make sure that you do so to avoid the cat ingesting the excess when it washes.

Some poisonous substances are positively attractive to cats, notably antifreeze, which many cats will drink readily if given the opportunity, but which contains ethylene glycol. This is converted in the body to oxalic acid, which will crystallize out in the cat's brain and kidneys, causing lack of co-ordination, difficulty with breathing, kidney failure and even coma. Prompt and intensive treatment is essential.

Cats are particularly at risk from toxic substances on their coats, which they may lick off or which may pass through the skin directly. Many common household agents which could be spilled onto the skin are poisonous to cats, including bleach, petrol, shoe polish, some crayons and pencils, many detergents and cleaning agents, and wood preservatives such as creosote or tar. When bathing wounds, use only disinfectants recommended as safe for cats, as the cat will almost certainly lick the injury after treatment. Many commonly used disinfectants contain phenolic compounds, which are especially poisonous to cats even in small amounts.

If the cat's coat becomes contaminated with any noxious substance, it is a good idea to muzzle the cat if possible to prevent it from licking the coat. Seek veterinary advice before attempting to clean the cat's coat, as incorrect treatment in some cases can have serious side-effects, and it may in any case be necessary to sedate the cat to facilitate thorough cleaning. Some substances can be removed with large amounts of water. Oil-based substances such as gloss paint should not be removed with turpentine or turpentine substitute, which is poisonous and an irritant in itself, but with a waterless cleansing agent or butter or vegetable oil, which should then be washed off.

Cats are sensitive to many drugs which are safe for other species including man. Aspirin and paracetamol are both highly poisonous to cats, which also react differently to other species with the sedative morphine, which causes excitation. It is vital to keep household drugs such as aspirin in a secure place, and never to give medicines prescribed for one animal to another. Never keep medicines after the course of treatment has been completed.

On the whole cats will avoid eating poisonous plants, but indoor cats may resort to chewing houseplants in the absence of grass and many of these are poisonous. Cats have occasionally been known to eat poisonous mushrooms such as Fly Agaric and False Blusher.

If your cat suddenly becomes very ill, and could have had access to poison, telephone your veterinarian immediately. If you can identify the source of the poison this will assist treatment. It may be appropriate to administer an emetic (a pea-size lump of washing soda, or a strong salt or mustard solution will serve) to induce vomiting if the poison has been recently ingested – within half an hour – but this is not recommended for all poisons so you must take veterinary advice. Do not administer an emetic if the cat is unconscious or if a corrosive or irritant substance has been swallowed; with irritant poisons, a demulcent mixture, such as milk and egg-white or olive oil, can be given to soothe the stomach.

Cats are well-known for their ability to climb and rarely become stranded in trees or similar locations. Left to its own devices, a cat will normally find its way down in its own time.

HOME NURSING

Specialist treatment for any illness or injury of your cat is the province of the veterinarian, but there will often be a certain amount of home nursing involved, and often this may be the most crucial factor in the cat's recovery. You may need to administer tablets, ear drops or eye drops, to coax a cat to take nourishment, or simply to persuade a cat that has lost interest in life to keep up the fight.

Knowing the individual cat helps. Many sick cats want solitude, which means you should find a warm, undisturbed site for a bed, but others will be comforted by human companionship, in which case the 'sick bed' needs to be in the midst of the family and time needs to be made for stroking and chatting to the invalid.

Loss of appetite is common in sick cats, especially in cases of cat flu, where a blocked nose prevents the cat from smelling the food and often a sore mouth makes it positively reluctant to eat. It may help to warm the food to body temperature to make it more attractive, or to mash it up to make it easier to eat. Strong-smelling foods such as pilchards or cheese may tempt a cat which will not look at an ordinary diet. Cats can survive quite a long time without eating, but the longer the period of starvation the more likely are nutritional deficiencies, and the convalescent diet should include Vitamin A to compensate.

More serious than a failure to eat is a failure to drink. Dehydration can kill, particularly if the cat is losing fluids through diarrhoea or vomiting. You can test for dehydration by gently pinching a fold of skin and releasing it: normally the skin will drop back into place, but if the cat is dehydrated the skin loses its elasticity and will remain pinched up for several seconds. Ensure that a drink is within easy reach of the cat and, if it does not take any, see if it will allow you to dribble water into its mouth with a teaspoon or even a medicine dropper. If the cat cannot keep down sufficient quantities of water or cannot be persuaded to accept any, it may be necessary for the veterinarian to administer a saline drip into a vein or under the skin.

Force-feeding of food or fluids may be possible with some cats but this will depend very much on the nature of the cat concerned. Do not administer food or fluids too quickly, or they may go down the windpipe into the chest where they can cause serious pneumonia. Food has to be administered in a liquidized form, and your veterinarian will be able to provide you with a syringe with which to administer it. The head should be held firmly upward and the food or fluids slowly dribbled into the mouth, pausing for the cat to swallow. Some cats will tolerate this fairly well, but others resent it violently, and you may do more harm than good if you have to use too much force.

If you are unable to force-feed your cat, and the lack of food and fluids is becoming critical, your veterinarian may decide to carry out a *pharyngostomy* operation to place a tube into the stomach from the side of the neck so that foods can be introduced through the tube. This is surprisingly well tolerated by most cats and can be continued over a period of several weeks if necessary. But the cat will probably have to be hospitalized while the tube is in place.

If your cat has to have an operation, it will not be released from the veterinary surgery until the vet is satisfied that it is in no immediate need of expert care, and you will be given information on aftercare. Any cat that has undergone surgery should be kept warm and under observation for at least 48 hours afterwards. If you have other cats or dogs, be sure they do not pester the patient. Generally, cats should be fed a light diet in small amounts after an anaesthetic. After some forms of bowel surgery, however, they may not be allowed to take food at all. It is vital to follow the directions you have been given in such cases.

Any appointments for re-examination at the vet's office must be strictly kept, and the wound checked regularly for any sign of undue swelling, pain, or discharge. Most cats will be sleepy for at least the first 24 hours after surgery, but if the patient does not seem to be slowly coming around

THE ELIZABETHAN COLLAR

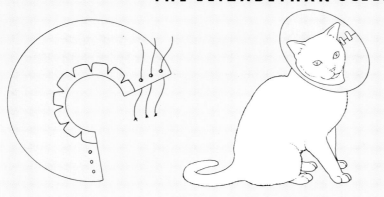

This is a device sometimes used to prevent a cat from worrying a wound. Made of plastic or card, it is very light and not uncomfortable, but many cats find them an imposition, at least at first, and it is probably best not to use one unless it is essential. Sedation may be necessary until the cat becomes accustomed to wearing the collar.

GIVING A TABLET

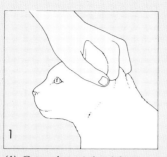

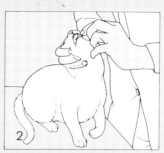

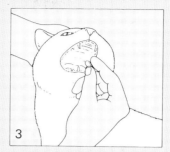

(1) *Grasp the cat's head firmly on either side of the jaw.*
(2) *Bend the head gently but firmly backwards until the lower jaw begins to drop open.*
(3) *Push the tablet onto the 'V' right at the back of the cat's throat. It may go down more easily if it is lubricated with a bit of butter.*

The cat should swallow

immediately, but if it does not, keep the held held back and gently massage the throat to encourage it to swallow. Most cats will accept the administration of tablets in this way without anyone holding the rest of their bodies. Generally speaking the more you restrain the cat, the more it will struggle. If, however, the cat keeps trying to

scratch with its claws, it may be necessary to wrap the act in a towel, so that only the head is sticking out.

Drops can be administered in a similar way, but be careful to dribble them onto the tongue slowly. Otherwise, the cat may choke.

or improves but then becomes dull and refuses to eat, you should contact the veterinarian for advice. Cats are generally excellent surgical patients, and usually seem to recover from even the most major surgery remarkably quickly.

If the cat has had stitches inserted, these may be the dissolving kind that do not have to be removed, or the cat may need to visit the surgery about seven to ten days later to have them taken out. The cat's natural instinct to lick its wounds means that it may remove the stitches itself before the wound has closed, necessitating further repair work, and in some cases an Elizabethan collar will be fitted to prevent the cat from reaching the wound. Most cats dislike such an imposition at first, but soon grow reconciled to it.

Your vet will normally give guidance on the administration of medicines. Sometimes a tablet will be accepted disguised in a titbit: never mix it in with a bowl of food, as you cannot be certain the cat has taken it. Otherwise tablets can be given as shown in the diagram. Eye and ear drops are most easily administered if the cat is already used to regular grooming which includes checking these organs – another benefit of daily grooming sessions. If you are asked by your vet to provide a specimen of your cat's urine, the simplest method is to shut the cat in with a clean litter box containing a little newspaper, so that urine not soaked up by the paper can be poured off into a clean jar.

When nursing a sick cat, never hesitate to ring your vet for advice. He will not mind you calling for such information during normal working hours, or even out of hours if it is very urgent.

EYE AND EAR DROPS

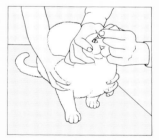

Ear Drops
Any dirt and wax should be gently cleaned from the ear before the drops are applied.

Hold the ear flap and use a cotton-tipped stick, but do not insert it deeper than the depth of cotton tip itself.

Then, keeping hold of the ear flap firmly, allow the drops to drip into the ear canal – the cat may resent it less if you warm the bottle of drops in your hand first.

Hold onto the ear flap long enough to allow the drops to run down deep into the ear.

Clean away any excess ointment.

Eye Drops
Hold the head of the cat as if administering a tablet, but do not bend it backwards.

Approach with the bottle or tube from above, and either allow a drop to fall onto the surface of the eye, or pull the lower eyelid downward and put a small amount of ointment between the lower eyelid and the eye.

Do not touch the surface of the eye with the bottle or tube, and do not allow the end of the bottle or tube to become contaminated.

THE AGEING CAT

Old age comes to pets as to their owners, and the ageing cat needs special care.

The average lifespan of the domestic cat is considered to be about 11 or 12 years. However, this is increasing as infectious diseases become more readily controlled and treated.

Many cats are old at the age of seven. At the other extreme, there are cats in their twenties which appear to be as lively as they did in their younger days. Any article in the Press about long-living cats will provoke a spate of letters from people claiming to have cats of 28 and 30.

A high proportion of such letter-writers always seem to be elderly folk who feed several visiting cats, indeed colonies of cats. Without wishing to seem unkind, the likelihood of any cat surviving for 30 years is remote.

Man spends an average of one-third of his life growing up, a third as an adult, and the remaining third in the gentle decline into old age. Cats, on the other hand, spend only about a tenth of their lives growing up, with eight-tenths in vigorous maturity, and a further tenth in the final slide.

Animals born to long-living parents are more likely to live longer themselves. It is also thought that a kitten born to a relatively old mother may have more defects and a shorter lifespan than those of younger mothers.

It is obvious that a cat with a stable home, regular meals and inoculations against disease, is more likely to reach a ripe old age than the unfortunate alley cat.

The signs of ageing may not be immediately apparent to the owner, mainly because the disabilities of old age do not seem to affect the cat's appetite. In fact, many senile cats eat with more gusto than ever.

However, like all elderly animals – and people – the ageing cat will be less active than before, spending more of its time asleep in comfortable spots and showing reluctance to go out in inclement weather. It will move more slowly and carefully. Instead of leaping up on to a chair, it will either climb slowly, or wait for a human friend to lift it up.

Closer examination will reveal the other signs of old-age deterioration, such as a dry, scaly nose, receding gums, blunted claws, harsh coat, and difficulty in manipulating the spin, head or neck.

The ageing cat will need some special care if it is to live out its lifespan in comfort. Its diet may need adjusting to allow for reduced activity; like a young kitten, it may need to eat several small meals a day rather than one full-size one to make digestion easier. Many elderly cats develop constipation, which can be alleviated by giving sardines in oil once or twice a week, or beef mince rolled in bran to give added fibre.

Additional help with grooming will be appreciated, as the elderly cat tends not to groom itself as regularly as it

once did. Stiffening joints make the process more difficult, and self-interest seems to lessen with the advance of the years and the decrease of energy. Regular grooming will help to maintain its own pride in its appearance and to keep the skin and fur healthy and clean.

As the cat becomes more reluctant to go out into the cold and wet, it may benefit from an indoor litter tray. Claws which the cat once kept in trim itself may become overgrown and need clipping.

As the cat's joints stiffen, so does its mind. Change of any sort is resented. Therefore, it is useless to try to brighten up your elderly pet's life by introducing a kitten or puppy. The cat will hate this.

Moving house is, of course, a real trauma for the aged cat. As long as familiar objects are available, it will settle comfortably within the confines of the house. It is the outdoor aspect of the move that causes problems. In its old home, it probably spent several years establishing superiority over the neighbourhood animals. It cannot do that in its new environment, for it is sure to lose any territorial fights with younger cats.

It is important to keep an eye on the ageing cat's general condition, looking out for waning alertness, loss of muscular tone, dull eyes and a lacklustre coat. Old age makes the animal more vulnerable to many diseases than in its youth, and there are a number of veterinary problems which are specifically associated with the elderly cat.

Warning signs include loss of weight, increased thirst, bad teeth and laboured breathing. Old cats may become progressively deaf or suffer failing eyesight, although both conditions are comparatively rare in cats and do not seem to cause a great deal of distress.

The most significant problem with old cats is kidney failure. Because the cat's kidneys are designed to conserve fluid and produce a highly concentrated urine, they are under considerable stress and are the cat's weakest physical point. The sufferer from kidney failure will show a marked increase in the intake of fluids and consequently in urine output. Other symptoms may include bad breath, lack of appetite, and sometimes vomiting and/or diarrhoea. The veterinarian will probably take a blood test to measure the blood urea levels if he suspects kidney failure.

Unfortunately, by the time signs of this disease develop in an elderly cat with kidney failure, a large part of both kidneys will have been irreversibly damaged and replaced with scar tissue. Therefore, any treatment that your veterinarian gives can only prevent further deterioration – kidney transplants are still a long way off for cats! Treatment for kidney disease may include an attempt to increase the amount of starchy foods the cat eats, but this may not be successful with a cat that is not eating well anyway. It is better for the cat to eat anything rather than nothing at all. Your veterinarian may well prescribe drugs

to try to support your cat. These often include *anabolic steroids*, which help to build up body weight and slow down muscle wasting. Under the guidance of your veterinarian, you should also administer a suitable vitamin

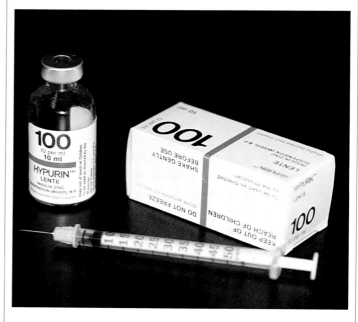

Diabetic cats may need to be injected daily with insulin (**ABOVE**). *They will need to be trained to use a litter tray so that the urine can be tested daily. With proper care a diabetic cat can live out its life without distress.*

BELOW: *This cat shows an obvious enlargement in the neck region suggesting a problem with the thyroid gland. A blood test will indicate whether thyroid hormone levels are normal or raised, and surgery may be needed.*

supplement, since cats tend to lose the water-soluble B vitamins through the kidneys when these are not functioning normally. It is always worth supplementing the intake of these particular vitamins in an elderly cat. Vitamin B12 appears to act as an appetite stimulant and may be given in the form of an injection by a veterinarian, to assist the overall condition of a geriatric cat.

While some cats do not respond at all well to treatment for kidney disease, there are many cats that do seem to respond and with treatment, have been able to live out a year or two of happy lives.

Although incontinence in an ageing and previously house-trained cat may be a symptom of kidney failure, it sometimes arises from other causes. It may simply be due to laziness, and the cat may respond to the provision of more litter boxes around the house for it to use, and to retraining as for a kitten. Unfortunately, some cats will still soil indoors. If a veterinary check-up establishes that there is no obvious physical cause such as urinary failure or infection, the reason may simply be senility. In such cases, the cat has either to be confined to an area where the soiling does not matter, or put to sleep.

Increased thirst and weight loss may also be caused by other diseases, for example diabetes, which sometimes occurs in elderly cats. Often a cat with this complaint will be over-weight at first and then lose weight as the condition progresses, and the breath may smell like nail varnish remover. The condition can be diagnosed either by a urine or a blood test, a test that should not be carried out following a large meal. Treatment may involve a change of diet together with regular injections of insulin. The owner will probably have to collect a urine sample to test regularly. While most owners will learn to cope with giving regular injections, they will also need to give a diabetic cat very regular care and attention for the rest of its life. Although the treatment of a cat with diabetes is not simple, many owners have enabled their diabetic cats to live out the final year of two of their lives in a reasonably normal and contented manner.

Another fairly common cause of weight loss and increased thirst is an over-active thyroid gland. This gland is situated in the neck, and when over-active may sometimes be felt as a lump or even seen as a swelling of the neck area. Affected cats are typically voraciously hungry, often suffering from diarrhoea, and may be hyperactive and nervous. The diagnosis can be confirmed by a blood test. While drugs can be used to control the problem, surgery provides the only cure, and although surgery on the thyroid glands is not without problems, many cats have now been successfully cured of this problem.

Cancer *(Neoplasia)* is unfortunately fairly common in cats of all ages, and is a common cause of weight loss in older cats, often despite a voracious appetite. In older cats it usually settles in the lymph nodes of the intestines or along the wall of the bowel, interfering with the absorption of food. If it affects the liver or kidneys, it may also cause increased thirst. Definitive diagnosis may be possible from the clinical signs or from a blood test, but it may be necessary to carry out an exploratory examination under the microscope. Anti-cancer drugs may be used to treat some mild cases of lymphosarcoma, but they only prolong life and do not cure the underlying problem. Other forms of cancer may affect the skin or any of the internal organs. Cancer is not one disease, but many different diseases that all result in excessive and uncontrolled growth of certain body tissues. Treatment will depend upon the type of tumour involved – it can include surgery, chemotherapy (drugs), or even radiotherapy.

The ageing cat may suffer from a degeneration of the heart muscle *(cardiomyopathy)*. This causes a build-up of fluid on the chest leading to laboured breathing; it can also cause blood clots to form in the arteries. The most likely place for such clots to form is in the arteries supplying the legs. This causes *iliac thrombosis* and results in severe cramps in the hind leg muscles. The outlook for cats with such symptoms is poor, since the underlying heart problem will remain, even if the blood clot is removed surgically. Some cats with cardiomyopathy are treated with aspirin to discourage blood clotting, but since the drug is very poisonous to cats, it must be given in very low doses under close veterinary supervision. Drugs may also be given to assist the heart and remove fluid from the chest. But, unfortunately, few cats survive with a weak heart.

Arthritis is not a severe problem in cats but degenerative

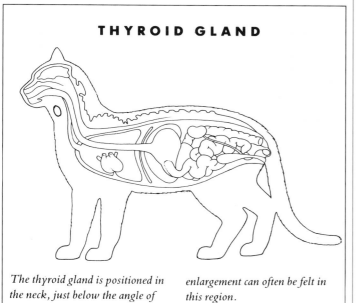

THYROID GLAND

The thyroid gland is positioned in the neck, just below the angle of the jaw. When it is over-active, an enlargement can often be felt in this region.

changes in the joints may result in intermittent lameness, typically after a period of rest. If the cat becomes noticeably handicapped, veterinary advice should be sought. Under no circumstances should human treatments be administered as they are likely to prove toxic. The cat's inability to metabolize many drugs successfully restricts the choice of drugs to alleviate the symptoms, and older cats can often not tolerate doses suitable for younger cats as the liver, which processes the drugs, become less competent with age.

Dental problems are common in old cats and may cause bad breath and a reluctance to eat because the mouth is painful. The problem arises from build-up of tartar on the teeth which pushes on the gums and makes them sore and inflamed (a condition known as *gingivitis*). If left untreated, the roots become infected, and the teeth become loose and painful. Removing the tartar by scaling the teeth under anaesthetic 'stops the rot' and allows the gums to heal. However, this does not prevent the further build-up of tartar with time, and regular scaling may be necessary. A diet that exercises the teeth – a little dry cat food, or even a piece of gristle to chew on – can delay the rate of build-up. However, even given identical diets, some cats seem to build up tartar more quickly than others, and there is

SCALING THE TEETH

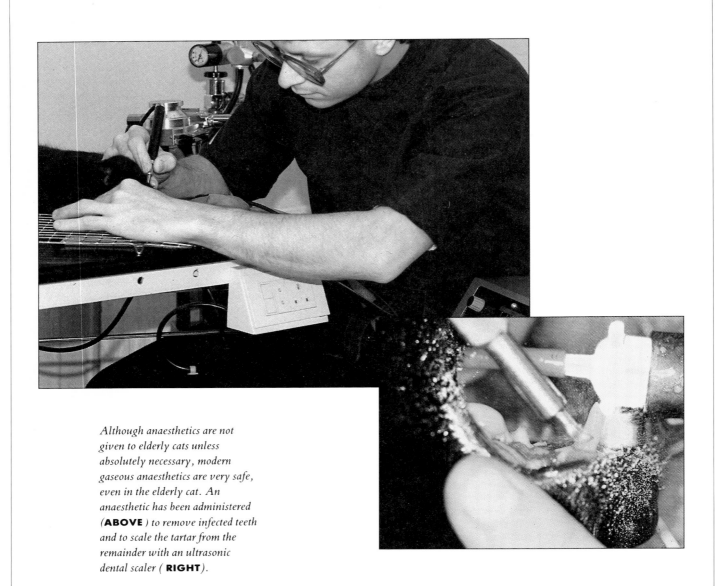

*Although anaesthetics are not given to elderly cats unless absolutely necessary, modern gaseous anaesthetics are very safe, even in the elderly cat. An anaesthetic has been administered (**ABOVE**) to remove infected teeth and to scale the tartar from the remainder with an ultrasonic dental scaler (**RIGHT**).*

INFLAMMATION OF THE GUMS

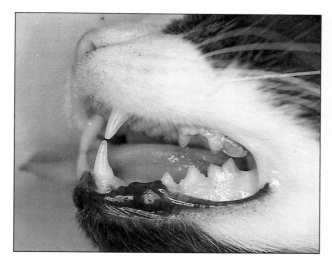

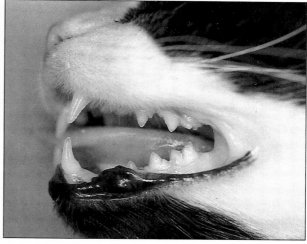

*Tartar is formed on the teeth from an accumulation of food, bacteria and substances in the saliva (**ABOVE LEFT**). Small amounts only discolour the teeth and possibly cause bad breath, but as it builds up it pushes on the gums and causes them to become inflamed, a condition which permits infection to attack the roots of the teeth. This is painful for the cat, and if left untreated will lead to the teeth loosening and eventually falling out. Removing the tartar under anaesthetic will allow the gums to heal (**ABOVE RIGHT**) and prevent a lot of discomfort. Naturally, the tartar will begin to accumulate again with time, and regular scaling may be necessary.*

probably a hereditary factor involved, associated with the composition of saliva.

EUTHANASIA

Loving care, and veterinary attention when appropriate, can prolong a cat's life and its enjoyment of life. Many a cat has lived for several contented years despite having an incurable condition, through the care of its owners and appropriate medication. However, there often comes a point where the responsible owner must decide whether life is becoming a burden to the animal and consider whether it is better to have it put to sleep. As an owner, you will be familiar with the normal behaviour pattern of your cat and will soon notice if there is a change. If your cat is eating normally, seems alert, and is going about life as usual, you can reasonably assume that it is not in any great degree of pain. If you are in doubt, do not hesitate to discuss the matter with your veterinarian.

It is usually kinder to find the courage to make a decision and ensure that your cat is put quickly and painlessly to sleep than to risk the possibility of a drawn out and painful death. Euthanasia is quick and painless and need cause the cat no more pain or distress than having an anaesthetic. The most widely used method consists of injecting a measured overdose of barbiturate, usually into one of the leg veins. The cat then quietly passes away in a matter of seconds with no distress. The procedure is identical to that carried out for anaesthetic purposes except that the barbiturate solution used for euthanasia is much stronger. Another means of euthanasia involves the use of a halothane mask, normally reserved for anaesthetic purposes.

While many owners prefer their pet to end its days in home surroundings, it is often better to make the final gesture of farewell and take the cat to the veterinary surgery. There is no need to be present at the end and the cat itself will probably be less distressed if left on its own. An emotionally charged atmosphere is likely to be detected by the cat and will serve to upset it unnecessarily. Discuss the matter with your veterinarian, who will advise you depending on the nature of your cat and his or her personal opinion of the issue.

Chapter Eight

BREEDING

SEX AND THE CAT

Sex plays an important role in the cat's life. Both male and female reach maturity usually at under a year old, and thereafter sexual activity is frequent, conspicuous and noisy, as well as prolific in kittens – the female can produce three litters a year with an average of four to five young in each. This trait is shared by wild felids; lionesses on heat mate every quarter-hour during the three-day period, and a pair of leopards were once recorded mating 100 times in 11 hours.

No responsible pet owner should permit uncontrolled breeding – thousands of unwanted kittens are put to sleep every year or lead wretched lives as strays. The pet cat is best neutered, not only for this reason but because otherwise the overpowering reproductive urge outweighs any social considerations in the cat's life, for most of the year in the case of the tomcat and during the regular breeding cycle in the case of the female. The un-neutered cat is at risk of being lost while roaming in search of a mate, or being injured in fights and, in the case of the queen, of being worn out by too-frequent kittening.

If you do not intend to breed from the cat, a basic understanding of its natural reproductive cycle nonetheless adds to your picture of the cat as a complete animal. If, after consideration of all the factors involved, you decide that you do wish to breed, kittens must be amongst the most delightful of responsibilities.

TO BREED OR NOT TO BREED

The decision to breed from your cat should not be taken lightly, for there are greater implications than the arrival of a litter of delightful kittens.

For one thing, you will be living with an un-neutered queen, which means a degree of responsibility and also putting up with a certain amount of inconvenience when she is in season. You must be in a position to control her breeding activities. Whilst many kittens become pregnant at their first oestrus – usually at around 7 months of age, but as early as 3 months in some individuals – and bear their own kittens successfully, it is advisable to allow your queen to mature before having her first litter. It is therefore recommended that she should not be bred until her second or third season, at around a year old. Frustrating her designs at her first season can be quite stressful for the human household, particularly with the strong-willed and highly vocal Oriental breeds.

This problem will recur after the first litter, as you will not wish to wear your queen out by allowing her to breed at every season. Even during pregnancy and lactation she must be guarded against undesired matings. If you are planning a purebred litter and have mated her to the selected stud, she must still be isolated from other toms as it is possible for her to conceive to separate matings by different toms – a process called 'superfecundation'. Since 10 per-cent of queens call and accept male cats while they are pregnant, it is even possible for a queen to be carrying two litters conceived at different times – most commonly about

RIGHT: *The queen is likely to be fertile from about seven months of age (or even younger) until she is fourteen or more years old, and may have three litters every year. Think carefully about finding homes for the kittens before you allow your queen to become pregnant.*

three weeks apart. After the kittens have been born, she may be ready to mate again as little as ten days after the birth. In fact, the breeding queen will have to be guarded from unplanned pregnancies for a high proportion of her life.

You must also consider whether you have the time to care for the kittens. Whilst pregnancy and birth are usually straightforward in the cat, your watchful presence will be needed just in case something goes wrong. Once the litter is born, the queen will take care of them exclusively in the early days, but once they leave the nest you will be letting yourself in for a certain amount of work – and also play, which is not only virtually irresistible with young kittens but also an important part in the socialization process, so that the kittens will grow up interacting happily with humans.

It goes without saying that you will also have a responsibility to find good homes for the kittens. Pedigree kittens can usually be sold by advertisement in the cat press, and often the breeder from whom you bought your queen will be helpful. Mongrel kittens may be harder to home since there is usually a superfluity of them. Do try to ensure that kittens go directly from your home to their new owner: they should not be passed on for sale by a pet shop or sent to a home for stray animals unless there is absolutely no alternative. It is stressful enough for a kitten to have to go to one new home without changing hands again, and if it is mixed with other cats and kittens, it may well contract a disease.

It is a common belief that a queen should be allowed to have one litter before she is spayed, for her health's sake. This is not so. If you genuinely want and are prepared to take responsibility for kittens, all well and good, but it will make no difference whatsoever to the queen's health whether she bears a litter or is spayed before having the opportunity to do so.

LEFT AND ABOVE: *Few creatures are more entertaining than kittens as they discover the delights of their brave new world – but they are also a responsibility.*

LEFT: *The queen may conceive by more than one mating, by more than one tom, so that individual kittens in a litter may have different fathers. The 'odd man out' in the litter shown here may be a genetic 'throwback', or it may be that the queen was multiply mated, making the white kitten only a half-brother or -sister to its litter-mates.*

THE REPRODUCTIVE CYCLE

THE REPRODUCTIVE SYSTEM OF THE MALE

The reproductive anatomy of the male cat is not very different from that of other mammals, in spite of its internal penis. This organ deposits semen in the female's reproductive tract, and swells with blood during periods of sexual excitement to facilitate penetration of the vagina. The penis of the cat, however, is barbed with small spines around the tip, or glans. These may serve to keep the erect penis in position, but also appear to stimulate ovulation in the female.

The testes, where the semen is produced, are located outside the body because body temperature is too high for spermatozoa to mature successfully. Prior to birth, the testes develop first in the abdomen of the kitten and then descend into the scrotal sac. On some occasions this may not occur and one or, rarely, both testes are retained in the body. Such cats are known as cryptorchids. The testicle will need to be removed surgically if it has not descended by the age of eight months. Castration alone is not recommended because the cat will continue to display the typical signs of male behaviour, including spraying.

In the testes, semen is produced in the seminiferous tubules, while the neighbouring interstitial cells are responsible for producing the sex hormone testosterone. This is sometimes known as the 'male' hormone, but can also be detected in females, who correspondingly possess relatively higher levels of oestrogen, the 'female' hormone, than males. Testosterone is responsible for the development and maintenance of the secondary sexual characteristics which, in the case of the cat, include the presence of thicker skin in the region of the neck, and prominent jowls around the face.

THE REPRODUCTIVE SYSTEM OF THE FEMALE

The uterus of the female cat has two relatively long 'horns' which connect to the ovaries by tubes known as oviducts. The horns meet to form the body of the uterus which terminates in the cervix and connects to the vagina, or birth canal, where the male inserts his penis. The reproductive cycle in the queen cat differs from that of the human female and indeed most mammals, in several fundamental respects. The most important of these is the fact that ovulation, the release of eggs from the queen's ovaries to her uterus where they can be fertilized, is brought about by mating, rather than following a regular cycle. The female cat is therefore said to be a 'reflex ovulator'.

Ovulation, as with other reproductive processes, is mediated by hormones released under the control of part of the brain called the hypothalamus. It triggers an adjoining region, known as the anterior pituitary, which in turn then produces and liberates follicle stimulating hormone (FSH) into the circulation. The hormone acts on the ovaries, stimulating the development of fluid-filled follicles containing ova. The ovaries contain masses of minute ova from birth, but only a relatively small proportion of these will develop and be released during the individual's lifetime. Oestrogen is produced within the follicles and this produces characteristic signs of 'heat' or sexual activity, as well as preparing the uterus to receive the fertilized ova.

The process of fertilization, when a male sperm fuses with an ovum, normally occurs in the uterine horns, with the sperm swimming up through the cervix from the vagina. The number of ova released will determine the maximum number of kittens which can be born; this number is usually between three and six. The fertilized ovum then moves down into the uterine horns where the process of implantation, or attachment to the uterine wall,

THE REPRODUCTIVE SYSTEM

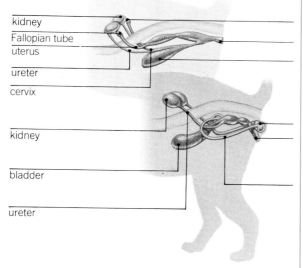

kidney
Fallopian tube
uterus
ureter
cervix
kidney
bladder
ureter

occurs, giving rise to the development of a placenta.

Although only one sperm can fertilize an ovum, it is possible for a queen to bear kittens by different sires in one litter if matings occur very closely together, a process termed 'superfecundation'. Certain queens will also mate while pregnant and can even conceive during this period, although such behaviour is unusual. The second set of kittens may be born prematurely at the same time as those from the initial mating. Under controlled conditions such events are not likely to occur.

THE BREEDING PERIOD

The house cat, like most domestic animals, has a more extended breeding period than its wild relatives, extending over the greater part of the year. Both males and females reach sexual maturity at under a year old and remain fertile for much of their lives.

The female normally enters oestrus for the first time at around seven months of age, although individuals may call as early as three months or as late as eighteen months of age. Oriental breeds tend to develop earlier, and Longhairs later. Queens which mature in the winter months may not come into season until the spring – although the presence of tom cats or other queens in season may bring their development forward.

Oestrus, or the fertile period, is often termed 'calling' from the characteristic loud cries uttered by the queen at this time. In many individuals, and notably in Siamese, it is unmistakable: the queen is noisy and demonstrative, rolling seductively on her back, rubbing herself against legs, and repeatedly licking the vulval area. Some breeds are less forward and vocal, such as the Russian Blue and some Longhairs, and the owner may hardly be aware that their queen is on heat. A sure way to check is by grasping the queen by the neck and stroking along her back by the base of the tail: she will react noticeably if she is in season, treading with her hind feet, raising her rump, and lifting her tail to the side.

The oestrus period lasts for three weeks, signs being especially noticeable for about one week. If the queen is not mated, she will come into season again. Throughout this period she will actively seek mates, and if it is not desired to breed from her great care should be taken to keep her in securely.

The young tomcat becomes sexually mature later than the female, at about a year old and sometimes not until his second year. From this time on the pursuit of females will be a major preoccupation with him, and he will wander considerable distances in quest of the alluring scent.

ABOVE: *The queen in oestrus often demonstrates extra-affectionate behaviour.*

MATING BEHAVIOUR

(1) *The roused tom approaches the female from behind, as she rolls provocatively and treads with her front paws.*

(2) *The tom grabs her by the scruff of the neck and, arching his back, mounts her, front legs first. The female twitches her tail aside.*

(3) *Afterwards, the queen pulls forward, crying out, and turns on the male, who beats a hasty retreat and washes.*

(4) *The female also washes voluptuously, and after some minutes she may well invite further advances and the process will be repeated.*

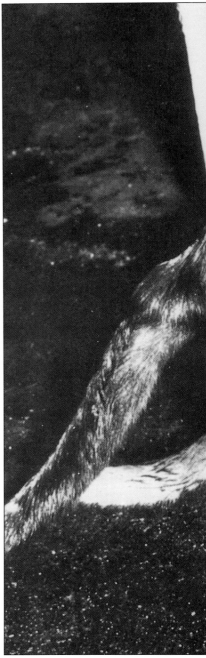

ABOVE: *The mounted male grips the queen's neck in his jaws to prevent her from rounding on him.*

COURTSHIP AND MATING

Although the actual mating lasts only a few seconds, the courtship of cats is protracted over hours and even days as the oestral queen seeks to attract as many suitors as possible before she is fully receptive, and when she is ready will repeat the act of mating several times, often with different males.

The queen in heat attracts toms from some distance by her scent and also by her behaviour, with characteristic loud 'calling'. In the first days she will reject advances but continues to attract the males, and by the time she is prepared to accept mating she will have acquired a number of followers. The males will fight to establish a ranking order, the owner of the territory having a moral edge over the others.

Eventually the queen is prepared to accept a closer approach and the dominant male will pursue his advances. After an initial repulse, she will choose her first mate – probably, but not always, the dominant tom. Mating is brief and noisy, even violent. The female demonstrates her receptivity by adopting a characteristic posture with raised hindquarters, and the tom mounts, gripping the queen by the scruff of the neck and sometimes even biting. The queen screams at penetration; the male's penis is barbed and may well prove traumatic to the vaginal walls. The significance of these barbs is not completely understood, but they may serve to stimulate the release of luteinizing hormone (LH) from the pituitary glands of the female, ensuring that ovulation takes place; the queen needs the stimulus of mating before eggs can be released from her ovaries into her uterus.

There is no 'tie', or locking together as occurs with dogs. Immediately after mating, the female will turn on the male who breaks away and beats a hasty retreat. The queen then rolls around and washes voluptuously, and after a few minutes she may be receptive again. Over the following period some or all of the other toms are likely to be accepted in turn. In the artificial situation of a breeding cattery, with a single male available to the queen, most male and female cats will mate about seven times.

Courtship and mating behaviour in all species of animals have developed to maximize the chances of young being born. The naturally solitary lifestyle of the cat means that it is advantageous to the female to be able to attract the males from a distance and in large numbers, and the long-drawn-out courtship period ensure the best chance of conception. Similarly, the non-cyclical ovulation pattern has benefits for creatures which are only drawn together for mating purposes. Regular releases of ova, as occurs monthly in human females, would not be advantageous for the female cat with no male regularly in the vicinity, and thus the future of the next generation would be threatened.

ABOVE: *Visiting cat shows is a good way of studying the characteristics of your chosen breed, seeing the winners and noting their points, and making contact with other breeders.*

STUD MATING

If you have a pedigree queen and you want her to produce pedigree kittens, you will have to select a suitable mate for her. The special needs of a stud tomcat are such that only the dedicated and large-scale breeder will wish or find it worthwhile to keep one (see page 90), and it is therefore usual for the small-scale breeder to pay a stud fee for the services of a tom owned by a larger cattery.

The prospective stud should be chosen with care to complement your queen's qualities. You can use any old male of the same breed, and the kittens will be 'pedigree' in that you can register and sell them as such to anyone who does not worry too much about quality, but the implication of pedigree breeding is that you are attempting to produce the best stock possible. If you want to produce top quality kittens and to build up a reputation as a breeder, you will want the best and most suitable tom you can find.

It is not enough to pick out a stud who is a good example of the breed and has won well at shows. His type and bloodlines should be such as will reinforce the queen's strengths and balance out her weaknesses to produce kittens of higher overall calibre than their dam. Look for a stud which excels in those points where your queen fails, and which is himself bred from a bloodline strong in those points. He needs to be of at least fair quality in those points where she is strong, or you may lose her virtues in the kittens.

Avoid any stud cat which appears to have a doubtful temperament, for this could be inherited by his offspring. If possible, it is advisable to see some of the stock he has already sired, to form some idea of the qualities he is likely to pass on.

Stud cats are advertised in the cat press, and many may be seen in the flesh at cat shows. For the novice, however, familiarity with pedigrees will take some time to acquire, and it is recommended that you seek guidance from the breeder from whom you obtained your queen, who will probably be able to recommend a suitable stud.

STUDYING SHOW POINTS

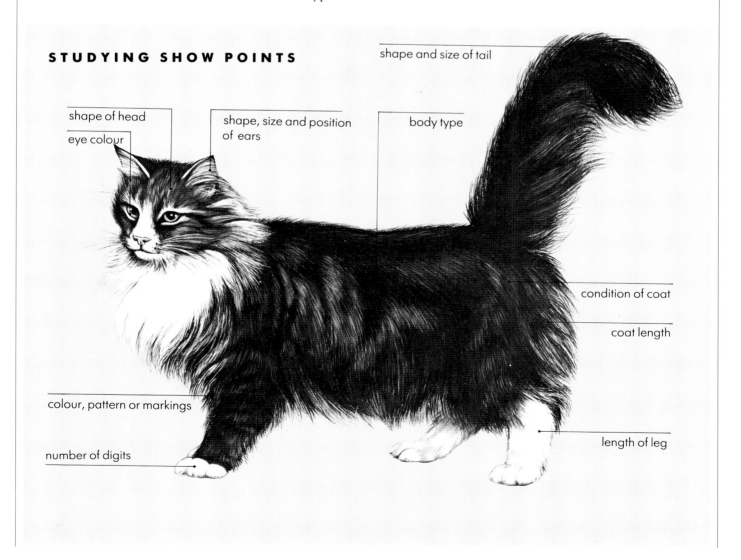

shape and size of tail

shape of head

eye colour

shape, size and position of ears

body type

condition of coat

coat length

colour, pattern or markings

number of digits

length of leg

249

Always try to see the stud before finalizing arrangements. Visiting the breeder beforehand is advisable in any case because, in addition to seeing the stud cat, you have the opportunity to inspect his quarters and assure yourself that a high degree of hygiene is maintained, with thorough disinfection between visiting queens.

It is also important to establish the stud fee; this will be influenced by the status of the male, with championship winners commanding correspondingly higher fees. There is no guarantee that mating will produce any kittens and some owners will permit a second mating period free of charge in the event of an initial failure.

When the queen starts calling, an appointment can be confirmed by telephone with the stud owner. The queen should then be taken to the stud with minimum disturbance, especially in the case of an uninitiated cat. Relevant papers must also be taken: the queen's pedigree, and vaccination certificates both for feline infectious enteritis and respiratory viruses are likely to be required, possibly together with the result of screening for feline leukemia virus. Many stud owners also like a diet sheet for the queen as she will remain in residence for several days.

It is quite normal for the stud owner to examine the incoming queen for any signs of illness and even to take her temperature. This is often slightly raised as a result of the journey. If the queen appears at all off-colour, it is preferable from all points of view to defer mating.

Naturally, it is essential that the queen should be in the best possible condition when she is sent for mating, both for her own sake and to avoid the risk of her passing any infection on to the male.

When the queen arrives, she may be disturbed by the journey, especially if she has not been bred before, in which case she may take a day or two to settle down before she can be introduced to the stud in his quarters.

Mating quarters consist of adjacent pens with a connecting door. The queen, still in her box, is introduced on one side of the partition and then released. The tom will already be on the opposite side; at first the door between the two will be kept closed. Some queens become very wild at the scent of a male; they should never be carried free into the enclosure for this reason.

After a period of adjusting to her environment, the queen will begin to acknowledge the male by rubbing along the bars to attract his attention. On rare occasions, the journey may have disturbed the queen so much that mating will have to be postponed until the next period of oestrus. The time taken to settle down in breeding quarters will vary greatly, largely according to the experience of the female; with previously unmated animals, it may take eight hours or so before they feel comfortable in their surroundings.

Once the signs of wanting to mate are evident, the cats can be allowed to mix together. After mating, the queen is likely to strike out at her mate and he must be allowed sufficient space to withdraw a safe distance. A shelf is often provided in stud quarters for this reason. The female's apparent resentment is normally brief; subsequently, mating may take place again.

The violent episodes which can occur during mating necessitate the constant yet discreet presence of the stud owner. Difficulties are especially likely to arise with inexperienced cats of either sex; pairings are usually arranged so that at least one partner knows the routine.

The queen is normally separated after one mating. Once she has settled down, she will be reintroduced to the tom for further matings. This procedure is carried out daily and should ensure successful fertilization of her ova. Most studs keep queens for at least three days and often longer.

After you have brought your queen home, she must be kept isolated from other cats until her oestrus is over. If she is allowed out, she will still be fully receptive to other toms and capable of conceiving by them whether or not she has already conceived by the approved stud.

PREGNANCY

The unborn kittens begin to develop some 16 days after fertilization. For the first two or three weeks, there are no apparent changes in the queen, apart from the fact that usually she will lose all interest in the opposite sex. Appetite, activities and appearance remain normal.

The first sign of pregnancy will probably be some enlargement and reddening of the queen's nipples, especially if this is her first litter, at around three weeks after mating; this change is often referred to as 'pinking up'. At this stage the foetuses will be about the size of peas and no enlargement of the queen's abdomen will as yet be apparent.

Apart from the slight swelling of the nipples, there are few signs that the queen is pregnant. Chemical tests and X-rays are not only too expensive but, in the latter case, may be dangerous to the embryo. The best diagnostic procedure for cats is still the loving eye of the owner, allied to the expert attention of the vet.

A veterinarian will be able to feel the cat's abdomen and make a fairly accurate guess as to whether she is pregnant or not, about four weeks after mating. You might like to take your cat for such an examination if you are impatient to find out, and take the opportunity to discuss how to cope with the arrival of the kittens if the pregnancy is confirmed.

You should also consult your vet about any possible conditions that the queen can transmit to her unborn young. All external parasites, including fleas, lice and ear-mites, can be eliminated at this stage. It is also thought quite safe to give the queen a booster inoculation against feline infectious enteritis.

By the time the queen is about six weeks into her pregnancy, she will begin to show her condition with a noticeably distended abdomen. From day 49 of the pregnancy, it is possible to feel the distinct outline of the kittens in the uterus, although the actual number present is hard to detect accurately. Their developing skeletal systems will also appear on X-rays from this stage onwards, although unnecessary exposure to such radiation should be avoided if possible. The major period of the kittens' physical growth takes place during the last third of pregnancy.

Gestation lasts for approximately 63 to 66 days after mating. Kittens born prematurely are unlikely to be sufficiently well developed to survive.

Not every mating is successful. The most obvious sign that a queen has failed to conceive will be her coming into season again. Occasionally an unsuccessful mating may stimulate the queen to undergo a false pregnancy, putting on weight, producing milk, and making a nest, and then failing to produce a litter. Most cases of false pregnancy will sort themselves out if left alone. But if there is a lot of milk, it may be necessary for your veterinarian to prescribe drugs to dry it up.

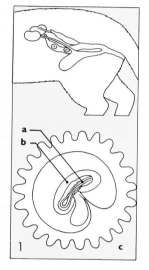

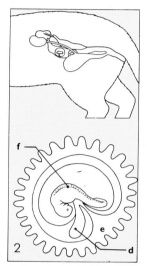

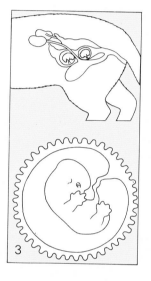

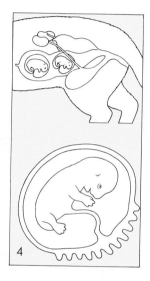

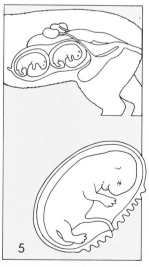

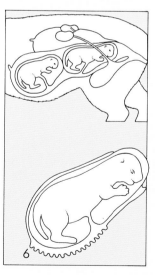

FELINE EMBRYOLOGY

Development of the unborn kittens begins 16 days after fertilization (1). The embryo (a) is surrounded by chorionic and amniotic sacs (b) and becomes attached to the uterine wall (c). A yolk sac (d) provides nutrients until the placenta (e) has developed.

At 18 days (2) the yolk sac is shrinking and an embryonic backbone (f) has formed.

Four days later (3) the embryo is receiving its nutrients from its mother across the fully developed placenta.

Four weeks after fertilization (4) a miniature kitten about 1 in (2.5cm) long has developed.

The foetus grows rapidly and at five to six weeks (5) it reaches a length of 3 in (7 cm).

By nine weeks (6) this has doubled, and the kitten will soon be born.

STAGES OF PREGNANCY

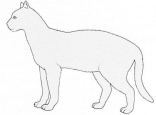

Non-pregnant queen

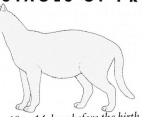

10 to 14 days before the birth

1 to 4 days before the birth

The first signs of pregnancy occur about three weeks after the queen has mated – a 'pinking up' of the nipples. Obvious signs such as a distension of the abdomen and a decrease in activity only become apparent in the sixth and seventh weeks of pregnancy.

CARE OF THE PREGNANT QUEEN

Cats cope with pregnancy well and need very little special care during this period, of about nine weeks. There is no need to restrict the activity of a pregnant cat, although she will need to be handled with extra care during the latter stages of pregnancy. The kittens, each weighing perhaps ¼lb (0.55kg), will be a considerable burden on a creature that normally only weighs 10lb (5kg) or so. About a week before the kittens are due, it is sensible to worm the queen so that she will be less likely to act as a source of infection. Treatment should be continued every week throughout the suckling phase.

The pregnant queen is not sick in the mornings, neither does she have a craving for crazy foods. Nature does not allow for such luxuries. She will not require significantly increased amounts of food until the unborn kittens have begun to increase rapidly in size, from about six weeks onwards.

At this stage she will need more food and can be fed to appetite – towards the end of the pregnancy she may be taking twice her usual amount of food.

Although her demands will not be outrageous, she will also beg or steal additional morsels. The wise owner provides a variety of minerals, greens and scraps for his cat to nibble at. Anyone who has had a pregnant cat in the house will know that his pet visits every potential source of food. Although science has yet to find a way of discovering why, the cat is driven by inner compulsion, beyond its conscious control, to find nourishment not provided by an apparently adequate diet.

During the later stages of pregnancy, because her enlarged womb will be restricting the space for her stomach, the queen may not be able to swallow her daily food requirements in a single meal, or even two. She will need to eat smaller meals more frequently than usual, say three or four times a day. It is helpful to offer her nibbles throughout the day, and privacy in which to enjoy them.

Be sure that she receives a balanced diet. She will certainly need additional calcium: milk is a good source, but if she cannot digest this, as many cats cannot, she should be given an alternative supply of calcium. Your veterinarian will be able to provide an appropriate supplement and will recommend whether or not she should be given vitamin and mineral supplements as well.

Some queens become constipated in the later stages of pregnancy. A little milk or oily fish may be helpful.

At least ten days before the kittens are due, you should give thought to where they are to be born and start directing the queen tactfully in the right direction. Cardboard boxes with paper towelling inside can be distributed in suitable warm, secure locations around the home. The queen will start looking for a safe place to give birth about a week before the kittens are due, and by preparing a choice of sites well beforehand you will reduce the likelihood of her electing to have her kittens somewhere unsuitable.

The boxes should be prepared by cutting away one side to allow easy access; later it can be taped back to prevent the kittens from walking off unsupervised. Paper towelling is preferable for bedding purposes because it can be easily discarded when soiled. If you are lucky, you cat will adopt your box as a suitable home for her kittens – if you are less lucky it could be your new bedspread!

You may be able to encourage her to choose your approved site by shutting her in the room concerned for a period, making sure that she finds it warm, quiet and comfortable.

It is best to keep her indoors in the period before she goes into labour to avoid her vanishing to get on with her job in peace behind the garden shed. Block off any inaccessible places where you don't want her to go to have her kittens and leave the nesting box in a quiet and sheltered place so she can discover it for herself. There is nothing more off-putting for an independent cat than to be told where to have her kittens!

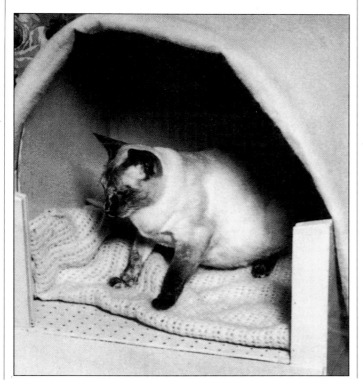

LEFT: *This is a suitable box for the mother and kittens, warm and enclosed. A heating pad has been provided for extra comfort.*

FAR LEFT: *Signs of pregnancy in the later stages are evident in the obviously enlarged abdomen and prominent breasts.*

BIRTH

Cats do not normally have difficulty in giving birth, but it is advisable to notify the veterinarian of the likely date of the kittens' arrival, in case problems do arise.

Two or three days before the birth, you may notice that the queen's abdomen 'drops' and becomes noticeably pear-shaped. It may be possible to express milk from her nipples. In the last 24 hours, she will probably pace around restlessly and refuse to eat. With the onset of labour, the contractions of the uterus will be visible against the cat's flanks and she will probably appear anxious and restless. However, even queens of the same breed can vary greatly in their reaction to giving birth. Once the movements in her sides are apparent, she must be confined to the room where the chosen box is located. Signs of a discharge in the vulval region may be evident; she will also start treading the paper to form a bed.

The amount of human attention required during labour will depend upon the individual queen. In most cases she will manage very well without help and the owner should not interfere – unnecessary interference will only make the queen nervous and therefore complications more likely. However, it is unwise to leave the queen entirely to her own devices, just in case some difficulty arises, so you should keep an eye on the labour from a distance, trying to disturb the queen as little as possible.

A very human-oriented cat, on the other hand, may make it clear that she wants her owner close at hand for reassurance and comfort. If your queen feels this way, you should be prepared to stay with her throughout the labour, although avoiding active interference.

After the first stage of labour, the cat will then actively strain and may cry out. This is quite usual and not a cause for concern. She should be left without interference throughout the whole birth process unless difficulties arise. The period of straining before the first kitten is born can vary, and is often longer in cats giving birth for the first time, but will normally be about 30 to 45 minutes.

As the first kitten is about to emerge, the queen changes her posture every few seconds. All her movements and positions appear to be particularly uncomfortable, but they are designed to relax the pelvis to ease the birth of the kitten. She will squat, crouch, scratch the floor of the nest, and may brace her body against any solid surface.

The kittens will normally be presented (born) head first. The fluid-filled sac in which each kitten is enclosed may burst before the kitten is born, or the kitten may be born still wrapped in its shiny bag. The mother will usually lick fervently at the newborn kitten and break the sac. But, particularly if it is her first litter, you may need to help clean the membranes away from the face of the kitten and wipe any fluid out of its mouth – you should, of course, always wash your hands before handling the kittens. The

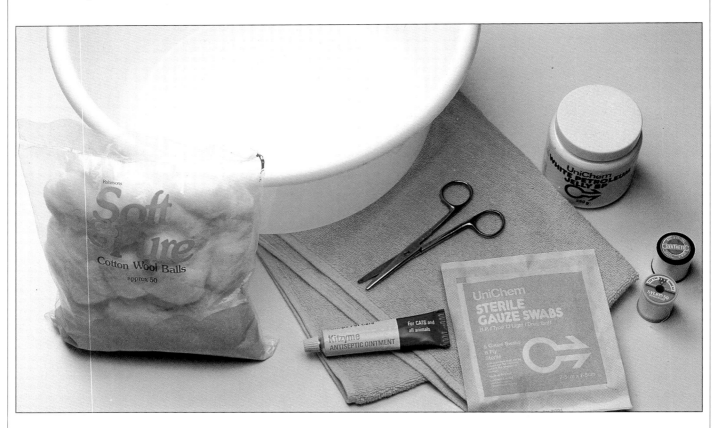

birth process may be fairly slow, so do not rush to pull on a kitten that is half-presented. Watch from a distance, and only help if it is obvious that the mother is getting nowhere with her own contractions, and the kitten appears stuck. In this case, you should clear the membranes away from the kitten's mouth so that it can breathe and pull downward gently on the kitten as the queen contracts. Do not use excessive force when assisting both and obtain veterinary advice if you are not rapidly successful.

Problems may occur if a kitten is presented backwards. If the hindlegs emerge first, there is usually no real cause for concern: unless the queen tires, she will normally be able to give birth unassisted. The most difficult position is a true breech presentation, with the hindquarters emerging first. This can be dangerous, since the head may become stuck; the kitten concerned is likely to start breathing while still in the vagina and may choke as a result. Careful manipulation, using a clean towel or piece of cotton sheeting, will be necessary to free the kitten. It must be handled gently, preferably as close to the shoulders as possible, so that the risk of injury is minimized.

The third or final stage of labour entails the passing of the placentae, one for each kitten. This may be interspersed with the birth of subsequent kittens, but more commonly the young cat emerges still attached to its placenta. The connecting umbilical cord should be cut by the queen and she may then eat the afterbirth. This behaviour is quite normal, but it is perhaps preferable to remove the placentae if she shows no interest in them. Most litters consist of about four kittens but larger or smaller numbers are not uncommon. The kittens are usually born at intervals of between 10 minutes and one hour.

There are no rigid rules governing the length of labour. Although a litter of six or eight kittens may be delivered in less than two hours, a total period of 12 hours is not unknown. If the queen is inexperienced, or very tired after giving birth, she might not cut the cord or break the amniotic sac enveloping the kitten. Without rapid assistance the young cat is likely to die. In such an emergency the sac can be broken with clean fingers and then, most importantly, the kitten's nose and mouth must be wiped clear of any debris, which may otherwise stop it breathing. Opening the jaws slightly with a finger should stimulate inflation of the lungs. If the kitten still does not respond after having been held upside down, its rib-cage should be rubbed repeatedly. Applying pressure to the chest is not

Sterilized accesories and implements **LEFT** – *surgical scissors, a bowl, cotton reels, antiseptic ointment, gauze swabs, petroleum jelly and a towel – should be at hand to help with the afterbirth. They should only be used if the queen fails to attend to the newborn kittens quickly. But, never interfere with the delivery – if there appears to be any problem, call the veterinarian.*

recommended in case internal organs are damaged. The remaining alternative is artificial resuscitation.

If the cord has not been cut by the queen, after a few minutes, it can be severed with your fingers, about 2 inches (5cm) from the kitten, or cut with surgical scissors that have been cleaned with disinfectant. The remaining length of cord will shrivel and drop off the kitten within a few days. Breaking the cord too near the kitten may cause bleeding, or an *umbilical hernia*. If the umbilical cord bleeds excessively when it is broken, it can be tied off with some strong cotton thread. A few drops of blood, however, are no cause for alarm. Once the cord is cut the kitten should be returned to its mother so that it can start suckling.

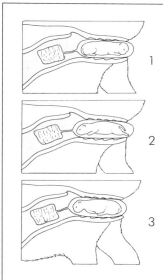

FOETAL POSITIONS

In terms of ease of labour, the optimum as well as the commonest position for the kitten to be born in is anterior, head first (1). Problems may arise if the kitten happens to be in the posterior, feet first position (2), but only if the queen weakens. The most difficult position is the true breach (3), when the kitten emerges hindquarters first.

If a kitten is not obviously moving and breathing, you may need to pick it up and rub it vigorously in a rough towel to stimulate it. If this doesn't do the trick, try holding the kitten in the palm of your hand and gently but firmly swinging the hand downward and back up again. Be careful – newborn kittens are as slippery as a bar of soap. Keep the kitten's head lower than the rest of its body so that any fluid in its airways can drain down and out of the mouth. Here the bowl of warm water may be vital. Immersing its body in warm water is the quickest way to warm up a kitten that may have become chilled. If the mother is not taking much notice of the kittens, perhaps distracted by the birth process, the kittens should be kept covered in a box on a warm hot water bottle wrapped in a blanket until she is ready to turn her attention to them.

You will need to call in veterinary assistance if the queen is in second-stage labour for more than an hour without producing any kittens – but remember, it is not unusual for there to be a gap of several hours, even days in rare cases, between kittens delivered normally.

Failure to give birth after straining probably means that

the first kitten is in an awkward position with its head causing an obstruction. Unfortunately, the birth canal of the cat is too small for a major manual correction of presentation. A Caesarean section may be required; providing surgery is begun without undue delay, there is usually a good prognosis for both mother and kittens. In some cases, such as a female with a fractured pelvis, the veterinarian may recommend simultaneous spaying, removing both kittens and uterus via an incision made in the abdominal wall. Abnormally large kittens, giving rise to the condition described as 'fetal oversize', are not common, but can sometimes be the cause of a hold-up in the birth process.

If a queen strains firmly at first, but does not produce a kitten, and then gradually strains infrequently and half-heartedly, she may be going into *uterine inertia*, where the womb becomes tired and unable to contract properly. Most such cases respond well to drugs that your veterinarian can give to stimulate the womb. If you are in doubt, seek advice too soon rather than too late.

After giving birth to all her kittens, the queen usually settles down and starts cleaning them while they suckle. Only now is she likely to take a drink to refresh herself; some queens stay with their offspring constantly for the first day. In rare cases, after the queen has finished giving birth and everything is proceeding normally she may enter labour again up to a day later and produce more kittens.

It is important to check that the number of afterbirths passed corresponds to the number of kittens. If any are retained within the body, the cat is likely to become ill. They can be detached by suitable drugs, often given in the form of an injection. Any signs of a brownish discharge from the vagina, coupled with a raised temperature, must also be treated seriously. The cat will appear sick and dull and rapidly lose interest in her kittens. Antibiotic therapy will prove effective in most cases.

Labour may begin at any time from the sixty-third day of the pregnancy onwards. Keep an eye on the pregnant queen in the later stages, and ensure that everything is ready for the birth.

LABOUR

(1) *The first signs that the queen is about to give birth include general restlessness and heaving movements of her flanks, indicating that contractions have begun. She will be seeking somewhere quiet and sheltered to give birth, and should now be confined to the room where a suitable box has been provided. You should be present in case of* any problems, but try to disturb her as little as possible.

(2) *After a period of active straining lasting normally 30 to 45 minutes, the first kitten should appear. The queen will free it from any retaining membranes and rupture the umbilical cord. Her licking will stimulate the kitten to breathe and clear its airways of mucous and fluid.*

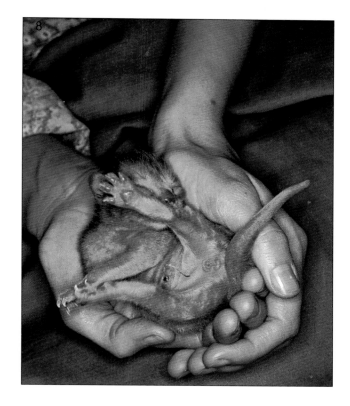

(3) More kittens will be born at regular intervals, and each one will need to be cleaned and stimulated to breathe by the mother's tongue.

(4) The first-born may find their way to the nipples and begin suckling before the rest of the litter have appeared. The suckling helps to stimulate the contractions of the uterus.

(5) After each kitten is born, its placenta or afterbirth will be passed and the mother will eat it if it is not taken away. This is normal behaviour, and she should be allowed to do so if she wishes.

(6) An average litter consists of about four kittens, but larger or smaller litters are not uncommon.

(7) When the whole litter has been born, the mother usually settles down and cleans them all thoroughly while they feed. She may stay with them constantly for the first day or even longer.

(8) The newborn kitten is small enough to cup in the palm of a hand, a helpless little creature with a light covering of fur and sealed eyes and ears. Normally it is best not to handle kittens at this stage for fear of causing alarm to the mother.

POST-NATAL CARE

Normally the queen will recover quickly from the stresses of pregnancy and labour and will rear her litter without complications. If she seems weak and unwell and displays little or no interest in the kittens you should contact your vet. She may have lost too much blood during the birth or may have retained an afterbirth.

Inspect her breasts from time to time for signs of mastitis, apparent in the form of hot and swollen nipples which will appear painful and the queen will resent any kittens attempting to suckle from them. The glands most commonly involved are those nearest the tail, but often only one will be affected. This condition will need treatment with antibiotics, and in addition some protection must be given to the gland itself to minimize discomfort.

Of the other conditions that affect a cat which has recently given birth, perhaps the most serious is prolapse of the uterus, where the uterus is expressed through the vagina. This is typically associated with a prolonged birth cycle or excessive straining: the uterus will hang out as a red, inflamed mass of tissue. Rapid veterinary attention is required to clean the uterus and reinsert it back in the abdominal cavity.

One of the most disturbing disorders of the lactating queen is lactation tetany or milk fever, seen predominantly in cats nursing large litters. Shaking, muscle tremors and collapse typically occur, but rapid treatment with calcium borogluconate, given by a veterinarian, will lead to a spectacular recovery. It is also advisable to reduce the number of kittens being suckled by placing a few with a foster mother, but they should remain with their mother for the first few days in order to obtain the 'first milk', or colostrum, a fluid containing vital antibodies.

The healthy lactating queen will need extra food while she is supplying her kittens' needs as well as her own. The kittens are likely to be growing at the rate of ½oz (15g) daily, which puts a considerable burden on the mother. She is likely to drink more when lactating, because of the loss of fluid in her milk. Mineral and vitamin supplementation may be advisable, depending on the diet concerned, and advice on this should be obtained from a veterinarian. Food must be offered three or four times a day during this period, to prevent the queen having to draw on her own body reserves to nourish the kittens.

Motherhood comes naturally to most cats without the need for human intervention, but occasionally one may panic and start to injure or even kill one or more of her youngsters. Immediately separate her from any injured kittens. Hold her and comfort her until she seems calm; then try to introduce her to her unharmed kittens again but do not leave her alone with them until all has been well for several hours. If she starts to attack them again, contact your veterinarian to see if a tranquillizer is called for – you might well need one too by that time! Even then, some female cats cannot adjust to raising a family, and hand rearing the kittens becomes the only alternative.

It is wise to isolate the mother and kittens from other cats to avoid the risk of infection while the kittens are at this vulnerable age. They receive antibodies from their mother via her blood stream before they are born and also from her milk in the first day or two after birth, which will protect them from all the diseases she has formed a protection against. However, they will still be vulnerable to other strains of infection.

The queen should be isolated from other cats in any case, as she may well come into season again as early as ten days after giving birth. If she does come on heat while she is still

FAR LEFT: *The cat is a devoted mother, and will dedicate all her time and energies to the kittens over the first three weeks, rarely leaving the nest.*

LEFT: *The blind and virtually helpless kittens spend their early days suckling, sleeping – and growing.*

MATERNAL CARE

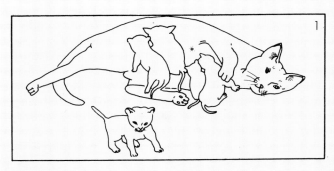

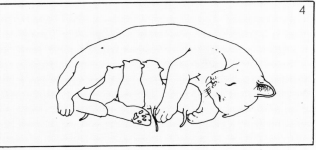

(1) *A nursing mother may reject one or more of her kittens, often weaklings. This rejection is almost irreversible, and rejected kittens will need to be hand-reared by the owner – a round-the-clock job.*
(2) *Like many other young mammals, kittens frequently lick their mother's mouths. This is partly a method of reinforcing the bond between mother and young, but it also helps the kittens to receive antibodies from their dam to fight disease.*
(3) and (4) *The kittens burrow underneath each other and underneath the queen until the anxious owner imagines they might suffocate, but there is no need for concern. The mother has two rows of nipples, and each kitten knows on which side it customarily feeds.*

raising the kittens, for her own sake you should ensure that she is not allowed to become pregnant again and undergo the strain of carrying a second litter while feeding the first. She will need a rest between litters to ensure that she is in the best possible condition. A maiden queen should only be allowed one litter in her first adult year. Subsequently, two litters a year is acceptable, although a queen may be pulled down by raising a particularly large litter and will need a longer rest.

Signs of oestrus may not be conspicuous while she is nursing her litter, so to avoid an unwanted pregnancy it is best to ensure that the queen has no contact with other cats.

If you do not wish to breed from your queen again, contact your vet to arrange a date for spaying. Most vets prefer to wait until the queen's milk has dried up before spaying, but if you have decided in favour of the operation make sure that she does not have a chance to mate again before it is carried out. Spaying can be performed on a pregnant female, but it is an easier and safer operation if the womb is in a dormant state.

It is important to keep a watchful eye on the suckling kittens to ensure that all are feeding successfully. Occasionally a weakling may be pushed away from the queen's nipples by stronger siblings, in which case you will need to intervene by helping it to a feeding place. If the whole litter appears distressed and is not thriving, there may be some-

thing wrong with the mother's milk supply and it may help to bathe the mother's teats gently with warm water and then checking to see if the milk is flowing properly. If she has insufficient milk of her own you may have to provide supplementary feeds.

Occasionally a queen may reject one or two kittens, often weaklings, whilst continuing to care for the rest of the litter. Such kittens may have some congenital defect which the mother has sensed, and even with human care they may well die. However, sometimes it is possible to save a rejected kitten by keeping it warm and assisting it to reach a nipple, perhaps also giving some supplementary feeding (see directions for hand-rearing kittens below). If it survives it will probably remain small and less sturdy than its siblings, but the extra human contact during its infancy may make it a particularly loving and affectionate pet.

While the kittens are still blind and helpless, they should be handled as little as possible to avoid agitating the mother. If you do need to disturb them, make sure first that your hands are warm. The queen will probably trust you in the presence of her youngsters, but her instinct at this time is for privacy and she should not be exposed to visits from strangers or other household pets, which may drive her to move her kittens to a more inaccessible site or even to destroy them.

You should however, with minimal disturbance to mother and babies, inspect the litter for any congenital abnormalities. Birth defects are fortunately fairly rare in cats, but occasionally a kitten may .be born with a cleft palate, a condition in which the roof of the mouth has failed to fuse together properly so that a hole is present from the mouth up into the nose. This prevents the kitten from suckling properly, and milk may actually be seen to run down the nose. It is not possible to treat this condition successfully, and affected kittens are best painlessly destroyed by the veterinarian.

Another condition for which young kittens should be inspected is *umbilical hernia,* which occurs sometimes when the umbilical cord has been severed too roughly by the dam. It can be recognized as a soft swelling around the navel where the tissue has been torn and abdominal material has slipped through the tear. In most cases the hernia is small and contains only a little fatty material, in which case it is unlikely to cause any problem; a larger hernia will require surgical treatment.

If the queen is completely confident in your presence, you may be able to sex the kittens within twenty-four hours of the birth. While not essential, this is a useful exercise because it is an easier task at this age than at a later stage, particularly in the case of Longhairs where, once the fur has begun to grow, you may find difficulties.

MOVING THE KITTENS

Some queens will feel impelled to move their kittens to another nest site as they grow, no matter how careful you are to avoid any disturbance that might make her feel insecure in the original box.

This is probably an atavistic instinct harking back to the lifestyle of her wild ancestors, who would have moved their precious kittens from time to time to avoid a build-up of telltale scent that might attract predators.

A contemporary cat who gives birth to her kittens outside the protection of the human home, such as a farm cat and even some cosseted pets who revert to their wild instincts when the time comes to give birth, may need to move her youngsters away from hazards such as combine harvesters, which can flatten a thousand acres before breakfast. Few rural nests can be considered inviolate. Unless the nursing queen responds immediately to the sound of advancing machinery, she will lose her litter.

In the domestic situation, the movement of kittens is seldom so pressing. The main reason for moving them may be the well-meaning but unwelcome attentions of the human family, the cat seeking greater privacy than she has been permitted. However, some queens will feel the urge to move their kittens around in any case.

One reason may be hygiene. As the kittens grow in size, so does the mess they make, and the fastidious queen may not be able to keep the original nest as clean as she wishes, so she moves house instead.

She will move the kittens one at a time, carrying each youngster by the neck in her mouth. This can look quite alarming to the inexperienced owner, but it is the most practical method. The neck and shoulder area has the great advantage of being near to the kitten's centre of gravity and provides a safe handle. The kitten is conditioned to hang limp when held like this and does not wriggle – the same instinct can be seen in the adult cat, which is most easily controlled by a grip on the scruff of the neck, but of course the adult's greater weight means that it can no longer be carried in this fashion without some discomfort.

When the kittens are old enough to start exploring, they will need more space and the queen will also be more enthusiastic about sharing them with her human family, so a move at this time is advisable as well as probable.

LEFT: *The cat may feel the need to move her kittens to a new nest, often because of well-meaning human interference. Her choice of a new site will not always meet with human approval.*

RIGHT: *Close contact with the queen is vital to ensure that the kittens are kept warm. At first she will hardly leave them.*

LEFT: *The experienced mother carries her kittens about with confidence and efficiency.*

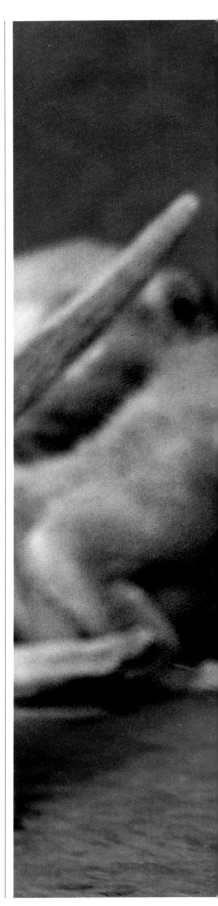

RIGHT: *Carrying kittens by the neck is not instinctive. It is, however, the most efficient method: the neck and shoulder area is near to the kitten's centre of gravity so that it is nicely balanced as well as under control. The mother cat soon learns by experience that this is the easiest and safest way to transport her youngsters.*

MOTHER KNOWS BEST

The domestic cat may feel the urge to move her litter for many reasons, although the most likely

is human interference. She will find a new site and transport the kittens one by one.

NORMAL DEVELOPMENT

The newborn kitten is a helpless creature totally dependent upon its mother for survival. Its eyes and ears are sealed shut, but the senses of smell and touch are well developed to aid it in finding the mother's nipple and in cuddling up to her and its litter-mates for warmth. Its limbs are about as useful as fins, enabling it only to flounder the limited distance needed to reach the nipple, using a sort of rock-and-roll shuffle accompanied by characteristic head-shaking. It crawls about in an apparently haphazard manner at first but within an hour or two after birth it will have located the nursing area and selected a nipple.

During the first few days the kitten's response seems to be to the same nipple. Later on, as it grows and becomes more hungry, it will be less fussy.

The kitten's eyes will begin to open from five days onward depending on the breed; Siamese, as always, are precocious in this respect and Longhairs typically somewhat later. This is a gradual process extending over several days; gentle bathing using cottonwool soaked in warm water may be necessary to remove any discharge. If the eyes become sealed again, they may be infected and an antibiotic ophthalmic preparation will be required to prevent any serious and lasting damage.

By the end of the first week the kittens should have doubled its birth weight and the stump of the umbilical cord will have shrivelled and dropped off. While it will still be unable to walk, it can crawl much more efficiently than at first, using its limbs as paddles. By two weeks of age the eyes should be fully open and the ears will have started to prick up.

By three weeks of age the kitten can stand and walk, somewhat unsteadily, and will soon start climbing out of the nestbox. You should make sure that a litter tray is within easy reach. Until now, they have had little control over their bodily functions and the mother cat has kept the nestbox clean, but once they can walk they are ready to start learning about proper toilet training. The queen will probably teach them what the litter tray is for, but you can assist the process by popping the kitten on to the tray first thing in the morning and at intervals during the day. Make sure that the tray is shallow enough for baby kittens to climb in without difficulty, and large enough to accommodate the whole litter. Regular changing of the cat litter is essential.

The kittens' milk teeth begin to grow at this age and they will begin to chew – teething kittens can be nearly as destructive as puppies. It is now time to think about weaning. The queen may start to encourage the kittens towards solid food, but it will be best to provide food designed for young kittens rather than allowing them to delve into their mother's food dish.

GROWTH AND DEVELOPMENT

The newborn kitten, with closed eyes and folded-down ears, is only capable of a paddling crawl to reach the nipple.

After a week the eyes begin to unseal.

At two weeks of age, the eyes are open and the kitten begins to crawl.

By three weeks the kitten can stand, unsteadily, and the ears have straightened up.

By six weeks the kitten is sturdy, mischievous and able to feed and groom itself.

So far the kittens' only source of nourishment has been their mother's nipples, and they have to learn a completely new technique of feeding in order to cope with lapping. Start with a very shallow saucer and a little warm milk – goat's milk is ideal – and, taking one kitten at a time, introduce it to the milk by offering a little on your finger. Once it has the idea, lower your finger gradually into the saucer until the kitten is lapping from that.

At first, feeding should supplement the mother's milk rather than replace it, so begin with tiny quantities and gradually increase the number and quantity of meals. There are now complete canned foods produced especially for kittens and these should be used if possible. Other palatable items for young cats include finely chopped mince and boiled fish. Milk, or a suitable substitute, should also be freely available. Remember that any new foods should be introduced gradually, for a kitten's stomach is easily upset.

By the time the kittens are six weeks old they are very much little individuals, able to run, climb, play and get into mischief. They explore their surroundings eagerly at this age, and socialization with people and other animals such as dogs is vital if they are to accept them readily when they are adult. The kittens are able to groom themselves and demand food, and they should be well on the way to being weaned.

The litter will be virtually independent of their mother at about two months old, although the more slow-developing Longhairs may need to be left with their mother for another month. In order to help the queen's milk dry up it is advisable now to limit the kittens' opportunities for suckling. Begin by removing them from her for the day-time and only returning them at night. By now she will be willing to leave them for longer periods; indeed, she may well show signs of beginning to feel fed up with them and to want some peace. Gradually the kittens can be separated from her at night as well. Some kittens are very reluctant to give up suckling, and if allowed to continue will keep up the habit long after they need it, which will be a drain on the queen.

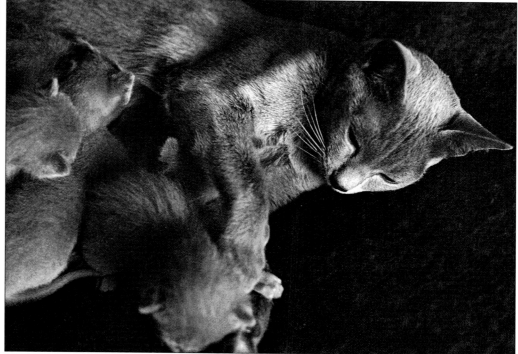

ABOVE: *The 'toddler' kitten explores unsteadily at first, but soon its physical co-ordination and confidence will develop to make it an athletic ball of energy.*

ABOVE: *These helpless kittens with their eyes just opening will soon be charging madly around the room with all their senses tuned to investigation.*

HAND REARING KITTENS

If kittens are orphaned or if the mother for some reason is unable to provide milk, it may be necessary to rear them by hand, but this is a demanding and time-consuming task, not to be undertaken lightly. If a foster-mother can be obtained, perhaps through your veterinarian, this will be preferable. Cats will readily foster other kittens alongside their own without difficulties, providing their litter is relatively small. One of two kittens from a large litter could be transferred usefully to a queen with only a couple of kittens herself. This is a potential advantage of having two cats expecting litters at approximately the same time. A vet may be able to help find a foster mother.

If a foster mother cannot be found, the necessary milk substitute powder can be obtained from a vet. Complete products which correspond exactly to the queen's milk are now available; alternatively, other general rearing foods sold in pet stores can be used.

Evaporated milk diluted in the ratio of three parts to one part of boiled water is also suitable. Cow's milk alone is inadequate because it contains insufficient protein to support the growing kittens. Special feeding bottles for kittens are also produced but in an emergency a simple eye-dropper or a 5ml syringe without a needle can be used.

HAND REARING

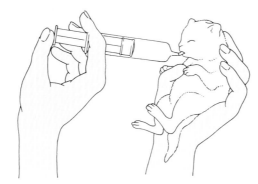

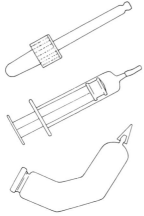

As a makeshift measure, a dropper (1) or a syringe (2) can be used to feed the kittens. But, once the kittens are able to suckle strongly, a proper feeding bottle and teat designed for kittens should be used (3). Ensure that you only feed slowly, so that milk is not inhaled by accident. In the case of very young, weak kittens, your veterinarian may be able to show you how to use a stomach tube for feeding.

BELOW: Hand-rearing a kitten is hard work, but such kittens are likely to grow up to be particularly human-oriented and affectionate pets because of the additional attention they received in infancy.

Good hygiene plays a very important part in successful rearing. Feeding bottles must always be kept scrupulously clean, and should be thoroughly washed and rinsed between feeds. The milk powder should be mixed fresh each time according to the instructions and offered at a temperature of 100°F (38°C). It is vital never to rush a feed; otherwise there is a significant risk of choking the kitten. Fluid entering the lungs is likely to lead to the development of inhalation pneumonia, with serious, often fatal, consequences. Kittens rapidly learn to suck and the feeding mixture should only be given a drop or so at a time.

Young kittens take small quantities of fluid at first, perhaps only 3ml per feed, and must be fed every two hours around the clock. Their food intake should have doubled by the age of a week and four-hourly feeds, certainly through the night, should then prove adequate. At three weeks old, they can be offered a little solid food on a spoon, such as a finely chopped boiled fish mixed with gravy. As soon as the kitten starts to lap, feeding will become much easier.

Hand-reared kittens must be kept very warm at all times – about 30°C (86°F) initially, cooling gradually to about 21°C (70°F) at six weeks – either by keeping the room they are in at a constant temperature, or by using an infra-red heat lamp suspended above the box. Models specifically produced for use with livestock, which emit predominantly heat rather than light, should be used if possible. The temperature on the surface of the bedding should be monitored with a thermometer; it is possible to overheat the kitten if the lamp is placed too close. A hotwater bottle can be placed in the bed, but will need frequent replenishing.

If the kitten's mother, despite lacking milk, is available to care for the kittens they should be left with her and only removed for feeding. She will be able to supply all the warmth and comfort they need and will also stimulate them to urinate and defacate by licking the ano-genital area. Most young mammals need this stimulus in the early days, and if you are rearing the kittens without the mother' aid you will need to simulate her action by gently wiping with a damp cloth or cottonwool soaked in warm water, although the first movement may not be passed until about four days after birth. Hand-reared kittens should be weighed regularly to check that they are getting enough food – a weight gain of about one-third of an ounce per day is satisfactory.

While completely hand-reared kittens will not have had the chance to gain the full amount of protection from disease by drinking their mother's milk soon after birth, it is nevertheless important that they socialize with other healthy, vaccinated cats while they are still quite young if they are to grow up to identify with other cats at all. Although hand-rearing very young kittens is an exhausting and time-consuming task, it is often very rewarding, since the kittens usually respond to the extra huan contact by growing up to become exceptionally affectionate cats.

LEFT: *Warmth is essential for young kittens. To conserve body heat, they huddle together; if they are too warm, they will spread further apart. An infra-red lamp suspended above their box is recommended as a safe and reliable way of ensuring that they do not become chilled.*

The young kitten is constantly investigating the potential of its own body and of its environment. Exploration and discovery are the business of its life as it learns what being a cat is all about.

THE GROWING KITTEN

The kittens are now independent of their mother, but still need the security of their siblings and of their familiar home before the litter is split up for sale. At this stage they need plenty of human company and handling to ensure that they are properly socialized. They should be accustomed to the noise and bustle of a typical human household and familiar with such potentially frightening household paraphernalia as vacuum cleaners so that they learn that such things are normal and harmless.

At this stage, although they will not apparently be in need of human grooming, it is a good idea to start daily grooming sessions to accustom them to the idea. Ears should be inspected daily, and the eyes wiped around with cotton wool, so that they learn to accept this treatment as customary.

This is the time when you must decide which kitten, if any, you wish to keep from the litter. If you want to keep one for exhibition or breeding purposes, you will need to select the one which shows the most promise, and this is not always easy for the novice. In the case of a number of breeds, kittens may diverge considerably from the way they will look when adult. Black kittens may have a rusty tinge to the coat which could well disappear in the adult; it may be difficult to pick out Smokes from Blacks. It is a good idea to ask the help of an experienced breeder, perhaps the one from whom you obtained your queen, in this matter.

BELOW: *These helpless kittens with their eyes just opening will soon be charging madly around the room with all their senses tuned to investigation.*

RIGHT: *A few weeks later, the kitten devotes every waking moment to the adventures of exploration and investigation.*

VACCINATION AND WORMING

The kittens are protected from many infections at first by maternal antibodies which they receive from their mother's milk. This is termed 'passive immunity' and is one reason why hand-reared kittens, lacking that protection, are more vulnerable to disease. Until this protection wears off, as it does when the kittens reach an age to begin manufacturing their own antibodies, it is not possible to vaccinate them against infection. By nine weeks of age, however, they are ready for the first vaccination, to be followed by the second three weeks later.

Also passed on from the mother may well be an infestation of internal worms, so it is usual to worm kittens at around the same time.

ABOVE: *Kittens are dependent on their dam both for physical care and security. Do not be tempted to remove them from their mother until they are fully able to cope with feeding and grooming themselves.*

RIGHT: *The infant kitten receives some immunity to disease from its mother. By about nine weeks this will have worn off and it will need a replacement protection in the form of vaccination.*

REGISTRATION

Pedigree kittens should be registered with the appropriate association at around six weeks of age. In Britain this is the Governing Council of the Cat Fancy, but in the United States there are no less than nine major organizations. It is possible to register each kitten in a litter individually or the entire litter together, in which case the individuals may then be registered independently for new owners.

The purpose of registration is to ensure that any particular member of the breed could be traced at a later date, and for this reason all registered cats must have a unique name. Most breeders have a prefix, usually relating to their stud, which they register for their own exclusive use. All kittens bred by them are then listed with this description, followed by another name. Advice on such matter should be sought from the organization concerned prior to submitting a formal registration application. Pedigrees trace the bloodline of a specific cat back over at least four generations, showing the ancestry of both parents. When a cat changes hands, it may be possible to add the suffix of the new owner, but there can be no confusion as to who initially bred the cat in question.

The pedigree kitten when sold should be accompanied by a copy of its pedigree and by its registration papers. All kittens should be accompanied by a diet sheet so that its digestion will not be upset by an abrupt change of food and by either a vaccination certificate or, it is under nine weeks, advice on vaccination. No kitten should be separated from its mother until it is independent of her and able to cope well with solid food.

LEFT: *The Longhair kitten bears little resemblance to the dignified adult.*

BELOW: *This litter of kittens is ready to leave the mother cat and delight new owners.*

RIGHT: *The independent kitten will be on the look-out for playthings in the absence of its litter-mates.*

GLOSSARY

ABSCESS A collection of pus below the skin, surrounded by inflammation.

ACA American Cat Association.

ACFA American Cat Fanciers' Association.

AGOUTI A neutral brown colouring of fur, made up by banded hairs in white, grey/brown and black, common in many wild species of mammal. In the cat it is associated with Tabbies (as the ground colour between the black markings) and Abyssinians.

AILUROPHILE A person who loves cats.

AILUROPHOBE A person who hates cats.

ALOPECIA Baldness, often localized.

ALTER To neuter.

ANAEMIA A reduction in the number of blood cells which may be due to a number of causes.

ANAL SACS Scent glands situated on either side of the tail, found in both sexes and used for territory marking.

ANGORA Old term used for Longhairs (Persians), now reserved for Turkish breed.

ANTIBIOTIC Chemical compound, e.g. penicillin, used to combat bacterial disease.

ANTIBODY A substance produced by white blood cells to neutralize foreign proteins such as bacteria and viruses.

AOC Any other class (show class).

AOV Any other variety (show class).

BACK-CROSS Mating back of offspring to parent.

BARBITURATE A type of drug used as a sedative, an anti-convulsant, or as an anaesthetic. It is also commonly used for painless euthanasia.

BLAZE A clear marking on the forehead, usually white.

BILE A substance excreted by the liver to aid the absorption of fats from the bowel.

BLOODLINE Relationship of cats to each other, through several generations.

BREED A class of cats with similar defined physical characteristics and related ancestry, eg Longhair, Siamese (see Variety).

BRITISH Belonging to the cobby-bodied, short-legged broad-headed type of shorthaired cats (termed Domestic in the United States).

BRUSH Tail, especially of a Longhair (Persian).

CALICO An American term for a Tortoiseshell-and-White cat.

CALLING Behaviour of a female in oestrus, so named from her characteristic yowling cries to attract males.

CANCER An abnormal, uncontrolled growth of a group of body cells.

CANINE TEETH The long sharp teeth near the front of the mouth used for catching and killing prey.

CARDIOMYOPATHY A degeneration of the heart muscle, fairly common in aged cats.

CARNASSIAL TEETH The specialized ridged and sharp-edged teeth used by carnivores for gripping and tearing; developed from upper premolars and lower molars.

CARRIER An animal which is able to pass on infection, but is not showing any clinical signs of that infection.

CARRY To possess a gene which is not evident in the external appearance.

CASTRATION Neutering of a male by surgical removal of the testes.

CAT FANCY Selective breeding and exhibiting of pedigree cats.

CAT FLU A respiratory disease caused by one of a number of viruses.

CCA Canadian Cat Association.

CFA Cat Fanciers' Association (USA).

CFF Cat Fanciers' Federation (USA).

CHAMPION A title awarded to a cat after winning three challenge certificates at championship shows under three different judges; neutered cats are not eligible.

CHARTREUSE A breed of blue shorthaired cat bred in France at least as early as 1558, now amalgamated with the British Blue in the United Kingdom but sometimes still classed separately in the United States.

CHESTNUT BROWN An American name for the Havana cat.

CLINICAL INFECTION A state of infection in which the animal shows the symptoms of the disease (see Sub-clinical infection).

COBBY Stocky and compact; the type exemplified by the British (Domestic) Shorthair.

COLOSTRUM A specialized milk produced by the mother cat in the first few days after giving birth, containing antibodies against disease to protect the newborn kittens.

CONGENITAL Present at birth (usually said of a congenital disorder).

CONJUNCTIVITIS An inflammation of the membranes around the eye.

CROSS-BREEDING Mating of two different breeds or varieties together (sometimes done deliberately to create a new breed or variety, as in the cross-breeding of Siamese and Burmese to produce Tonkinese).

CRYOSURGERY A surgical technique of freezing tissues with a liquid nitrogen probe to kill diseased areas; may be used to treat ulcers or tumours.

CRYPTORCHID A male whose testicles have failed to descent into the scrotum: the condition may affect only one testicle (unilateral cryptorchidism, sometimes called monorchidism) or both (bilateral cryptorchidism). In the latter case the cat will have the appearance of a neuter and will not be fertile, but will show the behavioural characteristics of an entire male.

CYSTITIS Infection and inflammation of the bladder.

DAM Mother cat.

DEHYDRATION A reduction in the water content of the body due to excessive loss or inadequate intake of water.

DERMATITIS An inflammation of the skin, sometimes called eczema.

DISPLACEMENT ACTIVITY An action carried out in response to conflicting stimuli – for example, simultaneous fear and aggression – when an animal literally does not know what to do. In the cat, washing, often a mere ritual licking of the lips, is a common displacement activity.

DOCTORING Neutering.

DOMESTIC See British.

DOMINANT CHARACTERISTIC One of a pair of contrasting characteristics (eg longhair/shorthair) which, when an individual inherits a gene for each of the two from each parent, will over-ride the other to express itself in that individual's appearance; for example black is dominant over blue.

DYSPNOEA Laboured breathing.

ENDOMETRITIS A bacterial infection of the uterus.

ENTIRE Unneutered.

ENTERITIS Infection and inflammation of the small intestine.

EUTHANASIA 'Putting to sleep': the painless destruction by a veterinary surgeon of an animal which is suffering from an incurable condition, to prevent a painful death, or of an unwanted animal which cannot be found a home.

EXOTIC SHORTHAIR A variety of cat bred from Longhairs crossed with American Shorthairs to produce a composite type with a medium length coat. The variety is growing in popularity in the United States but not yet recognized in Britain.

FALSE PREGNANCY A condition in which the female shows the signs of pregnancy without having conceived, generally as a result of sexual stimulation without fertile mating.

FCV Feline calici virus (linked with FVR) – a respiratory disease.

FELIDAE The family of cats, including the 'big cats' such as the lion as well as the smaller wild cats and the domestic cat.

FeLV Feline leukaemia virus.

FERAL Having reverted to the wild, after domestication.

FHV Feline herpesvirus – a respiratory disease.

FIA Feline infectious anaemia.

FIE Feline infectious enteritis.

FIFE Federation Internationale Feline.

FIP Feline infectious peritonitis.

FLEHMEN REACTION A reaction shown by the cat and some other animals to certain scents, particularly that of an oestral female: the mouth is opened and the upper lip curled back as if in a snarl, enabling scent particles to be drawn up on to the sensory organ called Jacobson's organ.

FOREIGN Belonging to the long-bodied, fine-boned, wedge-headed group of cats (sometimes called Oriental) exemplified by the Siamese.

FPL Feline panleucopaenia (alternative name for FIE, also sometimes called feline distemper).

FRILL Ruff round the face, in longhaired cats.

FSH Follicle stimulating hormone.

FUS Feline urological syndrome.

FVR Feline viral rhinotracheitis.

GASTRITIS Infection and inflammation of the gut.

GASTRO-ENTERITIS Infection and inflammation of the gut and intestines.

GAUNTLETS The white 'socks' on the hindlegs of Birman cats.

GCCF Governing Council of the Cat Fancy (Great Britain).

GENES The units of heredity which control all the physical characteristics with which an animal is born, eg hair length and colour.

GESTATION Period between conception and birth.

GHOST MARKINGS Faint tabby markings present in the coat of a self-coloured cat; may be visible in the young kitten and disappear in the adult coat, or may persist.

GINGIVITIS An inflammation of the gums, likely to lead to infection and subsequent loss of teeth if untreated.

GUARD HAIRS The longest hairs in an animal's fur, which form the outer layer of the coat.

HAW 'Third eyelid'; see Nictitating membrane.

HEAT Female's period of oestrus.

HEPATITIS An inflammation of the liver.

HETEROZYGOUS Possessed of a non-matching pair of genes, one from each parent, for a physical trait: one gene will be dominant and its effects will show in the animal's physical appearance, while the other will be recessive and will not show, but may be passed on to offspring if their other parent also carries this recessive trait. The offspring of a (dominant) black and a (recessive) blue cat will appear black but will be heterozygous with respect to blue.

HOMOZYGOUS Possessed of a matching pair of genes for a particular characteristic. A recessive characteristic, such as blue colouring, will only be apparent if the animal is heterozygous for that gene.

HOST The animal upon which a parasite lives.

HOT Term used to describe a reddish tinge to the fur, a fault sometimes found in Cream cats, especially along the back.

HYPERTHERMIA Overheating.

ICF Independent Cat Federation (USA)

IMMUNITY The ability of the body to protect itself against infectious disease.

IMMUNOSUPPRESSION Suppression of an animal's immune system by a virus.

INBREEDING Breeding closely related cats (eg mother/son) together: over a number of generations this can lead to concentration of the weaknesses of the strain. See Line-breeding.

INCISORS The small front teeth, used for tearing food and grooming.

INCONTINENCE An inability to control the passing of faeces or urine, or both.

INCUBATION PERIOD Period between contact with an infection and appearance of symptoms.

JACOBSEN'S ORGAN A specialized sensory organ located in the roof of the mouth and not found in man, which receives scent molecules from the air via the tongue and makes connection with the hypothalmic region of the brain to trigger an appropriate response.

JAPANESE CAT SCRATCH FEVER A rare human illness typically associated with cat scratches and thought to be caused by a virus. Symptoms include weakness, fever and swelling of the lymph glands. Despite the name, the illness is not confined exclusively to Japan.

JAUNDICE A yellow coloration of the body tissues, most noticeable in the whites of the eyes, and caused by a failure to excrete bile pigments, due to one of several causes.

JOWLS Prominent cheek folds, seen especially in male cats.

KHMER An early name for the Colourpoint cat.

KINK Malformation of the tail, sometimes occurring as a fault eg in Siamese.

LEUKAEMIA Cancer of the white blood cells.

LINE-BREEDING A form of inbreeding pursued deliberately to fix a desired type, usually avoiding the closest relationships such as mother and son.

LOCKET Patch under the chin, contrasting with the rest of the coat, usually white.

LONGY A Manx cat with a tail of almost normal length.

MALOCCLUSION Failure of the jaws, and thus teeth, to meet correctly.

MALTESE An American name for the Russian Blue cat.

MASTITIS An infection of the mammary glands.

MELANISM A variation from the normal coat colour to black.

MEMBRANE A thin sheet of body tissue.

METRITIS An inflammation of the womb.

MILK FEVER A disorder sometimes affecting nursing mothers, particularly those with large litters, arising from calcium deficiency and requiring veterinary treatment.

MILK TEETH The first teeth, which are shed and replaced by the adult teeth in the cat at about between five and seven months of age.

MOLARS The large chewing teeth at the back of the mouth next to the premolars.

MONGREL Cat of no recognized breed and with no fixed pedigree.

MUZZLE Jaws and nose.

NCFA National Cat Fanciers' Association (USA).

NEPHRITIS Infection and inflammation of the kidneys.

NEUTER Castrated male or spayed female.

NICTITATING MEMBRANE 'Third eyelid', membrane present at the side of each eye nearest the nose, which usually becomes apparent in cases of illness and debility when it partially extends across the eye.

NOSE LEATHER Skin of the nose.

NZCF New Zealand Cat Fancy.

ODD-EYED Having the two eyes of different colours.

OESTRUS Breeding cycle of the female.

ONCHYECTOMY The surgical removal of the claws to prevent destructiveness, not uncommonly practised in the United States where more cats are kept indoors, but generally frowned upon by veterinary surgeons in Britain as an unjustifiable mutilation.

ORIENTAL See Foreign.

ORIENTAL SHORTHAIR An American name for a Foreign Coloured cat.

OTITIS EXTERNA An inflammation of the outer ear.

OTITIS INTERNA An inflammation of the inner ear.

OTITIS MEDIA An inflammation of the middle ear.

PADS The leathery undersides of the feet.

PANCREATITIS An inflammation of the peritoneum, a membrane that lines the abdominal cavity.

PASSIVE IMMUNITY The immunity from disease which kittens receive from their mothers' milk and which protects them until their systems are able to build up their own active immunity.

PENCILLING Delicate markings like pencil lines on the face of a Tabby.

PHARYNGITIS Inflammation of the throat.

PHENOTYPE The appearance of an animal, including such factors as its colour or hair type, as opposed to its genotype or genetic make-up (which may include factors not apparent in the individual but capable of being passed on to its offspring).

PINKING UP Expression used to describe the enlargement of the pregnant queen's nipples.

PINNA The outer ear flap.

PNEUMONIA A lung infection.

POINTS Coloured extremities of the body (ears, muzzle, tail and feet), typically associated with Siamese.

POLYDACTYLISM The condition of having extra toes, not uncommon in cats and due to a dominant mutant gene. It does not usually cause any problems.

PRA Progressive retinal atrophy, a hereditary condition of the eye leading eventually to blindness. This condition may occur in all cat breeds, but is most common in Abyssinians, Longhairs and Siamese.

PREFIX Stud name used exclusively by a breeder for home-bred kittens.

PREMIER A title awarded to a neutered cat after winning three challenge certificates at championship shows under three different judges, comparable to the title of Champion for which entire cats are eligible.

PREMOLARS The large chewing teeth at the back of the mouth next to the molars.

QUEEN Unneutered female.

RABBIT CAT A nickname sometimes used of the Manx cat, referring to its rabbit-like gait, and sometimes of the Abyssinian, referring to the unusually (for a cat) ticked hairs giving its characteristic colour.

RECESSIVE CHARACTERISTIC One of a pair of contrasting characteristics (eg longhair/shorthair) which, when an individual inherits a gene for each of the two from each parent, will be over-ridden by the other and will not express itself in that individual's appearance. An animal showing a recessive characteristic (eg the colour blue) does not carry the other dominant characteristic (in this case black).

RECESSIVE WHITE A blue-eyed white variety of Siamese, lacking coloured points. Sometimes termed the Albino, but the true albino has red eyes.

RECOGNITION Approval of a breed for exhibition purposes by a governing body or association.

REGISTRATION The recording of a kitten's birth, giving appropriate details such as its ancestry, with a governing body.

REX Possessed of a short curly coat without guard hairs. Rexing occurs in several domestic animals, for example rabbits and gunea-pigs, and is responsible for two breeds of cat.

RHINITIS An inflammation of the nasal passages.

RICKETS A skeletal disorder arising from an inadequate diet, particularly from deficiency of Vitamin D. In young animals the development of the long bones is affected, causing characteristically bowed legs; in older animals it causes fragility of the bones, which will fracture easily.

RUMPY Completely tail-less Manx cat.

RUMPY-RISER Manx cat with a vestigial stump of tail.

SACRED CAT OF BURMA An alternative name for the Birman cat, not to be confused with the Burmese.

SELF Having a coat of one colour.

SEX LINKAGE The linkage of a genetic trait with the sex chromosomes. The classic example of sex linkage in the cat occurs with the tortoiseshell colour, the gene for which is located in the female chromosome and which is therefore only found in females (or very rarely in sterile males carrying a female chromosome).

SILVER GREY An early name for the breed now known as the Chinchilla.

SOMALI A longhaired form of the Abyssinian cat, developed in the 1960s from Abyssinian stock that possessed longhaired genes.

SPAYING Neutering of a female by surgical removal of ovaries and uterus.

SPRAYING Marking out territory with urine; largely a habit of males but occasionally occurs to a lesser extent amongst females and neuters.

SQUINT Deformation of the eyes giving a cross-eyed appearance.

STANDARD OF POINTS Points scale to which exhibition cats are judged.

STUD (i) Male cat kept for breeding, (ii) breeding premises.

STUD TAIL Skin condition sometimes occurring near the base of the tail in entire tomcats, due to over-activity of skin glands in that area.

STUMPY Manx cat with short (instead of absent) tail.

SUPERFECUNDATION The process whereby a female may conceive by multiple matings, often by different males, giving birth to a litter of mixed parentage.

TABBY Marked with stripes, spots or blotches.

TARTAR A hard mineral deposit that accumulates on the teeth.

TATTOOING A method of marking a cat for identification purposes, usually on the inside of the ear. At present there is no central agency in the United Kingdom carrying records of identification codes for all pets, although there are several commercial registration schemes.

TICA The Independent Cat Association (USA).

TICKED Having the individual hairs banded in different colours, as in Abyssinians.

TIFFANY A longhaired form of the Burmese recently produced in the United States from crossings with Longhairs; not yet officially recognized.

TIPPED Having the ends of the individual hairs a different colour to the rest, as in the Chinchilla and the Cameo.

TOM Un-neutered male cat.

TYPE The physical appearance of the cat (or breed).

UCF United Cat Fanciers (USA).

VARIETY Specifically colour form or other characteristic within a breed, but the term may be used for the breed itself.

VASECTOMY An operation to render the male sterile by tying off the tubes that carry sperm from the testes to the penis. Unlike castration, this does not affect the male's behavioural characteristics and is of little benefit to the pet-owner, but some breeders keep a vasectomized tom to mate with queens in season to prevent them from calling.

VIBRISSAE Whiskers on the head and behind the forelegs these are hairs modified for sensory purposes.

WEDGE Term referring to narrow head shape, especially significant in Siamese.

WHIP TAIL Thin, long tail tapering to a point at the end.

ZOONOSES Diseases which can be passed from animals to humans.

USEFUL ADDRESSES

The following is a list of the main cat fancy organizations and some general addresses of various councils and associations throughout the world. It is usually appreciated if you enclose a stamped, addressed envelope when writing for information.

AMERICAN CAT ASSOCIATION,
10065 Foothill Boulevard,
Lakeview Terrace,
California 91342, USA

AMERICAN CAT FANCIERS' ASSOCIATION (CFA),
PO Box 203,
Point Lookout,
Missouri 65726, USA

AMERICAN FELINE SOCIETY,
41 Union Square W,
New York, NY 10003, USA

AMERICAN HUMAN ASSOCIATION,
5351 S Roslyn Street,
Englewood,
Colorado 80111, USA

AMERICAN SOCIETY FOR THE PREVENTION OF CRUELTY TO ANIMALS (ASPCA),
441 East 92nd Street,
New York,
NY 10028, USA

CANADIAN CAT ASSOCIATION,
14 Nelson Street West (Suite 5),
Brampton,
Ontario L6X 1BY, Canada

CANADIAN SOCIETY FOR THE PREVENTION OF CRUELTY TO ANIMALS (CSPCA),
5214 Jean-Talon Street West,
Montreal,
Quebec H4P 1X4, Canada

CAT ACTION TRUST (CAT),
The Crippetts,
Jordens,
Beaconsfield,
Bucks, England

CAT FANCIERS' ASSOCIATION,
PO Box 430,
Red Bank,
New Jersey 07701, USA

CAT FANCIERS' FEDERATION,
2013 Elizabeth Street,
Schenectady,
NY 12303, USA

CAT PLAN INSURANCE,
Pet Plan Ltd,
32 Wood Lane,
London W12 7DU, England

CATS PROTECTION LEAGUE,
20 North Street,
Horsham,
West Sussex RH12 1BN, England

CAT SURVIVAL TRUST,
Marlind Centre,
Codicote Road,
Welwyn,
Herts AL6 9TV, England

CROWN CAT FANCIERS' ASSOCIATION,
1379 Tyler Park Drive,
Louisville,
Kentucky 40204, USA

FELINE ADVISORY BUREAU.
6 Woodthorpe Road,
London SW15 6UQ, England

FELINE ASSOCIATION OF SOUTH AUSTRALIA,
7 Athelney Avenue,
Brighton,
South Australia 5048, Australia

FEDERATION INTERNATIONALE FELINE (FIFe),
Friedrichstrasse 48,
6200 Wiesbaden, West Germany

GOVERNING COUNCIL OF THE CAT FANCY (GCCF),
Dovefields,
Petworth Road,
Witley,
Surrey GU8 5QT, England

NATIONAL CAT CLUB,
The Laurels,
Chesham Lane,
Wendover,
Bucks, England

KENSINGTON KITTEN AND NEUTER CAT CLUB,
Fairmont,
78 Highfield Avenue,
Aldershot,
Hampshire, England

LONG ISLAND OCELOT CLUB,
PO Box 99542,
Tacoma,
Washington 98499, USA

NEW ZEALAND CAT FANCY INC,
PO Box 3167,
Richmond,
Nelson, New Zealand

PEDIGREE PETFOODS EDUCATION CENTRE,
Waltham-on-the-Wolds,
Melton Mowbray,
Leics LE14 4RS, England

PEOPLE'S DISPENSARY FOR SICK ANIMALS (PDSA),
PDSA House,
South Street,
Dorking,
Surrey RH4 2LB, England

PETCARE INFORMATION AND ADVISORY SERVICE,
254 George Street,
Sydney,
New South Wales, Australia

PET HEALTH COUNCIL,
Walter House (4th Floor),
418–422 The Strand,
London WC2R 0PL, England

ROYAL SOCIETY FOR THE PREVENTION OF CRUELTY TO ANIMALS (RSPCA),
The Manor House,
Causeway, Horsham,
West Sussex RH13 1HG, England

RSPCA (AUSTRALIA),
Colter Road,
Canberra ACT 2600, Australia

SOCIETY FOR THE PREVENTION OF CRUELTY TO ANIMALS (SPCA),
Wellington, New Zealand

SPCA (SOUTH AFRICA),
PO Box 38035,
Johannesburg 2000, South Africa

SPILLERS PET ADVISORY SERVICE,
New Malden House,
1 Blagden Road,
New Malden,
Surrey KT3 4TB, England

THE INDEPENDENT CAT ASSOCIATION,
211 East Olive (Suite 201),
Burbank,
California 92111, USA

UNITED CAT FEDERATION,
6621 Thornwood Street,
San Diego,
California 92111, USA

WESTERN PROVINCE CAT CLUB,
PO Box 3600,
Cape Town 8000, South Africa

INDEX

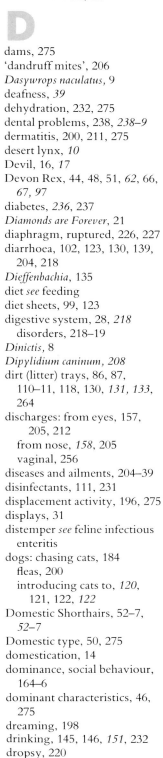

ACKNOWLEDGEMENTS

(t)=top, (l)=left, (r)=right, (c)=centre, (b)=below

Creszentia Allen: 40, 48, 50(t), 54, 56, 57(b), 75, 78, 79, 81(t, cr, ctl, ctr & br)

Animals Unlimited: 39, 50(c), 52, 53(t), 55(b), 59, 61(b), 62–4, 68–70, 71(b), 72–3, 74(l), 76, 77, 80(t), 81(cbl), 86(b), 87(t), 88, 96(l&r), 97(b), 98(t), 100–1, 155(r), 170, 248

Ardea London: 14(t), 23(b), 27, 31(t&b), 32

Mike Buselle: 41, 42(r), 89, 91(b), 92, 93, 96–7, 118(t), 120, 122, 130–1, 141, 151(t), 152, 153, 164, 166, 172–3, 176, 177, 183–6, 199(t), 202, 240, 261–3, 265(l), 168–71

Bruce Coleman Ltd: 106(t)

Anne Cumbers: 42, 60, 65, 67, 89(t), 118(b), 136, 158/9, 162, 273(t)

R. Estall: 192–3

Paul Forrester: 83, 254

Michael Freeman: 23(t), 30(t)

R.D. Hallman: 20, 197

Marc Henrie: 14(c), 20, 26, 33(r), 36(bl&r), 50(b), 53(b), 58, 61(c&t), 74, 135, 142, 155(bl), 161, 196(t), 204, 230, 256(l), 267

Mick Hill: 242

Popperfoto: 246–7

Science Photo Library: 215, 217

Spectrum: 182

Andrew Sydenham: 273(b)

Sally Anne Thompson: 29(l), 55(t), 66, 94, 132–3, 244, 260, 272(l), 273(c)

Trustees of the British Museum: 15, 18(b)

Victoria and Albert Museum: 19

Bradley Viner: 29(r), 33(l), 98(b), 103, 104, 125–7, 132(l), 148, 204(b), 205–7, 210–13, 216, 221–3, 225–6, 228–9, 236, 238–9, 272(r)

Trevor Wood: 174–5

Jon Wyand: 149

5/12/91